The Business Turn
in American Religious History

The Business Turn in American Religious History

Edited by

AMANDA PORTERFIELD

JOHN CORRIGAN

DARREN E. GREM

OXFORD
UNIVERSITY PRESS

OXFORD
UNIVERSITY PRESS

Oxford University Press is a department of the University of Oxford. It furthers
the University's objective of excellence in research, scholarship, and education
by publishing worldwide. Oxford is a registered trade mark of Oxford University
Press in the UK and certain other countries.

Published in the United States of America by Oxford University Press
198 Madison Avenue, New York, NY 10016, United States of America.

© Oxford University Press 2017

CIP data is on file at the Library of Congress
ISBN 978–0–19–028020–8 (pbk.)
ISBN 978–0–19–028019–2 (hbk.)

1 3 5 7 9 8 6 4 2

Paperback printed by WebCom, Inc., Canada
Hardback printed by Bridgeport National Bindery, Inc., United States of America

Contents

Preface: Business, Religion, History,
and Consilience—ROBERT E. WRIGHT   vii

Contributors   xxi

Introduction: The Business Turn in American Religious History—
AMANDA PORTERFIELD, JOHN CORRIGAN, AND DARREN E. GREM   I

1. Believing Within Business: Evangelicalism, Media,
   and Financial Faith—DANIEL VACA   20

2. Fundamentalism and the Business Turn—TIMOTHY E. W. GLOEGE   46

3. Godly Work for a Global Christianity: American
   Christians' Economic Impact Through Missions, Markets,
   and International Development—DAVID P. KING   72

4. Liberty and Order: The Mormon Struggle with
   American Capitalism—MATTHEW BOWMAN   108

5. A Business Turn in American Jewish Religious History:
   Women and the Emergence of Popular Philanthropy—
   DEBORAH SKOLNICK EINHORN   131

6. The Business of Asian Religions: Guru Entrepreneurs
   and Godmen CEOs—MICHAEL J. ALTMAN   155

7. Hunting Buffalo in Oklahoma: Native American Casinos, Constructed Identities, and Portrayals of Native Culture and Religion—ANGELA TARANGO   176

8. St. Homobonus Leads the CEOs: Doing Good Versus Doing (Really) Well—PAULA M. KANE   199

Afterword—JAMES HUDNUT-BEUMLER   223

Index   235

Preface

BUSINESS, RELIGION, HISTORY, AND CONSILIENCE

Robert E. Wright

CONSILIENCE WAS THE term Harvard University biologist Edward
O. Wilson used in 1998 to describe the "unity of knowledge," the quest to
link facts and theories across traditional scholarly disciplines, from the sciences
to the humanities, "to create a common groundwork of explanation."[1]
Raised a Baptist in southern Alabama but educated an empiricist in eastern
Massachusetts, Wilson portrayed science as a "continuation" of attempts by
the world's religions "to explain the universe."[2] Empirical evidence, he argued,
has already seriously eroded the notion "of a biological God, one who directs
organic evolution and intervenes in human affairs," but he leaves the fate of
a deistical or "cosmological God who created the universe" to future scientists
blessed "by forms of material evidence not yet imagined."[3] Religious and
ethical precepts, he insisted, following Scottish Enlightenment thinkers such
as David Hume and Adam Smith, can be assessed empirically, as products of
human biological and cultural evolution, or as sophisticated instincts mediated
by and through specific historical contexts. In a densely interconnected
universe such as ours, in other words, to understand one thing (text), one
must understand everything (context), and vice versa.

Wilson considered religions to be "superorganisms" that experience "a
life cycle" of birth, growth, competition, reproduction, and eventual death.[4]
Historiography also cycles as hoary ideas, themes, and emphases lose momentum
and fall out of favor while (ostensibly) new questions and topics arise,
capture the interest of researchers, readers, and students, and rise to prominence,
only to give way, eventually, to yet newer notions and interests. For

example, for the first time since the "linguistic turn" of the 1970s and 1980s, mainstream historians are (again) taking a serious interest in business and economic matters. After the global financial panic of 2008, the "history of capitalism" emerged as a legitimate subfield at prestigious universities such as Cambridge, Cornell, Harvard, and Wisconsin.[5] At the same time, a bevy of studies on American chattel slavery centered on the business of slave trading, slave mortgaging and insurance, and slavery's role in economic development.[6]

Religious historiography turns as it cycles too, partly due to its own internal dynamics, partly because of changes within religious discourse itself, and partly due to wider intellectual trends and the ever evolving social zeitgeist.[7] Unsurprisingly, then, historians of religion have also recently (re)turned to business, economic, and financial questions.[8] *The Business Turn in American Religious History* offers readers a view of religion better described as inter- or multidisciplinary than consilient but nevertheless interesting and an improvement over disciplinary insularity.[9] Here, religion confronts not physics and evolution but rather business and economics, and in sometimes surprising and controversial ways. The "turn" refers to the perception that a major shift in religious historiography is under way, that is, to the notion that religious historians have come to see the importance of investigating how the business of religion has changed over time and place.

In addition to the broader intellectual and historiographical trends and societal zeitgeist described in the previous paragraphs, the business turn can be traced to two books published by Oxford University Press, R. Laurence Moore's *Selling God: American Religion in the Marketplace of Culture* (1994) and *Sacred Companies: Organizational Aspects of Religion and Religious Aspects of Organizations* (1998), a collaborative, interdisciplinary effort edited by University of Massachusetts sociologist Jay Demerath.[10]

Moore, a historian at Cornell University, argued that religion remained a central component of American life despite the formal separation of church and state because American religious organizations essentially wedded themselves to commerce, not in the late twentieth century but from the nation's very beginning. Over time, Moore showed, "religion itself took on the shape of a commodity" as religious leaders "looked for ways to appeal to all consumers, using the techniques of advertising and publicity employed by other merchants" and a "boom market in religion" developed (6).

Sacred Companies examined both the influence of religion on businesses (e.g., the ubiquity of "mission" statements) and the influence of business on religions. It also issued a challenge to scholars of religion who, according to Demerath, had long tended to "avert their eyes from organizational phenomena of any sort." Even descriptive accounts of religious organizations, he complained, "are generally couched in religion's own terms" and assume the "singularity of the religious experience and the organizations that serve it" (vii). Demerath also claimed that "intellectual inbreeding" had created an "increasingly stunted" literature (viii). Moving beyond the hackneyed distinction between church and sect, Demerath and the volume's contributors, with help from organizational sociologists Charles Perrow, Paul DiMaggio, and Walter Powell, sought to recast religious institutions as a specific type of nonprofit association rather than as conceptually unique or distinct organizations.

Sacred Companies appeared at a propitious moment, a year after *New Directions in American Religious History*, which counted among its contributors Gordon Wood, Daniel Walker Howe, John Higham, and other high-profile historians, argued that "by building on the insights of organizational sociology, historians are in an ideal position to fill out the story of religion in modern America."[11] *Sacred Companies* came to the attention of religion historians in several ways, including through the mostly favorable review of it by sociologist of religion R. Stephen Warner that appeared in *Church History*.[12] In a review for the *Journal for the Scientific Study of Religion*, John A. Coleman, then a professor but later associate pastor at St. Ignatius Church in San Francisco, predicted that *Sacred Companies* would "enjoy a relatively long shelf-life" because it bristled "with a rich implicit and doable research agenda."[13] He was right, as the book has since been widely cited in business, sociology, religion, and history journal articles as well as numerous books, including the *Oxford Handbook of Church and State in the United States* (2010), *Christianity Incorporated* (2002) by political scientist Michael Budde and philosophy professor Robert W. Brimlow, Peter W. Williams's textbook *America's Religions* (2001), and Charles Lippy's massive *Faith in America: Changes, Challenges, New Directions* (2006).

As *Selling God* and *Sacred Companies* helped beget *The Business Turn in American Religious History*, so this volume may help to beget the next step on the road to consilience, a public choice "turn" akin to that which occurred in political science. Public choice is an economic view of government that posits that government employees, from the top to the bottom of the bureaucratic hierarchies they compose, can behave in self-serving ways when left unchecked. Public servants, in other words, are not always public-spirited.[14] While sundry Freudians and other skeptics of religion have long argued that religious organizations and their leaders are not always spiritually oriented, religion scholars are just beginning to consider carefully the implications of religious leaders more concerned with their own interests (be they spiritual, secular, or both) than those of their respective flocks.[15]

The application of public choice theory to religion may appear forced at first, especially considering that the study of the economics of religion (after Adam Smith's seminal contribution, discussed below) lay largely dormant until barely two decades ago.[16] After all, governments are essentially compulsory monopolies and hence subject to numerous foibles and failings that one would not expect to find in a pluralist society where church attendance is not mandatory and religious choices abound.[17] Of course, where competition was eliminated by edict, as in medieval Europe, church leaders could get away with murder, literally.[18] Reacting to religious monopolies that had rendered Europe and other parts of the world a living hell, Smith argued that governments ought to allow religious groups to proliferate so they would have to compete with each other for acolytes and funding.[19] Competition alone, he believed, would limit all sorts of evils, including self-serving behavior on the part of church leaders.[20]

The problem with the view of Smith and others who believe that competition will cleanse all is that religions are not perfect substitutes for each other.[21] Religion is a service industry that sells salvation, spirituality, and so forth, but religions vary considerably in how they deliver those services. Whether religious services are objectively genuine or not is beside the point. As with members of the "Nacirema" (*American* spelled backward) tribe, who believed in the alleged beneficial health and social effects of all sorts of "magic potions" that they safeguarded in special medicine boxes hung on the walls of their sacred porcelain throne rooms, what really matters is what acolytes believe is necessary to earn a happy afterlife.[22] Apparently, such beliefs were (and remain) rather "sticky," that is, difficult to change, so acolytes did not (and do not) change religions as readily as they shift toothpaste or deodorant brands. With competition thus somewhat dampened (more technically, the market for religious services, like the markets for automobiles, colleges, and many other goods, should be modeled as one of monopolistic competition rather than one of pure or Smithian competition),[23] room for self-serving behaviors on the part of church leaders was opened and maintained. This of course does not mean that all religious leaders always take advantage of their followers, just that competitive forces alone cannot be expected to prevent self-serving behaviors.

Perhaps the most disturbing implication of this line of reasoning is that church leaders in pluralist societies have incentives to render their teachings simultaneously as popular and as "sticky" as possible. Theology itself, in other words, could be distorted by market forces as church leaders seek to attract and retain followers, believers who willingly donate resources (time, money, goods) to the church over extended periods. Consider a situation in which church leaders must decide whether to preach the virtues of asceticism or socialism and receive $1 from each of a million poor acolytes or to preach the benefits of capitalism and receive $1 million from a single wealthy donor. The latter would be more profitable (much cheaper collection and many fewer souls to service) but infinitely more fraught (what if, God forbid, the big donor dies intestate—or converts to the Church of the Flying Spaghetti Monster?), so perhaps the best strategy is not to explicitly oppose anyone's material interests and to try to appear as "otherworldly" as possible by focusing on arcane questions of ritual or theology with no clear real-world implications. Is it miraculous, then, to discover that religions differentiate themselves on the basis of what they literally call their "services," which range from solemn Quaker affairs to the emotional, participatory atmosphere of many Baptist meetings,[24] as well as in myriad other minor ways, much the way that casual dining chain restaurants differentiate themselves on the basis of the "crazy crap"[25] on their walls as well as their menus?

Of course, distinguishing self-serving from selfless behaviors is not always, or even usually, easy. Consider, for example, the role of the Catholic Church in the urban renewal movement of the 1970s. In a statement entitled "The Right to a Decent Home," the National Conference of Catholic Bishops lambasted redlining and other urban disinvestment practices and argued that "we must insure fair and equal access to available credit."[26] Surely the bishops were concerned about issues of social justice and for the welfare of their parishioners, but they also must have realized that the hollowing out of urban centers threatened parish finances.

Clergy must have resources to live, so the behavior of ex-slave preacher Boston King, who fled Nova Scotia after discovering his followers there were so poor that they lived in stick huts and subsisted at times off their own dogs and cats, is understandable.[27] Clearer examples of self-serving behavior occurred when churches with resources neglected the needs of impoverished acolytes, as in the moving death scene of the "tramp" in Charles M. Shelton's 1897 novel *In His Steps*. Just before breathing his last, the "dusty, worn, shabby-looking young man" appeared in a wealthy downtown church and asked the Reverend Henry Maxwell, in the middle of his Sunday service, "What does following Jesus mean? I understand that Christian people own a good many of the tenement houses. A member of the church was the owner of the one where my wife died, and I have wondered if following Jesus all the way was true in his case?"[28] That was dramatized fiction, but clearly some real-world churches with ample resources spiritually shortchanged those short of change, like the Protestant denominations that provided "lame service" to white sharecroppers in the interwar U.S. South because "the typical farm tenant . . . [had] no money for the collection plate" or with which "to entertain the preacher at a meal now and then."[29]

Similarly, the revelation that all of the world's major religions developed theologies that can be used by church leaders to either support or reject the enslavement of human beings is as unsurprising as it is reprehensible. Before the great emancipations of the nineteenth century, proslavery sentiments typically prevailed because most slaves had no money of their own. Only where abolitionist sentiments were strong and slaveholders were not a major source of donations did church leaders have sufficient material incentive to support the enslaved with anything other than platitudes. Unsurprisingly, Boston ministers and Pennsylvania Quakers led the antislavery movement in the New World.[30] It is no miracle that today, in a world where only ISIS admits to holding slaves, or even to harboring proslavery thoughts, and images of trafficked and prostituted children open wide the pocketbooks of acolytes, religious leaders declaim mightily against slavery.[31]

Public choice theory also easily explains why free blacks in antebellum northern cities, most of whom were poor, were discriminated against even on Sundays. In addition to segregated pews, communion offerings, and burial grounds, black acolytes were usually not allowed to preach or take part in church governance, even in denominations, such as Methodism, that ostensibly opposed slavery and the racism it bred.[32] "We are bold in declaring," the free black Reverend Samuel E. Cornish lamented in 1838, "the professed christians [sic] in the city [in this case New York] have been to us as hypocrites and heathen." Yet black men of the cloth such as Cornish created their own congregations, to chastise bigoted church leaders and to help their downtrodden brethren but also to provide themselves with pulpits and even bishoprics. When income from the new benefices proved insufficient, Cornish and other black clergy complained to churchgoers that they could not afford to buy books, let alone the time to read them, and urged members to put quarters instead of coppers into collection plates by forgoing expensive clothes and postservice treats such as ice cream.[33] Some black political leaders, including William H. Holtzclaw, a student of Booker T. Washington and founder of the Utica Institute in Mississippi, considered many rural clergymen mere entertainers who, like the Gypsies in Cher's song "Gypsies, Tramps, and Thieves," would just as well dance or sell patent medicine as deliver a fiery but unlearned sermon.[34]

Theology and church coffers connect even more directly in "prosperity theology," which preaches that donations made to churches are actually investments that will be repaid many times over. In a single generation, Pentecostals replaced their traditional antimaterialist message with one that promised not just spiritual salvation but financial salvation—payable, of course, in weekly installments. For neo-Pentecostals such as Oral Roberts, Creflo Dollar, Joel Osteen, and T. D. Jakes, the almighty dollar became a sign of the Almighty's favor, much as wealth signaled membership in the elect for Calvinists. The difference was that the Pentecostal preachers portrayed themselves as the only proper intermediary between donors and the material bounty certain to follow.[35] Unsurprisingly, prosperity theologies have grown quickly, spreading into Brazil via the Universal Church of the Kingdom of God,[36] the Philippines through the Catholic El Shaddai movement,[37] and South Korea in the form of the Heavenly Touch Ministries.[38] Although originally pitched to poor African Americans and Latinos, who disproportionately believe that personal income is a function of God's will,[39] prosperity theology has recently found followers among America's growing population of creativity workers eager as much for fame (and hence job security) as for fortune.[40]

To point to the obviously self-serving nature of a theology that claims "the more you give, the more God promises in return" is not to deny that acolytes do not receive services in return (including hope or empowerment),[41] but it does suggest that to fully understand theology one must understand the reasons that church leaders stress one message over others. Many evangelicals remain uneasy with the tenets of prosperity theology and reject the notion that there is a direct link between business success and faith. Ironically, however, if those evangelicals do not donate enough, church leaders may find it desirable to preach prosperity anyway to lure in acolytes more willing to give often and generously.[42]

To link theological tenets to church coffers in a convincing, comprehensive, or at least systematic way, a researcher would have to understand both theology and church financing and to follow carefully how they coevolved over time. The role of endowments would also have to be carefully evaluated. Like universities, churches have incentives to accumulate income-generating assets to protect themselves from recessions and other economic shocks as well as to create revenue streams independent of the weekly collection plate. Thus insulated from the pressures of even monopolistic competition, such institutions can adhere to dead languages and defunct social theories in direct proportion to the size of their investment incomes. The Catholic and Mormon churches come immediately to mind, but may the religion without significant assets to protect cast the first aspersion. After World War II, for example, to help pay salaries, the Church of England replaced low-yielding assets, such as agricultural property, with more remunerative commercial and office developments. It has since shifted many of its assets from Britain to the United States and its investment strategies have become nearly indistinguishable from those of similarly sized financial intermediaries.[43] The leaders of one (unfortunately unidentified) church group presumably calculated that maintaining high returns on the group's investment portfolio was a safer strategy for them individually than winning acolytes, and accolades, for their church by lending to developers interested in building desegregated housing tracts. They explained to researchers "that FHA-insured mortgages were unacceptable because of interest-rate limitations: 'We must earn a maximum return on investments.' The committee also stated that the trustees were not in a position to invest money on the basis of social concern if it conflicted with sound investment policies."[44]

One irony of the church group's position was that, as a U.S.-based religious organization, it did not have to pay taxes on its investment income, so it could have taken on additional risk or accepted a lower return and still matched market benchmarks. While one might hope that churches would make socially responsible investments, and many do[45] (as when the World Council of Churches divested from South Africa because of apartheid),[46] it is not a requirement for the tax exemption, which also covers most other church revenues. Rooted in First Amendment protections of religious freedom, the tax exemption is salutary on balance, but it, along with the secrecy with which churches can invest, has long attracted to the "industry" leaders seemingly more interested in profits than prophets.[47]

More than a century ago in tiny Epiphany, South Dakota, for example, a defrocked Catholic priest named William Kroeger used his reputation as a faith healer to launch a quack health clinic and patent medicine factory that made big bucks, inadvertently healing some but speeding others to the afterlife, before Kroeger himself met his Maker in 1904.[48] The most notorious recent example of a religious organization behaving like a for-profit enterprise I refrain from mentioning by name for fear of being sued, or worse, but its investment portfolio is reputedly valued at over $1 billion and one of the main services it provides to its acolytes bears the same name as an important accounting function. Thanks to its sizable tax-free endowment, this organization may persist, with nary a remaining acolyte, to fulfill the billion-year contracts that it signed with some of its employees.

An article published by Harvard Business School in 2001 asserted that "chances are good that someone will take offense" if anyone dared to utter "the words religion and business in one breath . . . It's a common conviction within most Western societies that the two do not and should not be mixed—ever."[49] The appearance of this book suggests that such attitudes are history, so to speak. Serious study of the business aspects of religious organizations and even theology is here, at least until the historiography cycle turns once again. Although Wilsonian consilience, which seems to require the omniscience of a deity, does not appear even on the horizon, inter- and multidisciplinary approaches to important questions and subjects are becoming increasingly common and sophisticated and proving themselves in both the business[50] and policy spheres.[51] There is no reason to expect the business of religion will be any different.

Notes

1. Edward O. Wilson, *Consilience: The Unity of Knowledge* (New York: Alfred A. Knopf, 1998), 8.
2. Ibid., 6–7.
3. Ibid., 263.
4. Ibid., 280.
5. Larry Neal and Jeffrey Williamson, eds. *The Cambridge History of Capitalism* (New York: Cambridge University Press, 2014); *The History of Capitalism Initiative*, http://hoc.ilr.cornell.edu; *Program on the Study of Capitalism*, http://studyofcapitalism.harvard.edu/home; *History of Capitalism*, http://www.historyofcapitalism.net; Jennifer Schuessler, "In History Departments, It's Up with Capitalism," *New York Times*, April 6, 2013.
6. Edward E. Baptist, *The Half Has Never Been Told: Slavery and the Making of American Capitalism* (New York: Basic Books, 2014); Robin Blackburn, *The American Crucible: Slavery, Emancipation and Human Rights* (New York: Verso, 2013); Sharon Murphy, *Investing in Life: Insurance in Antebellum America* (Baltimore: Johns Hopkins University Press, 2010); Calvin Schermerhorn, *The Business of Slavery and the Rise of American Capitalism, 1815–1860* (New Haven: Yale University Press, 2015); Robert E. Wright, *The Poverty of Slavery: How Unfree Labor Pollutes the Economy* (New York: Palgrave, 2017).
7. Philip Goff, "Revivals and Revolution: Historiographic Turns Since Alan Heimert's *Religion and the American Mind*," *Church History* 67, no. 4 (December 1998): 695–721; John F. Wilson, *Religion and the American Nation: Historiography*

and History (Athens: University of Georgia Press, 2003); Kevin M. Schultz and Paul Harvey, "Everywhere and Nowhere: Recent Trends in American Religious History and Historiography," *Journal of the American Academy of Religion* 78, no. 1 (2010): 129–162.

8. Classics from earlier waves of interest in business and economic matters influencing religious leaders include Liston Pope, *Mill Hands and Preachers: A Study of Gastonia* (New Haven: Yale University Press, 1942) and Paul E. Johnson, *A Shopkeepers' Millennium: Society and Revivals in Rochester, New York, 1815–1837* (New York: Hill and Wang, 1978), as well as studies of the Men and Religion Forward movement such as Harry Lefever, "The Involvement of the Men and Religion Forward Movement in the Cause of Labor Justice, Atlanta, Georgia, 1912–1916," *Labor History* 14, no. 4 (1973): 521–535. See also Michael Shirley, *From Congregation Town to Industrial City: Culture and Social Change in a Southern Community* (New York: New York University Press, 1994), for a nuanced discussion of the interactions between Moravian congregations, evangelical religious camp meeting revivals, and business development in nineteenth-century North Carolina.

9. Jon Butler, "The Future of American Religious History: Prospectus, Agenda, Transatlantic *Problématique*," *William and Mary Quarterly* 42, no. 2 (April 1985): 167–183.

10. *The Churching of America, 1776–1990: Winners and Losers in Our Religious Economy* (New Brunswick, NJ: Rutgers University Press, 1992), by sociologists Roger Finke and Rodney Stark, also deserves mention, though I believe it was somewhat less influential because less carefully done. One important reviewer, for example, found the authors "sloppy with their language and loose with their pronouncements" and believed their argument a victim of the *post hoc, ergo propter hoc* fallacy. The same reviewer lauded Moore for carrying "readers into several virtually uncharted areas" and other virtues. Stephen J. Stein, "Buyer Beware! Provocative Literature," *American Studies* 36, no. 2 (Fall 1995): 119–125. Finke and Stark were also chastised for ignoring the finer points of theology. Bryan F. Le Beau, "Why Upstarts Win in America: Religion in the Market Place," *American Studies* 36, no. 2 (Fall 1995): 111–117.

11. Harry S. Stout and Robert M. Taylor Jr., "Studies of Religion in American Society: The State of the Art," in *New Directions in American Religious History*, ed. Harry S. Stout and D. B. Hart (New York: Oxford University Press, 1997), 15–47, quotation on 35.

12. R. Stephen Warner, "Review," *Church History* 68, no. 1 (March 1999): 233–235.

13. John A. Coleman, "Review," *Journal of the Scientific Study of Religion* 39, no. 2 (June 2000): 256–257.

14. For a readable overview of the public choice literature, see Dennis C. Mueller, "Public Choice: An Introduction," in *The Encyclopedia of Public Choice*, ed. Charles

K. Rowley and Friedrich Schneider (New York: Kluwer Academic Publishers, 2004), 32–48.

15. By contrast, public choice theory has long since been applied to social work. See, for example, Michael B. Katz, *In the Shadow of the Poorhouse: A Social History of Social Welfare in America* (New York: Basic Books, 1986). "In the end," Katz wrote, "the reformers' path to professionalism tied the management of social change to the development of their own careers" (170).

16. Rodney Stark, "Economics of Religion," in *The Blackwell Companion to the Study of Religion*, ed. Robert E. Segal (Malden, MA: Blackwell, 2006), 47–68; Laurence Iannaccone, "Introduction to the Economics of Religion," *Journal of Economic Literature* 36, no. 1 (September 1998): 1465–1496; Sriya Iyer, "The New Economics of Religion," *Journal of Economic Literature* 54, no. 2 (2016): 395–441.

17. Edward Stringham, *Private Governance: Creating Order in Economic and Social Life* (New York: Oxford University Press, 2015); Peter Schuck, *Why Government Fails So Often: And How It Can Do Better* (Princeton: Princeton University Press, 2014).

18. Barbara Tuchman, *The March of Folly: From Troy to Vietnam* (New York: Knopf, 1984).

19. Gary Anderson, "Mr. Smith and the Preachers: The Economics of Religion in the Wealth of Nations," *Journal of Political Economy* 96, no. 5 (October 1988): 1066–1088.

20. Adam Smith, *An Inquiry into the Nature and Causes of the Wealth of Nations*, Book V, Chapter 1, Part III, Article 3, "On the Expense of the Institutions for the Instruction of People of All Ages."

21. Like "philosophical banker" Alexander Bryan Johnson, who told his father-in-law and second president of the United States, John Adams, that he would "rejoice to see everywhere a toleration in which the mosque and the synagogue, the pagoda and the church, should be harmoniously located alongside of each other" because if any one "denomination of Christians" became "sufficiently numerous to control," he feared, they "would not have charity or philosophy enough to tolerate dissenters." Charles L. Todd and Robert Sonkin, *Alexander Bryan Johnson: Philosophical Banker* (Syracuse, NY: Syracuse University Press, 1977), 120.

22. Horace Miner, "Body Ritual Among the Nacirema," *American Anthropologist* 58, no. 3 (June 1956): 503–507.

23. Joan Robinson, *The Economics of Imperfect Competition* (London: Macmillan, 1933); Edward Chamberlin, *The Theory of Monopolistic Competition* (Cambridge, MA: Harvard University Press, 1933).

24. Leonard P. Curry, *The Free Black in Urban America, 1800–1850: The Shadow of the Dream* (Chicago: University of Chicago Press, 1981), 184.

25. Peter B. Orlik, *Electronic Media Criticism: Applied Perspectives*, 2nd ed. (London: Lawrence Erlbaum Associates, 2001), 367.

26. Gale Cincotta and Arthur J. Naparstek, *Urban Disinvestment: New Implications for Community Organization, Research and Public Policy* (Washington, DC: National Center for Urban Ethnic Affairs, 1976), 6.

27. Jacqueline Jones, *A Dreadful Deceit: The Myth of Race from the Colonial Era to Obama's America* (New York: Basic Books, 2013), 92–93.

28. As quoted in Peter Dobkin Hall, *Inventing the Nonprofit Sector and Other Essays on Philanthropy, Voluntarism, and Nonprofit Organizations* (Baltimore: Johns Hopkins University Press, 1992), 124.

29. Arthur Raper and Ira De A. Reid, *Sharecroppers All* (Chapel Hill: University of North Carolina Press, 1941), 22–23.

30. David Brion Davis, *The Problem of Slavery in Western Culture* (Ithaca, NY: Cornell University Press, 1966); Joel Quirk, *The Anti-Slavery Project: From the Slave Trade to Human Trafficking* (Philadelphia: University of Pennsylvania Press, 2011).

31. Julia O'Connell Davidson, *Modern Slavery: The Margins of Freedom* (New York: Palgrave Macmillan, 2015).

32. Curry, *The Free Black in Urban America*, 174–195.

33. Rhoda Golden Freeman, *The Free Negro in New York City in the Era Before the Civil War* (New York: Garland Publishing, 1994), 281–304.

34. Jones, *A Dreadful Deceit*, 220.

35. Shayne Lee, "Prosperity Theology: T. D. Jakes and the Gospel of the Almighty Dollar," *CrossCurrents* 57, no. 2 (Summer 2007): 227–236.

36. Devaka Premawardhana, "Transformational Tithing: Sacrifice and Reciprocity in the a Neo-Pentecostal Church," *Nova Religio: The Journal of Alternative and Emergent Religions* 15, no. 4 (May 2012): 85–109.

37. Katharine L. Wiegele, "Catholics Rich in Spirit: El Shaddai's Modern Engagements," *Philippine Studies* 54, no. 4 (2006): 495–520.

38. Sung-Gun Kim, "The Heavenly Touch Ministry in the Age of Millennial Capitalism: A Phenomenological Perspective," *Nova Religio: The Journal of Alternative and Emergent Religions* 15, no. 3 (February 2012): 51–64.

39. Ted M. Brimeyer, "Religious Affiliation and Poverty Explanations: Individual, Structural, and Divine Causes," *Sociological Focus* 41, no. 3 (August 2008): 226–237.

40. Gerardo Marti, "Ego-Affirming Evangelicalism: How a Hollywood Church Appropriates Religion for Workers in the Creative Class," *Sociology of Religion* 71, no. 1 (Spring 2010): 52–75.

41. Premawardhana, "Transformational Tithing."

42. Shirley J. Roels, "The Business Ethics of Evangelicals," *Business Ethics Quarterly* 7, no. 2 (March 1997): 113–114.

43. C. Hamnett, "The Church's Many Mansions: The Changing Structure of the Church Commissioners Land and Property Holdings, 1948–1977," *Transactions of the Institute of British Geographers* 12, no. 4 (1987): 465–481.

44. Eunice Grier and George Grier, *Privately Developed Interracial Housing: An Analysis of Experience* (Berkeley: University of California Press, 1960), 118.

45. Peter Luxton, "Ethical Investment in Hard Times," *Modern Law Review* 55, no. 4 (July 1992): 587–593.

46. Richard E. Sincere Jr., *The Politics of Sentiment: Churches and Foreign Investment in South Africa* (Washington, DC: Ethics and Public Policy Center, 1984).

47. C. Stanley Lowell, "Church Wealth and Tax Exemptions," *Phi Delta Kappan* 50, no. 9 (May 1969): 534–537.

48. James Marten, "A Medical Entrepreneur Goes West: Father William Kroeger in South Dakota, 1893–1904," *South Dakota History* 21, no. 4 (Winter 1991): 333–361.

49. Martha Lagace, "Can Religion and Business Learn from Each Other?," *Working Knowledge: Research and Ideas,* November 12, 2001, http://hbswk.hbs.edu/item/can-religion-and-business-learn-from-each-other.

50. John Cantwell, Anke Piepenbrink, and Pallavi Shukla, "Assessing the Impact of *JIBS* as an Interdisciplinary Journal: A Network Approach," *Journal of International Business Studies* 45, no. 7 (September 2014): 787–799.

51. Catherine Lyall, Ann Bruce, Joyce Tait, and Laura Meagher, *Interdisciplinary Research Journeys: Practical Strategies for Capturing Creativity* (New York: Bloomsbury Academic, 2011); Linda Hantrais, Ashley Thomas Lenihan, and Susanne MacGregor, "Evidence-Based Policy: Exploring International and Interdisciplinary Insights," *Contemporary Social Science: Journal of the Academy of Social Sciences* 10, no. 2 (2015): 101–113.

Contributors

Michael J. Altman
Assistant Professor of Religious
Studies, University of Alabama

Matthew Bowman
Associate Professor of History,
Henderson State University

John Corrigan
Lucius Moody Bristol Distinguished
Professor of Religion and Professor
of History, Florida State University

Deborah Skolnick Einhorn
Associate Dean of Jewish Education,
Hebrew College

Timothy E. W. Gloege
Independent scholar

Darren E. Grem
Assistant Professor of History and
Southern Studies, University of
Mississippi

James Hudnut-Beumler
Anne Potter Wilson
Distinguished Professor of
American Religious History,
Vanderbilt University

Paula M. Kane
Professor and Marous Chair of Catholic
Studies, University of Pittsburgh

David P. King
Assistant Professor of Philanthropy
and Religious Studies, Indiana
University–Purdue University in
Indianapolis

Amanda Porterfield
Robert A. Spivey
Professor of Religion and
Professor of History,
Florida State University

Angela Tarango
Associate Professor of Religion,
Trinity University

Daniel Vaca
Assistant Professor of Religious
Studies, Brown University

Robert E. Wright
Nef Family Chair of Political
Economy and Director of the
Thomas Willing Institute for
the Study of Financial Markets,
Institutions, and Regulations,
Augustana University,
South Dakota

Introduction

THE BUSINESS TURN IN
AMERICAN RELIGIOUS HISTORY

Amanda Porterfield, John Corrigan, and Darren E. Grem

FOUNDER OF THE world's most profitable company, Steve Jobs did not pinch pennies or care mainly about money. Notoriously cavalier about cost, he insisted that circuit boards sealed inside Apple computers be beautifully laid out. He installed staircases designed by I. M. Pei in company buildings and demanded perfectly spaced, white-toned interiors. Picky about material objects, he lived for years in a house with almost no furniture. A self-proclaimed artist with a revolutionary vision for the world, Jobs wedded the groundbreaking utility of computers to a simple aesthetic that made computers seem natural and inviting. The design of Apple's Macintosh computer derived from the friendly presence of the sunflowers his wife planted in their backyard, with big open faces leaning out over their stems.[1]

Jobs developed his highly profitable aesthetic through the study of Asian art, engagement with Buddhist and Hindu teachings, and hallucinogenic experiences he credited with opening him to spiritual enlightenment. After studying calligraphy at Reed College, he became an early member of the Los Altos Zen Center and a longtime student of the Soto Zen priest Kobun Chino. On many visits to Japan, he admired the curated naturalism of the Kyoto gardens, calling them "the most sublime thing I've ever seen." As his vision for computers developed, Jobs imagined himself as a kind of high-tech samurai fighting against the dark power and suffocating aesthetic he thought IBM represented. And like other Bay Area Californians of his generation, Job's appreciation of Asian spirituality was eclectic, not limited to Japanese Zen. He toured India seeking insight from Hindu teachers and often returned to a book that had inspired him as a teenager, Paramahansa Yogananda's *Autobiography of a Yogi*. When Jobs died in 2011, attendees at his memorial service received copies of the book.[2]

Steve Jobs is one spectacular example of the complementarity between religion and American business described in this volume. If his ambition to revolutionize the world exceeded that of many entrepreneurs, the interpenetration of religious aesthetics and business acumen he exemplified was not so unusual. His contemporaries at International Business Machines may not have admired Yogananda or sought enlightenment through LSD, but many of them revered the vision of IBM promoted by Thomas J. Watson, the company's strict Methodist founder. Dubbed "the world's greatest salesman," Watson imbued his company with principles of moral integrity derived from his religion, with a dynamic mix of commitment to individual responsibility and centralized organization similar to that of his Methodist Church. As his father's successor as head of IBM and a great admirer of military organization, Thomas J. Watson Jr. restructured the company during the Cold War into corporate divisions under central command. He also codified the three core "beliefs" that made IBM great, beginning with a "respect for the individual" that the younger Watson called "bone deep" in his father. Upholding a secular variant of Trinitarian doctrine, IBM promised respect for individual employees, service to customers exceeding that of other companies, and "insistence on perfection" in the fulfillment of every task.[3]

IBM's reputation for dynamic growth declined during the 1980s, at the same time that America's enormous denominational churches began their decline in wealth and membership. In 1993, in an outburst of free market pique, the *Wall Street Journal* even complained that the company had succumbed to the dull, bureaucratic mentality of "Soviet-style central planning." But at the apex of its greatness in the 1950s and 1960s, IBM stood out as a leading exemplar of the powerful combination of pragmatism and business ethics that typified—and continues to typify—many aspects of economic and religious life in the United States.[4]

The essays in this volume approach the complementarity between religion and business by examining the business side of religious organizations. Considering business activities supporting religion that historians of religion often overlook, these essays explore the financing, production, marketing, and distribution of religious goods and services such as worship, charity, philanthropy, and missionary work. Illustrating the role of business in a variety of different religious traditions, this volume lays important groundwork for understanding the parity and symmetry between religious and business life in America, opening the way for further study of religious elements in businesses such as Apple and IBM.

The interdependence between Christian religions and commercial activity in North America dates to the earliest days of European exploration and colonization. In the sixteenth century, Christian missionaries accompanied explorers seeking gold and trade routes through the continent. With religion operating as an arm of imperial authority, mercantilist nations sought to accumulate wealth by importing goods, acquiring new territories, and protecting trade within imperial territories from rivals. Through a variety of different legal and political arrangements in the seventeenth century, European powers established colonies in the New World that harnessed ambitions for material and spiritual gain.

In the thirteen colonies that eventually became the United States, commercial enterprises sustained religious community, and religion operated as a disciplinary force for commerce. With religious institutions and policies operating as extensions of government, colonists expected religion to be involved in government efforts to regulate commerce. When entrepreneurs ventured beyond direct government oversight, colonists found that religious affiliation could enhance business. Huguenots in British America built commercial alliances with Anglicans across several colonies. Quakers built their reputation for honest enterprise by engaging in business arrangements as "Friends."[5]

Religion and commerce changed together in colonial America, with developments in each area supporting developments in the other. Enlightenment theories about the rational order of the world dovetailed with growing enthusiasm for free trade and with rationalist trends in religion, lending support for economic theories about an invisible hand at work in free markets. Similarly, an upsurge in demand for consumer goods in the American colonies coincided with the growing popularity of traveling ministers, as the market revolution of the 1740s dovetailed with the rise of evangelicalism and the breakdown of parish boundaries. Communal bonds weakened over time as individualistic behavior became more acceptable, but religion and commerce changed together in this historical process, with developments in religious belief and practice stimulating commercial development as well as justifying it. As historian Mark Valeri showed in an important study of religion and commerce in colonial New England, government regulation of selling loosened over time in colonial New England as the religious status of successful merchants increased, along with trust in their moral virtue.[6]

In the decades following the American Revolution, lawmakers reworked this complementarity between religion and commerce by formulating ground rules to encompass both that enabled them to develop more symmetrically. Revising colonial systems at the state level and constructing an entirely new federal government, American lawmakers confirmed the centrality of contract law, clarifying the legal status of both religious and commercial organizations to ground these two arenas of civic life on much the same legal footing. As self-governing private entities, operating under contractual agreements protected by law, religion and business continued to influence each other, but more through informal horizontal sharing and less through the vertical authority of state-established religion. The new dispensation of legal parity between religion and commerce facilitated innovation in both spheres and reciprocity between the two.

A further reworking of the relationship of religion to commerce followed. Though still subject to expectations that they serve the common good, organizations in both realms increasingly defined that good in terms of their own interests. Thus advocates for business expansion in early nineteenth-century America claimed that new industries served the common good simply by virtue of their economic productivity. This shift in expectation meant that direct correlations between business expansion and responsibility for public welfare, such as increasing or even preserving public access to water, fell away. Evolving along a similar trajectory, early nineteenth-century religious groups enjoyed protection as presumed sources of civic welfare increasingly independent of state government, while diversity and competition among religious groups intensified, often at the expense of social harmony.[7]

Early decisions by the U.S. Supreme Court appealed to contract law to support both private commercial enterprise and the autonomy of eleemosynary institutions, including churches, as private organizations. In a dispute between the state of New Hampshire and the trustees of Dartmouth College, the trustees contested the state's takeover of the college, appealing to the college charter, issued in 1769 by King George III, as a charitable institution. In the 1819 ruling that confirmed the sanctity of contracts and denied the state's act to seize Dartmouth as a public institution, Chief Justice John Marshall affirmed the legality of the private institution established by the contract of the original charter: "An artificial immortal being was created by the Crown, capable of receiving and distributing forever, according to the will of the donors, the donations which should be made to it." While precedents for Marshall's respect for contracts existed in British common law, the evacuation of monarchical authority in the new American republic heightened the implications of that respect. In the absence of other authority, Marshall's decision "confirmed the supremacy of liberal contract-law doctrine in all of the United States," according to legal historian Mark McGarvie. "Once expressed as the supreme law of the land, these ideological and legal principles" separating public and private institutions "could then govern the design of American civil society."[8]

Thus the new legal system disestablishing religion and separating church and state also confirmed the sanctity of contract law, and in so doing, made religious and business organizations more similar to each other than in the past. As the church's role as an arm of the state withered, religion's role as a form of free enterprise expanded, opening give-and-take between religion and commerce, stimulating innovative forms of outreach and marketing in both arenas, and blurring the boundaries between sacred and profane. Through the legal status they came to share as private organizations, business and religious organizations became free to operate as parallel forms of private enterprise, with contracts protected by the state.

By the time of the *Dartmouth* decision in 1819, the expansion of evangelical organizations was already well under way. An early sign of explosive growth in both supply and demand for religion in the first decade of the nineteenth century, a mass rally in 1801 at Cane Ridge, Kentucky, drew thousands of people, with eighteen Presbyterian preachers vying with Methodists and Baptists for converts, calling sinners to Christ from log stands or the backs of wagons with promises of salvation. In regions famous for partisan conflict and territorial disputes, camp meetings signaled a new era of social formation along denominational lines.[9]

The Methodist Church expanded greatly in this competitive environment, becoming the fastest-growing and most broadly inclusive religious organization in the country. Methodists reached out to blacks and women, excluded from many forms of political participation, advancing their religious organization through innovative exercises in singing and prayer, attention to poor and dislocated people in urban areas, and ministers who traveled to new settlements on horseback in monthly circuits. With a commitment to individual participants, service to others, and demand for perfection that Thomas J. Watson inherited and developed later at IBM, Methodists succeeded through an effective combination of small group participation and overarching, hierarchical governance.[10]

Organizational innovation in the early Republic continued in the period following the War of 1812. Especially during the presidency of Andrew Jackson (1829–1837), the rapid development of commerce and finance brought precipitous change with consequences for religion. The swings in social and class demographics and the advent of a puissant language of trade led to fresh conceptualizations of the religious body as an organizational unit and to new understandings of how a religious organization could be secured in a changing world. Whether we take the early nineteenth-century coalescence of key market components to be what historian Charles Sellers termed a "revolution" that tore up valuable social institutions and customs like a tornado cutting unpredictably and uncontrollably through the countryside or, as Daniel Walker Howe and John Lauritz Larson have proposed, as an invention somewhat more susceptible to human steering, it is clear that the materializing market of scale profoundly affected religion.[11]

Religious groups in some cases drew explicitly upon financing models and organizational blueprints arising from the development of business, and in other cases explicitly rejected them. In a few instances groups did both. For some, the breakneck expansion of commerce, including the integration of industrial farming, labor, the factory system (including its "mill girls"), and the machineries of capital management and lending signaled the imminent collapse of a ruined world. Groups such as the early Mormons, Millerites, Shakers, and various revivalist followings imagined membership in a heavenly kingdom apart from the dirty business of business. Other groups, while less millennial, likewise sought refuge in communalism, trading what they deemed the worsening rational-legal strictures of a society hypnotized by commerce for the bucolic, seemingly more fluid, and nostalgic setting of Oneida (New York), Economy (Pennsylvania), Brook Farm (Massachusetts), or the Amana Colonies (Iowa). There they experimented with self-sufficiency and new models of social order, often while denouncing the acids of capitalism. Ironically, they sometimes proved the salutary effects of an intertwining of business with religious communalism. By the time of their demise, Oneida had built a silverware business into one of the oldest corporations in the nation, and the Rappites at Economy had established an integrated economy of factories and processing plants that manufactured textiles and whiskey, engaged in international commerce, and proved such a business success that by the 1850s they were able to make large investments in railroads, oil wells, and mines. Even the millennialist Mormons early on played with the possibilities of constructing themselves partly as a business, forming in 1837 the Kirtland Safety Society, a joint stock company in Ohio—although its immediate failure prompted Joseph Smith to flee Kirtland under threat of mob violence. The revivalistic stylings Charles Grandison Finney unleashed upon Rochester in 1830, while millenarian, similarly led to an evangelical plan of church growth that historian Paul Johnson has characterized as a calculated process relying on artisans, merchants, and other entrepreneurs organizing to bankroll churches in poor communities. Historian R. Laurence Moore has filled in some of the story here by pointing out that it was during this time that religion in America transitioned to a matter of "selling God," something that continued for decades afterward. Entrepreneurs increasingly took religion as a commodity that could be pitched to an audience much the way entertainments such as books, theater, lectures, and other performances were.[12]

Those who stayed in the cities joined religion to business in other ways. Most impressive among the many antebellum performances of that collaboration was the Businessmen's Revival. In the wake of the financial crash of 1857, many cities experienced a Protestant religious revival distinguished by the unusually robust participation of businessmen. Leaving their offices for noontime gatherings, the men participated in prayer meetings built around personal requests for help (often written on slips of paper and deposited in a box at the commencement of services) and around collective prayer undertaken to hasten divine delivery of that help. The revival incorporated explicit language about contractual relationships with God, spiritual capital and its investment, the rationality of providence, the predictability of consequences, the economics of faith, and other linguistic signifiers of business activity and market awareness. It advanced the construction of a more comprehensive vision of a religious corporation by providing concepts that bridged the notion of church as a community of believers and the idiom of church as a business organized along rational-legal lines.[13]

The nascent Gospel of Wealth elaborated ideas incubated during the Businessmen's Revival. The gradual but relentless infusion of Enlightenment ideas about laws of nature and social order into the mainstream of American Protestantism produced a view of religion and business as intrinsically joined. When revivalist Presbyterian preacher Francis Poage Hunt explained in *The Book of Wealth* (1836) that "no man can be obedient to God's will, as revealed in the Bible, without . . . becoming wealthy," and Baptist minister Francis Wayland spoke to a Providence congregation in 1837 about "the moral law of accumulation," they captured the mood of one end of the antebellum Protestant spectrum with regard to religion, money, and the role of business. Russell Conwell's *Acres of Diamonds* (1870s) and Andrew Carnegie's *Gospel of Wealth* (1889) subsequently not only refined the argument about the brilliant prospects of the Christian businessman but also fueled optimism for the future of the business of religion itself. In 1869 the *Methodist Quarterly*

Review already had acknowledged: "The Church has become a vast business organization." It was manifest then that Methodists were "acting in harmony with providence when we are seeking to combine into one grand working unity all the spirituality, wisdom, wealth, and business ability of Methodism." By the 1880s the notion of a church as an organization that systematically managed quantifiable material assets in conjunction with managing its spiritual business was well established.[14]

Washington Gladden, a Social Gospel leader whose views of religion, capitalism, and business differed from those of Conwell and Carnegie, nevertheless favored a similar view of the church as an organization that integrated the financial with the spiritual. The "church, as an organization, is constantly entering into contracts," he observed, noting that the late nineteenth-century call to "Christianize business" had its reciprocal other in the churches' clarifying the business of religion. Discussing the "business of the mart" and the "business of the church," Gladden concluded that when the financial management of the church was conducted on Christian principles, it amounted to "no less genuine Christian work than is the conduct of the prayer meeting or teaching of the Sunday school." Church treasurers and trustees "may also put so much the spirit of Christ into the methods of church business that it shall be a means of grace to them and to the whole brotherhood."[15]

As James Hudnut-Beumler has pointed out, Protestant churches "reinvented" the tithe during the mid-nineteenth century, transitioning to the practice of stewardship in the early twentieth century. Gladden, Josiah Strong, John Wesley Duncan's *Christian Stewardship* (1910), and especially Harvey Reeves Calkins's *A Man and His Money* (1914) all played a role. All contributed components to the argument for tithing while also formulating a view of stewardship as the allocation of resources not only to maintenance of the local community but also to evangelical outreach, especially abroad. That important step—envisioning the church as a business with global reach—was crucial to the development of the idea of the Protestant church as an international business organization in the twentieth century.[16]

Roman Catholicism well before the foundation of the United States had a suite of ecclesiastical directories to oversee the financial affairs of the Church. Moreover, church resources long had been strategically applied to global proselytization. In America, once the problems of the shortage of clergy and unreliable trusteeship had been overcome—and the neofeudal structuring of early Catholic Maryland reformed—the Roman models for church organization were systematically implemented. From the mid-nineteenth century onward, through the initiatives of Pio Nono and others in Rome, the financial structure of the Church was refined and the flow of money broadened by reinventions of old charitable customs such as Peter's Pence as well as by new emphasis on weekly giving. Roman Catholicism in America distinguished itself by its organizational efficiency, scale, and coordination top to bottom. As John Beal has observed, the strong emphasis on centralization in the business model of the nineteenth-century Catholic Church in America established the priority of diocesan "administration" over diocesan "governance." From the time of the Third Plenary Council in Baltimore in 1884 and forward through a succession of initiatives in the early twentieth century, the Catholic Church increasingly came to picture its role as a "central service bureaucracy" rooted in an "ecclesial corporate culture."[17]

During the nineteenth century, and especially after the Civil War, many black churches were founded. The intertwining of spirituality and commercial enterprise within African American Christianity, vigorous and explicit, was visible immediately. The entrepreneurial approach of African Americans to church founding—gathering people, often from white-led churches, to build communities where certain styles of worship could be practiced, a sense of belonging fostered, and commitments made to equality and justice—had its counterpart in the business initiatives of the churches. From the nineteenth century onward, black churches served as launching points for commercial ventures large and small. Booker T. Washington's National Negro Business League, partially funded by Andrew Carnegie, in the early twentieth century brought together business leaders and clergy with a view to advancing economic progress through church-managed commercial projects. Over the course of the twentieth century and into the twenty-first, the "prosperity gospel" emerged most impressively within black churches that had matured against that entrepreneurial background. The practical and ideological mingling of business and religion in African American churches, as well as in popular expressions of religious belief—as historian Kathryn Lofton has shown in writing about Oprah Winfrey—are deeply rooted in the details of African American religious history.[18]

Because of the Great Depression, many churches were thrust into more clearly defined roles as service organizations. Groups across the denominational spectrum stepped in to address the material needs of the poor, unemployed, and homeless. The spirit of the earlier Social Gospel informed much of the work done by Jewish and Christian groups during this time. However, New Deal spending on social programs eventually crowded out church efforts, leading to substantial declines in religious expenditures for social programs and less financial wherewithal for religious organizations generally as memberships plummeted. For historian Kevin Kruse, the ripening opposition of many Americans, especially in the South, to New Deal policies that appeared to undermine business initiative, hard work, and unregulated capitalism was harnessed by the business community to the advance of their own interests. Making "one nation, under God" came to mean an even more powerful joining, at the level of ideology, of religion to business, through corporations' promotion of religious values and virtues that could be exploited in service to capitalist economics and consumerism.[19]

Although the social tumult of the 1960s registered some opposition to the braiding of religion with business, the notion of a religious body as a corporate venture continued to develop in most denominations. The overweening efforts of white middle-class Americans during the 1950s to conform to a vision of shared religious and cultural frameworks—typified by the social behavior of the "man in the gray flannel suit"—gave way to tie-dyed T-shirts and criticism of "worldly" religion. Beatnik literature previously had cast spirituality and business as diametric opposites, and the hippies, seekers, and spiritual adventurers who subsequently migrated from urban to rural settings did so as much to escape the gravity of corporate culture as to invest in alternative religious styles. Multiracial Christian communes of the 1960s, for example, shared some of the visions of the abovementioned nineteenth-century analogues but were significantly more antithetical to organized commercial enterprise than their forebears. In spite of such acts of protest, which were short-lived for obvious reasons, the integration of business and religion continued, and the 1970s ushered in a period of coordination previously unseen in America. As it matured, the coordination of business and religion was driven partially by the growing ambitions of religious groups to project themselves overseas. With its sharp focus on fund-raising for missions and its aspirations to international influence, the global project—for Christian evangelicals, Mormons, African American religious bodies, Catholics, and others—was a key gear in the machinery driving the late twentieth-century corporatization of religion.[20]

The founding of the Willow Creek Church outside of Chicago in 1975 represented how thinking about religion and thinking about business were interwoven in the practical activity of Christian worship, evangelization, and social organizing. Bill Hybels, the founder of the church, collected data on people's religious likes and dislikes through a door-to-door survey. He then fashioned a product in response to that data. Keeping in mind the corporate culture of bedroom communities in suburban Chicago, he embarked on a project that eventuated in the construction of an office park—for religion. In an auditorium lacking religious iconography and fitted with state-of-the-art sound boards and lighting systems, and tuned to the feelings and priorities of a white corporate culture, Willow Creek religion both embodied and fostered a realization that religion was business and could be advanced as such.

Willow Creek's location in South Barrington, an affluent suburb northwest of Chicago, also signaled the arrival of a new landscape for religion and business. The suburbanization of American religion first began in the late nineteenth century but revved up after World War II. For the most part, suburbia was a majority-white zone of social, commercial, and religious enterprise. Urban cores, increasingly poorer and nonwhite due to a combination of residential "white flight" and cost-effective "business flight" to the suburbs, became symbolic and actual landscapes of social exclusion and economic deprivation. Religious interpreters of the midcentury American Dream, such as Norman Vincent Peale, granted Cold War capitalism a soft-focus soul. Peale's *The Power of Positive Thinking* (1952) was a best seller, and millions read his weekly newspaper columns on how positive thinking supposedly secured material, spiritual, emotional, and social well-being. Billy Graham, far and away the most public and influential religious figure in postwar American life, updated the corporate evangelicalism of the Businessmen's Revival, D. L. Moody, and Aimee Semple McPherson for a postwar audience. Graham used savvy marketing to promote stadium-filling "crusades" that attracted the support of media bigwigs and Wall Street insiders. Both Peale and Graham enjoyed close relationships with dozens of businessmen who supported their gospels of Cold War capitalism. Many of the same businessmen served as intermediaries between the anti–New Deal business conservatives of the 1930s and 1940s and the business-backed "new American right" of the 1960s and 1970s.[21]

As historians Lisa McGirr and Darren Dochuk have shown, suburbanization laid the groundwork for the emergence of a politicized conservative Christianity that favored privatization, antistatism, and lower taxes. But countercultural sentiments also shaped right-wing religious politics and consumerism. The Jesus People, a movement of younger, mostly white evangelicals captured by the religious implications of countercultural "rebellion" and identification, forged the musical and material culture of late twentieth-century evangelicalism. An evangelical-led market in "Christian" consumer goods emerged soon thereafter in the 1970s, attracting buyers by the millions and, more recently, the investments and support of evangelical businessmen (such as Lee Atsinger and Stuart Epperson of Salem Communications, whose holdings today include dozens of Christian radio stations) and nonevangelical businessmen (such as Rupert Murdoch of NewsCorp, which owns Zondervan, a major evangelical book and Bible publisher). Thousands of evangelical small business owners served as the new purveyors of faith-based enterprise, advertising their wares and services in alternative directories such as *The Christian Yellow Pages* while linking the profit margin to public identification against social and political liberalism. Questions of "What Would Jesus Do?" in the consumerist ethos of Christian bookstores, Christian record labels, and Christian televangelism largely came with a simple and alluring answer: Jesus would buy goods and services marked and marketed as "Christian," not only as a means of privately affirming one's faith but as a way of publicly representing it.

Enterprising television and radio stars also redefined the experience of religion and joined consumerism to conservative cultural politics. Empowered by changes in federal laws regarding paid-time and public-service on-air programming, white televangelists Pat Robertson, Jim and Tammy Faye Bakker, and Jimmy Swaggart—later joined by black televangelists such as T. D. Jakes—built media empires fueled by millions of dollars in donations from like-minded devotees. Service companies, such as ServiceMaster, Walmart, and Chick-fil-A, similarly represented the conjoining of Christian profit to Christian labor, with the pursuit of the former through the disciplining and direction of the latter. Evangelical financial counselors (such as Larry Burkett), corporate "leadership" gurus (such as John Maxwell), and revivalistic inspirational speakers (such as Zig Ziglar) affirmed the union of Christian business and Christian striving. Prosperity preachers from Oral Roberts to Joel Osteen coupled economic well-being to Pentecostal measures of transcendence. Along with dramatic physical healing or positive self-image, a gradual or dramatic bump in one's paycheck equated the blessed life for millions of believers in the American prosperity gospel.[22]

In the 1970s, derivative lessons regarding work, drawn from various religious traditions, supplemented race and gender as measures of access and improvement in corporate America. Thanks to the civil rights and women's rights movements, explicit barriers to employment and executive offices faltered as each came under increasing state purview. The "opening of the American workplace," as Nancy MacLean has put it, did not end discrimination against racial minorities or women, but it did create a new context for what work and business could or should mean in American private and public life. Changes in the regulatory environment on matters of race and gender coincided with the corporate embrace of non-Christian religions, thereby laying the legal groundwork for corporate religious pluralism. A late-stage religious disestablishment in corporate America, encouraged by state laws barring discrimination and federal law via Title VII of the Civil Rights Act of 1964, undercut implicit and explicit forms of Protestant privilege in American business life. If one aspired to bring faith into the workplace, then a wider array of faiths seemed to promise new meaning(s) for corporate work beyond the Protestant ethic. Exposure to Asian religions was particularly poignant for some corporate executives and business writers. For instance, Robert Pirsig's bestselling *Zen and the Art of Motorcycle Maintenance* (1974) joined Greek philosophical reflections regarding the primacy of end-product quality in high-tech and low-tech work to simplified Buddhist teachings on mindful awareness. Work of any kind, in Pirsig's assessment, was more meditative than redemptive. Like Buddhist meditation, remaining fully present and focused on the job was the key to personal fulfilment in the private sector.[23]

In the 1970s and 1980s, the American business—large, midsized, or small—had become yet another site where the twin movements toward a more pluralistic and "spiritual but not religious" America aligned, not surprisingly at the moment the New Deal order fell apart and the neoliberal persuasion took hold. Evangelicals also crafted their own take on "Christian free enterprise" in the small towns and suburban communities of the Sunbelt as an emerging service economy melded low-church revivalism with Jeffersonian populism in the aisles and checkout lines of companies such as Walmart. Walmart's populist auspices depended on the infusion of new corporate theories, particularly Robert Greenleaf's advocacy of "servant leadership." First promoted in a 1970 essay of the same name, "servant leadership" advocated that "greatness"—in any organization, but especially in the private sector—was ensured when the servant leader made "sure that other people's highest priority needs are being served." Greenleaf was hardly original in his thinking about employee well-being or corporate social responsibility. Supported by the National Council of Churches, the nation's foremost liberal Protestant body, Howard R. Bowen's *Social Responsibilities of the Businessman* (1953) advocated social stewardship on the part of blue-chip corporate executives and small businessmen alike. So too did Peter Drucker, the postwar era's most influential managerial theorist. Drucker viewed the corporation as a new form of community in American life, one imbued with a mission to do the most good possible. Taken together, such academic and popular writers reframed corporate executives as "leaders" or "stewards" of society, and, therefore, hardly the authoritarians of Carnegie's age. Disciples of "social stewardship" or "servant leadership" ideally sought cults of beneficent corporate personality, inspiring the hourly employee and middle manager alike to emulate the service to employee, God, company, and country that executive stewards and servant leaders ostensibly modeled.[24]

In the 1990s, religious individuals and experiences continued to shape the cultural milieu of corporate America. Financial advisors such as the Baptist Larry Burkett taught Christianized lessons on saving and investing, while the popular writer Stephen R. Covey, a Mormon, sold millions of copies of *The 7 Habits of Highly Effective People* (1989). More broadly, in business schools and in the books lining the shelves of Barnes & Noble, business "values," "ethics," and "character" became watchwords, each supposedly based in selective readings of various religious texts. With the proliferation of the personal computer and rise of Silicon Valley, hardware and software companies at times embraced and endorsed the alignment of technological transcendence and individual faith. Steve Jobs's corporate cult of personality worked to transform his CEOship of Apple into a story of godlike genesis and revelation, with new products "appearing" seemingly ex nihilo out of his own imagination and often premiered through artful onstage productions and advertising that mirrored rituals of religious revelation and notions of the transcendentalist or Buddhist simple life. More broadly, the spread of the PC and Mac enhanced the personal, customizable experience of technology while driving American religious experience further into the hyperprivate spaces of smartphones and tablets. That debates over religion at work have grounded legal battles over "religious freedom" at companies such as Hobby Lobby and have become more prevalent at neoliberal fanfests such as Davos in Switzerland speaks to the continuing enchantment of global corporate capitalism. It also requires a new scholarship on how religion has been made in a corporate America and how corporate America has been made in a religious nation. It requires the business turn in American religious history.[25]

This business turn involves revisiting and revising scholarly discourse on the relationship between religion and business activities, ideas, places, and pursuits. Evangelical contributions to capitalist enterprise have been a prominent, if often secondary, concern of American religious historians; hence, this book's first chapters reexamine the Protestant persuasion in for-profit companies and contexts. Daniel Vaca reconsiders past debates over who counts (and doesn't) as an "evangelical" before showing that such authoritative definitions largely became commonplace through business interests and pursuits, particularly in the first evangelical enterprise of religious book publishing. Timothy E. W. Gloege traces a similar path to evangelical influence in modern American public life, detailing the creative, bottom-line aspirations of fundamentalists. Hardly world-denying ascetics or self-segregating antimodernists, fundamentalists ran headlong into the consumerist, corporatist future, building not only viable print enterprises but also a wide array of institutions and businesses. Well-branded leaders convinced millions that a newly invented "old-time religion" was not just a consumerist-religious good worth buying but a bedrock faith for any "good" political agenda. Broadening the Protestant business framework further, David P. King considers the postcolonial entanglement of American Christians—particularly Protestants of various theological and social stripes—with the post–World War II global economy. As King shows, American Christians have a multifaceted approach to global capitalism, one that includes humanitarian efforts, nongovernmental organizations, international development agencies, and "business as mission" groups.

The majority of this volume's contributors treat the business turn as an important historiographic shift for all scholars of American religion, not just scholars of American evangelicalism. American Mormons, as Matthew Bowman shows, developed a complicated theological and political relationship with American capitalism, one that included an array of ethics: communitarian, utopian, individualist, reformist, and accumulationist. The course of Jewish history suggests a similarly diverse approach to markets and the state, as Deborah Skolnick Einhorn details. Focusing primarily on Jewish women's philanthropic efforts in the early twentieth century, Einhorn presents their efforts as a form of participatory subversion, both challenging assumptions regarding male authority in Jewish communities and creating self-sufficient networks of giving and social welfare that forged a new vision of Jewish public involvement through efficient fund-raising campaigns. Michael J. Altman's study of Hindu businessmen and interests historicizes the notion of a "business guru" as capitalist mystic and grounds the emergence of "Hindu" as a religious category. Hindus in America were politicized capitalists, Altman argues, as appeals for Indian-Hindu nationalism often came through market exchanges, fund-raising, corporatism, and marketing. Angela Tarango's visit to Native American casinos in Oklahoma similarly considers how the presentation and categorization of tribal identification and religious identity operate in accordance with the pursuit of profit and a midwestern landscape of freewheeling, bet-your-bottom-dollar risk. Sacred notions of "Native American–ness" coincide with selling a tourist experience grounded in an admixture of political, ethnic, and religious sovereignty, all framed by postmodern presentations of what it means to live and buy as "Cherokee" and "Choctaw." The recent rush to sacralize free market enterprise is also a relatively new phenomenon among Roman Catholics, as Paula Kane shows in her examination of wealthy Catholic businessmen. Unlike their immigrant forebears, the Catholics behind interest groups such as Legatus and the Napa Institute have recently gained traction among socially conservative bishops and prominent politicians in the Republican Party. The result, Kane concludes, is a Catholic politics at odds not only with historical ties to the Democratic Party but with papal authority as well. It is also a brand of religious politics that demonstrates—contrary to Weber's long-standing views on the centrality of the Protestant ethic in modern capitalism—the diverse and multifaceted religious ethics behind contemporary capitalism and the nation's political economy.

In parts and sum, this book argues that a fresh methodological framework is necessary to make sense of America's contemporary religious landscape. Today, Americans routinely turn to corporate modes, private enterprises, and consumer goods to craft religious experiences and religious categories. Similarly, they turn toward—or against—religious leaders, organizations, and sites that enhance or challenge their commitments to the for-profit or non-profit business as a viable embodiment and enabler of their social and political aspirations. This book, therefore, seeks to understand the religious turns that Apple, IBM, Walmart, and myriad other businesses have made while providing insight into the worlds of business that religious Americans have wrought, past and present.

Notes

1. Walter Isaacson, *Steve Jobs* (New York: Simon and Schuster, 2015), 223–225, 446.
2. Ibid., 136, 527, quotation from 128.
3. Thomas J. Watson Jr., *A Business and Its Beliefs: The Ideas That Helped Build IBM* (1963; New York: McGraw Hill, 2003), quotations from 13, 29, and 34; John Greenwald, "Thomas Watson Jr.: Master of the Mainframe," *Time*, December 7, 1998, 170–172.
4. Paul B. Carroll, "The Failures of Central Planning—at IBM," *Wall Street Journal*, January 28, 1993, quotation from A14.
5. Elizabeth Mancke, "Chartered Enterprises and the Evolution of the British Atlantic World," in *The Creation of the British Atlantic World*, ed. Elizabeth Mancke and Carole Shammas (Baltimore: Johns Hopkins University Press, 2005), 237–262.
6. Mark Valeri, *Heavenly Merchandize: How Religion Shaped Commerce in Puritan America* (Princeton: Princeton University Press, 2010). Also see T. H. Breen, *The Marketplace of Revolution: How Consumer Politics Shaped American Independence* (New York: Oxford University Press 2004); John Lauritz Larson, *The Market*

Revolution in America: Liberty, Ambition, and the Eclipse of the Common Good (New York: Cambridge University Press, 2010).

7. Morton J. Horowitz, *The Transformation of American Law, 1780–1860* (Cambridge, MA: Harvard University Press, 1977), 63–210; Nathan O. Hatch, *The Democratization of American Christianity* (New Haven: Yale University Press, 1989), 49–124.

8. Chief Justice John Marshall, "Opinion of the Court," *Trustees of Dartmouth College v. Woodward*, 17 U.S. 518 (1819), quotation from 643, https://www.law.cornell.edu/supremecourt/text/17/518; Mark Douglas McGarvie, *One Nation Under Law: America's Early National Struggles to Separate Church and State* (DeKalb: Northern Illinois University Press, 2004), quotations from 152 and 173.

9. Ellen Eslinger, *Citizens of Zion: The Social Origins of Camp Meeting Revivals* (Knoxville: University of Tennessee Press, 1999); John B. Boles, *The Great Revival: Beginnings of the Bible Belt* (1972; Lexington: University Press of Kentucky, 1996).

10. Dee E. Andrews, *The Methodists and Revolutionary America, 1760–1800: The Shaping of an Evangelical Culture* (Princeton: Princeton University Press, 2000).

11. Charles Grier Sellers, *The Market Revolution: Jacksonian America, 1815–1846* (New York: Oxford University Press, 1991); Daniel Walker Howe, *What Hath God Wrought: The Transformation of America, 1815–1848* (New York: Oxford University Press, 2007); Larson, *The Market Revolution in America*.

12. Paul Johnson, *A Shopkeeper's Millennium: Society and Revivals in Rochester, New York, 1815–1837* (New York: Hill and Wang, 1978).

13. John Corrigan, *Business of the Heart: Religion and Emotion in the Nineteenth Century* (Berkeley: University of California Press, 2001).

14. Thomas Poage Hunt, *The Book of Wealth: In Which It Is Proved from the Bible, That It Is the Duty of Every Man to Become Rich* (New York: Ezra Collier, 1836), w6; Francis Wayland, *The Moral Law of Accumulation: The Substance of Two Discourses Delivered in the First Baptist Meeting House, Providence, May 14, 1837* (Boston: Gould, Kendall and Lincoln, 1837); J. T. Peck, "Art. V—Methodism; Its Method and Mission," *Methodist Quarterly Review* 51 (April 1869): 255. Russell Conwell's *Acres of Diamonds*, which he began delivering as a speech in the mid-1870s, was first published in Philadelphia by the John Y. Huber Company in 1890.

15. Washington Gladden, *The Christian Pastor and the Working Church* (New York, Charles Scribner's Sons, 1898), 206, 208.

16. James Hudnut-Beumler, *Pursuit of the Almighty's Dollar: A History of Money and American Protestantism* (Chapel Hill: University of North Carolina Press, 2007), 47–75.

17. John Beal, "Weathering 'the Perfect Storm': The Contribution of Canon Law," in *Common Calling: The Laity and the Governance of the Catholic Church*, ed. Stephen J. Pope (Washington, DC: Georgetown University Press, 2004), 171, 170, 168.

18. "The American Dream and the American Dilemma: The Black Church and Economics," in *The Black Church in the African American Experience*, ed. C. Eric Lincoln and Lawrence H. Mamiya (Durham, NC: Duke University Press, 1990), 236–273; Kathryn Lofton, *Oprah: The Gospel of an Icon* (Berkeley: University of California Press, 2011).

19. Jonathan Gruber and Daniel M. Hungerman, "Faith-Based Charity and Crowd-Out During the Great Depression," *Journal of Public Economics* 91 (2007): 1043–1069; Alison Collins Greene, *No Depression in Heaven: The Great Depression, the New Deal, and the Transformation of Religion in the Delta* (New York: Oxford University Press, 2015); Kevin M. Kruse, *One Nation Under God: How Corporate America Invented Christian America* (New York: Basic Books, 2015).

20. Sloan Wilson, *The Man in the Gray Flannel Suit* (New York: Simon and Schuster, 1955).

21. Kenneth T. Jackson, *Crabgrass Frontier: The Suburbanization of the United States* (New York: Oxford University Press, 1985); Thomas J. Sugrue, *The Origins of the Urban Crisis: Race and Inequality in Postwar Detroit* (Princeton: Princeton University Press, 1996); Lawrence R. Samuel, *The American Dream: A Cultural History* (Syracuse, NY: Syracuse University Press, 2012); Carol V. R. George, *God's Salesman: Norman Vincent Peale and the Power of Positive Thinking* (New York: Oxford University Press, 1993); Darren Dochuk, *From Bible Belt to Sunbelt: Plain-Folk Religion, Grassroots Politics, and the Rise of Evangelical Conservatism* (New York: W. W. Norton, 2011).

22. Lisa McGirr, *Suburban Warriors: The Origins of the New American Right* (Princeton: Princeton University Press, 2001); Dochuk, *From Bible Belt to Sunbelt*; Eileen Luhr, *Witnessing Suburbia: Conservatives and Christian Youth Culture* (Berkeley: University of California Press, 2009); Larry Eskridge, *God's Forever Family: The Jesus People Movement in America* (New York: Oxford University Press, 2013); Shayne Lee, *T. D. Jakes: America's New Preacher* (New York: New York University Press, 2003); Jonathan Walton, *Watch This! The Ethics and Aesthetics of Black Televangelism* (New York: New York University Press, 2009); Kate Bowler, *Blessed: A History of the American Prosperity Gospel* (New York: Oxford University Press, 2013); Phillip Sinitiere, *Salvation with a Smile: Joel Osteen, Lakewood Church, and American Christianity* (New York: New York University Press, 2015); Darren E. Grem, *The Blessings of Business: How Corporations Shaped Conservative Christianity* (New York: Oxford University Press, 2016).

23. Nancy MacLean, *Freedom Is Not Enough: The Opening of the American Workplace* (Cambridge, MA: Harvard University Press, 2008); R. John Williams, *The Buddha in the Machine: Art, Technology, and the Meeting of East and West* (New Haven: Yale University Press, 2012), 174–198.

24. Angus Burgin, *The Great Persuasion: Reinventing Free Markets Since the Depression* (Cambridge, MA: Harvard University Press, 2012); Bethany Moreton, *To Serve God and Wal-Mart: The Making of Christian Free Enterprise* (Cambridge, MA: Harvard

University Press, 2009); Howard R. Bowen, *The Social Responsibilities of the Businessman* (Iowa City: University of Iowa Press, 2013); David W. Miller, *Faith at Work: The History and Promise of the Faith at Work Movement* (New York: Oxford University Press, 2006); Lake Lambert III, *Spirituality, Inc.: Religion in the American Workplace* (New York: New York University Press, 2009).

25. Larry Eskridge, "Money Matters: The Phenomenon of Financial Counselor Larry Burkett and Christian Financial Concepts," in Larry Eskridge and Mark A. Noll, eds., *More Money, More Ministry: Money and Evangelicals in Recent North American History* (Grand Rapids, MI: Wm. B. Eerdmans, 2000), 311–350; Stephen R. Covey, *The 7 Habits of Highly Effective People* (New York: Free Press, 1989); "Religion Comes to Davos Forum," Associated Press, January 26, 2013.

I

Believing Within Business

EVANGELICALISM, MEDIA, AND FINANCIAL FAITH

Daniel Vaca

"THERE'S ONLY ONE way to go, and that's up." With this elevatory objective, Peter Kladder summarized the business model and mission of the Zondervan Corporation in 1984. The corporation's president, Kladder made this comment with a view toward Zondervan's future. But his comment also could have served as an assessment of the evangelical company's past. Since its founding in 1931, Zondervan's fortunes had risen steadily. The 1970s in particular had secured its position as one of the leading publishers and distributors of Christian books and music in the United States. During that decade, for example, Zondervan not only published the best-selling book *The Late Great Planet Earth* (1970) but also released the New International Version of the Bible (New Testament in 1973; full Bible in 1978), which would become the most popular version among American evangelicals. The company's roster of authors included many of the most well-known evangelicals of the day, including Joni Eareckson Tada, Philip Yancey, and the renowned revivalist Billy Graham. Insofar as it provided evangelicals with their Bibles, taught evangelicals how to think about their world, and cultivated evangelical celebrities, Zondervan served as a veritable font of evangelical culture.

Prior success notwithstanding, Kladder insisted that his company would continue to grow. He expected Zondervan to double its sales within five years, for example, even though the company's gross sales of $92 million in 1983 already surpassed its closest competitor's by $31 million. Kladder also hoped to add to its chain of eighty-nine bookstores, bettering its rank as the fourth-largest chain in the United States by surpassing Waldenbooks, B. Dalton Bookseller, and Crown Books. To secure continued growth, Zondervan had begun stepping away from its "lackadaisical business practices." Kladder boasted about the firm's new computer systems, its acquisition of smaller companies, its new corporate divisions, and its use of a headhunting firm to recruit executives with experience outside of evangelical publishing.[1] "We are becoming more sophisticated," Kladder remarked. "We have been inbred for too long, operating more from tradition instead of from results."[2]

Although this brief account of Zondervan's corporate activities and aspirations offers just a glimpse of American religion and business in the early 1980s, it solicits the question that this chapter addresses: namely, what is the relationship between evangelical Christianity and business in American religious history? Any number of other stories, about other institutions or individuals, could solicit the same question. But Kladder invites this question especially with his contrast between "tradition" and "results." What kind of tradition did Kladder hope to subordinate to results? How did he imagine that realignment? Although Kladder would address such questions by insisting that his company would "retain the same religious tone that has marked Zondervan from the beginning," the ambiguities of "religious tone" ultimately amplify potential questions.[3]

An interpretation of Kladder's desire for results requires a historical hermeneutic. The historiography of American evangelicalism provides at least one, and this chapter develops another. To develop a hermeneutic for interpreting the relationship between evangelicalism and business, this chapter begins by reviewing and extending prevailing approaches to conceptualizing evangelicalism and narrating its business history. Focusing especially on the business of evangelical book publishing, the chapter then examines evangelical business attitudes and practices across the nineteenth and twentieth centuries, ultimately returning to Zondervan's experience in the 1980s. By revisiting both historiographies and histories of evangelicalism and business, I present business as more than a sphere of economic activity that evangelicals have embraced, either through evangelical tradition or at its expense. If "capitalism" names shifting paradigms of economic activity premised upon capital accumulation, and "the market" serves as shorthand for systems of capitalist activity and valuation, then "business" denotes the institutions and practices that markets comprise.[4] Through business, evangelical ideas, behaviors, and sensibilities continually have taken shape, manifesting market logic. In turn, evangelicals have evangelized on business's behalf.

Conceiving and Constituting Evangelicalism

Writing in a New York–based newspaper in 1861, an editorialist explained why the Boston-based American Tract Society (ATS) "enjoys the respect and confidence of evangelical Christians." In addition to applauding the ATS for finally publishing "testimony upon the sinfulness of slavery"— after avoiding the divisive issue for decades—the writer praised the ATS's business behavior above all else.[5] "What we like in the American Tract Society in Boston," the editorialist remarked, "is, that it conducts its business upon business principles." Noting that the ATS not only "employs the regular channels of trade both in the manufacture and in the distribution of its books" but also "aims to pay the cost of manufacture by a small profit on its publications," the writer presented financial responsibility and self-sufficiency as the primary reasons that the ATS succeeded in "the work of circulating a fresh and vigorous evangelical literature throughout the land."[6] During the nineteenth century, evangelicals increasingly expressed the same confidence in business that these comments conveyed. But why? This editorial helps account for that confidence by distilling the subjectivity, mediation, and business basis that have animated evangelicalism as a historical phenomenon.

What is evangelicalism? While most fields of scholarly inquiry regularly reexamine the abstractions that prompt or license their endeavor, scholars of American evangelicalism have obsessed especially over the task of defining evangelicalism. The reasons for this are numerous; while some historians use definitions to delimit the scope of their narratives, for example, other historians use definitions as a means of amplifying the historical presence and social profile of a tradition that they see as their own. Whatever motivates a definitional enterprise, a fundamental complication is that the term *evangelical* is, in its essence, not a noun. It is an adjective, and adjectives signify whatever qualities the speaker or writer has in mind. Based on the Greek word *evange-lion*, or "good news," the root *evangel-* refers not only to the "gospel" message of salvation through Jesus Christ but also to the biblical documents that carry that message. Drawing upon this root, Christians since the sixteenth century have used *evangelical* and its variants to describe people and activities that they have seen as true to their own understandings of the gospel texts, the gospel message, or the general spirit of either. This adjectival impulse lay behind Martin Luther's notion of an "evangelische Kirche," for example, as well as the nineteenth-century historian Robert Baird's list of "evangelical" and "unevangelical" denominations.[7] That impulse also determined which literature our editorialist deemed "evangelical" in 1861; many Christian supporters of slavery, after all, would have wielded the adjective differently.[8]

Especially since the 1970s, historians of American religion regularly have transformed the adjective *evangelical* into a noun that denotes what they have perceived as a distinct religious group. Portrayals of this group often have hewed to the conception of evangelicalism that the fundamentalist founders of the National Association of Evangelicals claimed for themselves in the 1940s.[9] Acknowledging that "evangelicalism is certainly not a denomination in the usual sense of an organized religious structure," George Marsden explains, it is "a denomination in the sense of a name by which a religious grouping is denominated."[10] Conceiving evangelicalism as a social unity and often describing that unity through metaphor, Marsden and other avowedly evangelical historians inspired a tradition of historiography that focused especially on identifying the theological or institutional criteria that situate Christians within that unity's boundaries.[11] Often repeated definitions have included such criteria as conversionism, activism, biblicism, and crucicentrism.[12] This emphasis on bounded grouping can be seen as an artifact of the approach to religious history known as "church history," which privileges denominational or ecclesiological affiliation and accordingly tends to fit other religious activity into that conceptual paradigm. At its best, however, this approach to evangelicalism has inspired illuminating questions about the means through which social groups take shape, cohere, and persist. Marsden noted, for instance, that evangelicalism operates in at least three senses: as "a grouping of Christians who fit a certain definition," as a collection of self-described evangelicals, and as a "more organic movement . . . with some common traditions and experiences."[13] But what makes a "movement," what do "traditions" comprise, and how do people come to hold any experience in "common"?

Addressing these latter questions, recent studies of evangelicalism often have used evangelical adjectives and nouns less to denote bounded social unities or fixed religious traditions than to gesture toward orientations that take shape recurrently and processually. Turning their attention to the varied social problems or processes that cultivate cultural styles and sensibilities, scholars have emphasized such varied themes as fear, intellectual disagreement, and urban unrest.[14] In addition to deemphasizing nodes of coherence like churches and denominations, recent scholarship has cut across binaries such as "conservative" or "liberal" Protestantism. Conceiving evangelicalism in broad terms, for example, Kathryn Lofton explains that "the only test to determine whether a Christian is an evangelical is whether he or she possesses a strong Christian identity that supersedes denominational location."[15] Emphasizing evangelical disregard for ecclesiological authority, Timothy Gloege contrasts "evangelical" and "churchly" Protestant orientations. Noting that evangelical orientations historically have achieved prominence cyclically, Gloege argues that evangelicals invariably have shifted "the primary locus of authentic faith from the communal context of church membership to an individual's personal relationship with God."[16] Inasmuch as particular doctrines and institutions help characterize evangelical orientations in any given era, the broadest conception of "evangelicalism" describes transdenominational constituencies of Protestants that identify the practices, ideas, anxieties, and social opportunities of other ostensible evangelicals as their own, subordinating institutional authority to an idealized individualism.

Throughout American history, circulations of media—and especially print—have conjured such evangelicalisms by diffusing reformist agendas, theological teachings, social narratives, behavioral norms, and more.[17] As Candy Brown writes about nineteenth-century evangelicalism, print "mediated and structured seemingly private experiences," generating an "evangelical textual community."[18] Conceptualizing evangelicalism as a larger social phenomenon than the notion of "community" colloquially conjures, John Modern explains that "evangelical media practices . . . made possible particular conceptions of the self, the social, and the means to understand them both." Media had this effect, in part, by generating "sensual criteria for evaluating the true, the good, and the beautiful—for others, to be sure, but, more importantly, for themselves."[19] Large and ambitious publishing enterprises, like the American Bible Society (founded in 1816) and the American Tract Society (1825), produced much of the media that Brown and Modern have in mind.

But if antebellum evangelicalism took shape largely through print culture, both evangelicalism and its print culture also developed through business. This fact helps explain why our editorialist not only expressed evangelical admiration for the ATS in 1861 but also insisted that evangelical publishing initiatives that relied financially upon voluntary contributions should hear a censorious message from their benefactors: " 'Dismiss your costly agencies; reduce your expenses; and conduct your business *as a business*, and according to the times.' "[20] While historians often have viewed evangelicalism as a bounded religious group that consistently has drawn business into its service, an emphasis on evangelicalism's processual creation highlights the business institutions, practices, and market logics that have animated evangelical sociality.

A Business Basis

Interpretations of evangelicalism's relationship with business rely upon conceptions of evangelicalism. Traditionally, notions of evangelicalism as a discrete "denomination" or "tradition" have presented evangelicalism and business as separate spheres that variously operate in conflict or collaboration. If holding evangelicalism and business conceptually apart, for example, Peter Kladder's decision to correct Zondervan's tendency to operate "more from tradition instead of from results" will appear to subordinate evangelical tradition to business results, enshrining both separateness and antagonism.

Less antagonistically, but drawing upon a similar model of separation, evangelicalism and business regularly have appeared in a collaborative partnership. Describing the range of possible ways that religious groups respond to "modernity" and "consumer society" as "withdrawal, resistance, or accommodation," the historian Douglas C. Abrams argues that twentieth-century fundamentalists simultaneously resisted and "utilized mass culture to spread and defend what was most important to them." Abrams notes that "their adjustments to mass culture did not alter the essentials of the Christian message." A similar framework has oriented many studies of evangelicalism's relationship with "secular culture." In attempting to discredit the notion that evangelicalism can be seen as a "throwback" that opposes the "thrust of mainstream society," for example, Joel Carpenter suggests that "it is more accurate to see evangelicalism as a religious persuasion that has repeatedly adapted to the changing tone and rhythms of modernity." Other scholars have insisted that evangelicalism's ability to adapt to modernity does not evidence its steady "accommodation" or the triumph of "secularization"; to the contrary, R. Laurence Moore argues, "much of what we usually mean by speaking of secularization has to do not with the disappearance of religion but its commodification, the ways in which churches have grown by participation in the market." While each of these studies and others have illuminated the inventive ways that evangelicals have "commodified" aspects of their religious activity and treated business as an instrument of faith, such instrumental approaches have highlighted collaboration but reified conceptual separation between evangelicalism and business.[21]

Viewing evangelicalism less as a religious tradition with distinct essentials than as a mode of transdenominational identity and activity that takes shape continually, business appears less as an instrument that evangelicals merely have used than as a social field, comprising shifting sets of ideas, practices, and institutions, through which evangelicalisms have evolved.[22] Rather than developing in collaboration with business or in spite of it, evangelicalism has developed through business. And insofar as "business" names the prevailing economic practices and institutional paradigms of the day, both business and evangelicalism have developed together.

During the first half of the nineteenth century, for example, advancing technologies, expanding markets, and proliferating business practices fueled evangelical ambitions.[23] "Our view here of the prospects of the two confessions in America," the Swiss historian, theologian, and emigré to the United States Philip Schaff explained to a German audience in 1854, "is based chiefly on the vital energy of Protestantism . . . and on the conviction that the evangelical truth, . . . as well as the evangelical freedom, which springs from this truth, can never perish, but, in spite of all hindrances, must spread in ever enlarging circles."[24] Viewing the other of two "confessions" as Roman Catholicism, Schaff shared a common American sentiment in hoping that Protestantism would triumph despite "all hindrances" over a growing Catholic presence. Convinced that economic initiative imbued "the minister, the missionary, the colporteur, the tract and bible societies" with just as much "zeal" as "the business man," Schaff suggested that industrial endeavor and business behavior could help secure the ascendance of "evangelical truth."[25] Promising developments in industry and business abounded. New industrial machinery, for example, facilitated new techniques for extracting natural resources, for transforming those resources into finished goods, and for transporting both resources and goods across greater distances.[26] In both the North and South, evangelical ideas and biblical hermeneutics portrayed prevailing economic paradigms—including the institution of slavery—as divine designs.[27] Yet with steam power not only fueling textile factories and canal boat engines but also powering paper mills and printing presses, few industrial developments generated as much metaphysical imagination and ambition as the possibilities of print.

Capitalizing upon those possibilities, organizations such as the ATS developed an array of business techniques designed not only to produce unprecedented quantities of religious literature but also to distribute it everywhere, reaching Americans without regard to regional location or denominational loyalty. Business techniques included cutting production and distribution costs through volume and centralization, manipulating consumer demand through differential pricing, and devising new sales tactics. While those tactics were not designed to generate profit, they did generate surplus revenue. Revenue became important largely because voluntary, charitable contributions increasingly had failed to keep pace with the high production and distribution costs that ambitions demanded. As a result, interdenominational publishers sold literature to readers who seemed capable of paying; their payments subsidized free literature for readers less able to pay.[28]

Through the dynamic and continual process of mediation that business tactics effected, evangelical print cultivated collective identity and elevated the authority of the individual. To be sure, an emphasis on rational reading, volitional piety, and shared Protestant identity predated the nineteenth century; it was, in a way, the logic of Protestant doctrines of *sola scriptura* and lay priesthood. But industrial changes and business developments transformed reading, choice, and common Protestant cause into ideals that seemed tantalizingly achievable.[29] To compensate for postal delivery networks that did not grow at the same pace as publishers' printing capacity, for example, evangelical publishers developed the figure of the "colporteur," a traveling agent who visited customers door-to-door. Colportage extended and complemented the activity of itinerant preachers, who also would serve as colporteurs. In addition to delivering evangelical literature to geographically diffuse consumers, colporteurs also collected information about their buying and reading habits. Such information enabled colporteurs to distribute more books, Bibles, and tracts. "When we find a family that has no book," one ATS colporteur explained in 1852, "we generally have to grant one: at the next visit they will usually buy one; and at the next a number, and so on, increasing their purchases as a thirst for knowledge and habits of reading increase." Although the task of the colporteur might be seen as an exercise in constraining individual choice by teaching people to value particular literature in the service of a particular moral and religious mode, the colporteur theoretically expanded choice. "After the colporteur left," the general agent of the ATS in western Pennsylvania boasted in 1852, "the gentleman where he deposited his books received so many calls that he was induced to fill a part of his store with books; and since then another bookstore has opened in the same town—both apparently owing to the demand created by the colporteur. Other book-merchants here bear testimony to the fact that the supply increases the demand."[30] If the integration of mass production and mass distribution defines the modern business enterprise—whose emergence historian Alfred Chandler located in the nineteenth century's final decades—firms such as the ATS not only heralded such developments but also circulated evangelical priorities through those endeavors.[31]

To be sure, publishers and patrons recognized that a kind of Faustian bargain lay in expanding evangelical Christianity both through and against the market.[32] Convinced that the market's laws of supply and demand had generated what David Nord describes as the "cheap trash of print culture, the literature of wickedness, sensation, dissipation, and error," evangelical publishers reasoned that business tactics might allow them to "turn the market on its head."[33] Virtually from the start, however, critics aired anxiety that business might undermine the objectives that it ostensibly served. As early as 1836, for example, a critic pointed out that "the methods of business-doing" had ensured that the "treasures of all the benevolent societies are full." But the critic also diagnosed a widespread "bias of the heart toward money-making," lamenting what he saw as "too much *trust* in money." In his view, this trust in money and business led both benevolent societies and churches "to substitute [money] for holiness."[34] As Kate Carté Engel illustrates in her study of early American Moravians, this anxiety about money belongs to a longer tradition; other Protestant communities also had preoccupied themselves with concerns about the proper relationship between money, business, and their gospel goals.[35] But even if nineteenth-century evangelicals stood in a longer tradition, their anxieties reflected the dramatic expansion of business that industrial developments heralded. As business increasingly became the technology through which social relationships formed and social activities occurred, evangelical leaders lost the ability to curate their communities' relationships with business, as Moravian leaders had in the eighteenth century. Business became an engine of evangelical identity, due in part to the social formations that evangelical media generated through business.

Throughout the nineteenth century, business in general and business wealth in particular would continue to elicit evangelical anxiety, even as business helped circulate Philip Schaff's "evangelical truth." Increasingly, however, business not only inspired perceived social problems but also promised apparent solutions. In the late 1850s, for example, the business districts of cities such as New York, Chicago, and Boston became sites of what later became known as the "Businessmen's Revival." Famous especially for their noontime prayer meetings, the movement developed partly as a response to the social instability that economic changes, market volatility, and business behavior had wrought. And yet prayer meetings ultimately enshrined the idea that a business sensibility could strengthen both individual piety and Christian society by wedding robust emotions to strict self-control, in the name of an optimized relationship with God. As John Corrigan explains, revival participants came to see "an emotional relationship with God as a contractual, transactional matter." Blamed for the instability to which the meetings responded, business also became a solution to that instability.[36]

This business-based faith found no more prominent advocate in the nineteenth century than the revivalist Dwight L. Moody (1837–1899). Born and raised in New England, Moody relocated to Chicago in 1856, where he worked initially as a traveling shoe salesman and credit account collector.[37] He also became involved in revival prayer meetings and the work of the Chicago branch of the Young Men's Christian Association (YMCA). Founded in London in 1844, the YMCA emerged out of the "deep concern and anxiety" its founders reported feeling in response to "the almost totally neglected spiritual condition of the mass of young men engaged in the pursuits of business."[38] Moody adopted the YMCA's mission as his own, making himself the model Christian businessman. By 1860, he decided to leave the shoe business in order to devote himself entirely to a ministry that ultimately would see him organize large revival meetings with attention to detail and savvy use of business techniques and commercial media.[39]

Amid an expanding northern economy after the Civil War, the growing unrest of working people who increasingly believed that economic expansion did not benefit them, and the proliferation of department stores premised upon consumer choice, Moody developed an evangelicalism that addressed economic disparities through business logic. Avoiding doctrinal details and divisive issues, Moody presented his version of Christianity as a simple choice, with profound moral, soteriological, and practical benefits. Equipping businessmen and volunteers with logistical and rhetorical techniques to reproduce his message and empirically measure its diffusion, Moody encouraged his supporters and his audiences to "work" in the service of achieving spiritual results. Prioritizing accessibility and disavowing denominational loyalty, he taught his listeners and readers to understand God as a being who communicated plainly and desired a personal and transformative relationship with each person. To be sure, as Heath Carter notes, antebellum evangelicals similarly had encouraged working people to accept their economic circumstances by viewing "industriousness as a vital expression of godliness." This tradition suggested that "freedom in Christ fit naturally with the freedom of markets." But Moody and his evangelicalism went further, not merely endorsing business in spite of its potential perils but even presenting the business principles of individual choice and responsibility as the sanctified solution to both individual and social suffering. While liberal Protestant notions of higher criticism and a "social gospel" tended to place broader populations and historical processes ahead of individual authority, Moody presented individuals as the source of social ill and the primary means of potential change.[40]

Although Moody recognized that business activity and its acquisitive emphasis could disorient and distract people who might otherwise choose righteousness, Moody did not condemn moneymaking or business. He simply taught that money and business had the potential to distract individuals from placing Jesus first, and he sought to present himself as an utterly undistracted model of righteousness and personal engagement with God. Both for Moody and for his evangelical collaborators, the primary problem with business lay not in business, money, or any systemic qualities of capitalism but rather in particular businessmen. Around the turn of the twentieth century, this understanding of business regularly reached sermon listeners and readers throughout the United States. "There is no war between religion and business," Thomas De Witt Talmage (1832–1902), minister of the Brooklyn Tabernacle, explained in an 1891 sermon that newspapers as far away as Nashville reprinted. Talmage not only claimed that "religion accelerates business" but also insisted that "business life was intended of God for grand and glorious education and discipline." Through business, Talmage promised, Christians acquire energy for Christian service, patience with life's annoyances, useful knowledge, and moral integrity.[41] Routinely speaking about money and business through metaphors, Moody compared an individual's spiritual journey to a ride in a hot air balloon. Just as a balloon rises only when its occupant removes the bags of sand that serve as ballast, Moody explained, "there are some Christians who, before they rise higher, will have to throw out some ballast. It may be money, or any worldly consideration."[42] Evidence of business's essential goodness came from the wealthy businessmen whose patronage bankrolled Moody's activities.[43] Both Talmage and Moody's understandings of business can be seen as popular expressions of nineteenth-century political economists' attempts to champion market capitalism while also acknowledging that flawed individuals occasionally took advantage of that system for condemnable purposes. All the more reason, evangelicals insisted, to highlight the deep alignment of business and the true gospel.[44]

While Moody and organizations such as the ATS illustrate how business tactics circulated evangelical media and cultivated evangelical identities throughout the nineteenth century, expanding commercial markets and rapidly proliferating multi-unit business enterprises not only positioned the idea and practice of business as a primary mode of social activity but also led evangelicals to speak that social vernacular. Evangelicals would invest business identity and behavior with spiritual authority, and their institutions and literature would manifest that investment in both word and deed. During the 1880s and 1890s, for example, the for-profit publishing firm Fleming H. Revell

Company would become the dominant publisher of "evangelical literature." Operating in competition not just with not-for-profit denominational publishers including the Methodist Book Concern but also with for-profit trade publishers such as Harper and Brothers, Revell Co. benefited from its status as Moody's official publisher—a privilege it enjoyed largely because Fleming Revell and Moody were brothers-in-law. During the 1870s, Fleming Revell had taken charge of publishing the sermons and musings of Moody and many of his associates, after consumer demand dramatically began to outstrip supply. Testifying to Revell's close relationship with Moody—while also criticizing that relationship—the Baptist minister J. H. Gilmore remarked in 1888 that "the pastor should not confine his reading to the Bible; nor, as Mr. Moody recommends, to 'books illustrative of the Bible.'" The minister joked that "many a book which does not bear the imprint of our good brother Revell, and which Mr. Moody would utterly condemn, may . . . be eminently helpful and suggestive in fathoming the meaning of the Book of Books."[45] As this remark suggests, Moody may have emphasized the importance of individual choice, but he also labored to "recommend" the choices that his listeners and readers might make. By using the consumer market to provide potential readers with his recommendations and teachings, Moody presented himself and his fellow authors as authorities that consumers should choose to engage.

In addition to developing a business model that served Moody's personal interests and complemented his style of evangelical ecumenism, Revell Co. also helped constitute Moody's expansive evangelical public, which would include future members of the fundamentalist coalition, avowed liberals, and participants in what would become known as pentecostalism.[46] As a Revell Co. executive later recalled, explaining the firm's strategy: "There were at least thirty other and minor denominations and sects, and as most of these had their beginnings in evangelical zeal and were relatively small and struggling, they could not produce their own literature. Here was a fertile and fruitful field for the independent evangelical publisher." By creating business relationships with a wide range of Protestant denominations, associations, and churches, Revell Co. simultaneously multiplied its profit potential by taking advantage of those groups' extensive distribution networks and cultivated a network that transcended both region and denomination. Business made sense to Moody, and Moody's evangelicalism made business sense.[47]

Inasmuch as Revell Co. provides a glimpse of Moody's mode of corporate evangelicalism in practice, it also illustrates how for-profit corporations and their leaders experienced and expressed elevated authority at the end of the nineteenth century. Business and businessmen increasingly acquired authority not simply to participate in evangelical movements but to engineer evangelical constituencies. To be sure, prominent businessmen had bankrolled revivals and other evangelical initiatives earlier in the nineteenth century. Most famously, for example, Arthur and Lewis Tappan supported Charles Finney, and John Wanamaker helped finance some of Dwight Moody's activity. These businessmen also provided more than money; they advocated for causes that they associated with their own interpretations of evangelicalism. Lewis Tappan, for instance, called persistently for the abolition of slavery. John Wanamaker and other turn-of-the-century businessmen saw Moody's evangelicalism as a potential means of securing proper moral comportment among the working classes. Yet in Moody's era, business expertise became more than a collaborative asset to ministers or ministerial initiatives; with business enterprise in ascendance, businessmen became ideal evangelical leaders.

During the first decades of the twentieth century, evangelical businessmen increasingly embraced the authority that evangelicalism invested in them. While publishers such as Fleming Revell had helped to model the evangelical businessman-as-leader, others would take prominent positions in virtually every organization that aspired to develop a wide reach. Insisting that they could contribute uniquely to the moral and economic fortunes of the United States, businessmen treated business expertise and success as greater evidence of spiritual authority than theological knowledge. " 'The preachers can tell us that Christianity works,' " the entrepreneur R. G. LeTourneau, who manufactured earth-moving machinery, explained, " 'But unless we business men . . . testify that Christianity is the driving power of our business, you'll always have doubters claiming that religion is all talk and no production.' "[48] Both modern business and modern evangelicalism promised to enable effective choices in individuals' lives, generating the prosperity that liberal religion and liberal politics had promised and seemingly failed to deliver.

Businessmen such as LeTourneau would fund, lead, and receive support from many of the institutions at the heart of twentieth-century evangelicalism's cultural infrastructure. Early in the 1940s, for example, LeTourneau joined other prominent evangelical businessmen in serving a term as president of the Gideons International. One of the founders of Zondervan Publishing House would serve several terms during the 1950s. Best known for placing Bibles in hotel rooms, on the logic that hotel guests might read the Bible and choose Christianity, that endeavor initially emerged out of the organization's broader mission of creating fellowship and evangelism opportunities among traveling Christian businessmen. The organization originally used the institutional subtitle "The Christian Commercial Traveling-Men's Association."[49] In the speech he gave upon his election to the presidency, LeTourneau insisted that "Christianity and business *will* mix, if given the chance, and that too many people think that they must keep their work and their Christian life as far apart as possible."[50] Throughout the 1940s and 1950s, LeTourneau shared similar messages at popular evangelical conferences and family retreats, including Winona Lake Christian Assembly, where he served as chairman of the board of directors. Such retreats always offered visitors the opportunity to buy books at exhibit tables, book stalls, and bookstores; beginning in 1941, visitors to Winona Lake might have purchased a hagiographic biography of LeTourneau himself, published by Fleming H. Revell Company. Or they might have purchased a copy of *Christianity Today*, which the evangelical oil executive and "Christian Libertarian" J. Howard Pew provided with funding, articles, and even editorial guidance.[51] Through the efforts of Moody, Revell, LeTourneau, Pew, and many more evangelical leaders, both prominent and ordinary Protestants experienced business as much more than a set of tools to use in the name of the gospel; instead, business figured as an organizing principle and animating impulse of evangelical activity and identity.

Financial Faith

When Peter Kladder announced in 1984 that Zondervan was turning away from its "inbred" business practices and "becoming more sophisticated," that statement proved only partially accurate. To be sure, the company had set about implementing new business tactics; but it had done so throughout its corporate history. Zondervan had proven innovative in a variety of ways; most visibly, it had developed a chain of bookstores that proliferated along with the shopping malls that increasingly appeared in American suburbs. Less visibly, the company made an initial public offering of its corporate shares in 1976. This offering ultimately inspired the steps that Kladder took in 1984. Rather than reflecting an embrace of business "results" at the expense of evangelical "tradition," both of Kladder's business steps fundamentally reflected the development of tradition through results. Over the course of the nineteenth and early twentieth centuries, shifting techniques of production and distribution had enabled evangelicals and evangelical media initiatives to conjure transdenominational constituencies, and evangelicals increasingly had invested the business practices and impulses that animated their endeavors with social and soteriological authority. By the second half of the twentieth century, as Zondervan's example illustrates, evangelical objectives and business strategies did not merely align; they often elided.

In the early 1970s, Zondervan found itself in a moment of transition. In addition to a corporate restructuring that saw people outside the Zondervan family begin to dominate the company's executive leadership, Zondervan undertook a costly expansion. Between 1969 and 1975, the number of company-owned retail stores expanded from twelve to forty.[52] In 1971, Zondervan had agreed to begin paying advance royalties on the New International Version of the Bible, in exchange for exclusive rights to publish it. And in 1973, the firm broke ground outside Grand Rapids on an 80,000-square-foot new plant for production and warehousing. To support itself through this transition and beyond, Zondervan's executives began considering a public offering of its shares. Zondervan would become a public company.

What is a public company? Fundamentally, public companies are not private companies, which private individuals or groups own. Private proprietorships belong to a single owner; private partnerships distribute ownership and liability between partners; and private corporations divide ownership of the company into any number of shares. Although companies have incorporated for centuries, the process became widely available to ordinary businesses in the United States only in the second half of the nineteenth century, when "general incorporation" replaced an earlier paradigm that required legislatures to grant all corporate charters.[53] By incorporating, companies become independent entities, protecting both companies and their shareholders from each others' legal liabilities and debts. Incorporation also allows a company to raise money by selling securities, essentially trading shares of ownership for shareholders' money, which serves as investment capital. While private corporations sell or allocate their shares privately, public corporations offer shares to the public. Offering investors nothing less than a promise to seek financial return on their investment, public companies do not demand that investors share the company's ostensible principles. Due both to the sense that securities generated money without hard work and to elites' fear that lower-class investors might meddle in their affairs, nineteenth-century businesspeople generally organized their companies as either proprietorships or private corporations.[54]

But if one definition of a public company emphasizes forms of ownership, another definition highlights the logic at the heart of public ownership. Insofar as public companies trust public shareholders to make choices not only in their own best interests but also in the best interests of the company in which they share ownership, public companies manifest market ideals. As the economic historian Ron Harris explains, Anglo-American general incorporation procedures developed due in part to a free market ideology whose "underlying principle was to replace the discretion exercised by state officials with one exercised by investors."[55] Since the early twentieth century, Julia Ott argues, the idea that "mass investment democratizes corporate capitalism" has become a central tenet of "shareholder democracy."[56] But a version of this free market ideology reaches back at least to the eighteenth century. "Every individual necessarily labours to render the annual revenue of the society as great as he can," Adam Smith explained in *The Wealth of Nations* (1776), adding that each individual serves society unwittingly, by "pursuing his own interest."[57] This notion that general social benefit flows from self-interested economic activity not only became a founding principle of free-trade policy but also came to serve as a kind of operating logic for the public corporation and stock market. Read out of the context of his broader discussion of mercantile monopolies, Smith almost could have been writing about public companies and public shares when he suggested that "every individual, therefore, endeavours as much as he can both to employ his capital in the support of domestic industry, and so to direct that industry that its produce may be of the greatest value."[58]

This kind of market conviction lay behind Zondervan's own decision to become a public company in 1976. " 'We believed that, over the long term,' " Zondervan CEO Peter Kladder explained following the public offering, " 'the majority of our stock will be in the hands of people who can relate to us personally.' " Speaking for the board of directors, Kladder explained: " 'We felt that there were many people who were investment-minded, but who were also like-minded spiritually and would be eager to see their money working two ways: first, to grow in an investment situation, and second, to be supportive of a kingdom cause.' "[59] By inviting public investors, Kladder suggested, Zondervan expected the market not just to effect the company's mission but to do so through profit-seeking investors, who could proverbially eat their financial cake and still have it spiritually. Zondervan's annual financial reports from the early 1980s emphasize this elision of spiritual and financial investment. As one 1982 profile of Ruth Peale (the wife of Norman Vincent Peale) explained, "Ruth believes so deeply in the ministry of publishing that when Zondervan offered the public a chance to participate in its publishing ministry by becoming a shareholder, she jumped at the opportunity. . . . Ruth Peale is a fine example of the kind of investors that the Zondervan Corporation attracts. Many of them share with the company a desire to strengthen the ministry."[60]

To be sure, the logic that lay behind Zondervan's public offering reflected more than market metaphysics. It also reflected the company's need for cash and capital. Both in 1973, when Zondervan originally planned to make its initial offering, and in 1976, when it ultimately went public, the *Wall Street Journal* explained the offering the same way: the sale would help Zondervan "reduce bank debt."[61] And in 1979, when the company split its stock by offering three shares for every two, it also offered 300,000 new public shares "to retire bank debt and to provide general working capital."[62] Fundamentally, however, the ability of Zondervan's executives to narrate all of the company's influences and objectives together into a seamless evangelical vision both expresses and evidences the elision between evangelicalism and business that evangelicalism's business basis had made possible.

To see both the ease with which Zondervan collapsed its evangelicalism and its business behavior, consider Zondervan's attitude toward its consumer audience. In 1984, a newsletter produced by and for Zondervan's employees asked them to answer a simple question: "Who are our customers?" Virtually every response published in the newsletter avoided bounded theological interpretations of Zondervan's audience, focusing instead on the supremacy of any potential consumer. Bruce Ryskamp, president of the company's Bible division, answered the question by quoting a passage from Earl Nightingale's *The Customer*: "The Customer is the one person who pays everyone's salary and who decides whether a business is going to succeed or fail." Ryskamp added, "The people who ultimately will pay our salaries and determine the future success of Zondervan's are not our distributors, our dealers, our salesmen, our advertising, our executive, etc. These people are all important as vehicles in helping us reach the final decision maker with our product—*the consumer*." Meanwhile, other employees emphasized a strategically vague understanding of those consumers. "Zondervan's customers are *every living person*," Dave Kok, an employee in the print shop, explained, "whether rich or poor, healthy or sick. From the baby who can only look at pictures to the elderly who can only read large-print . . . Zondervan customers are *unlimited*."[63]

True, an "unlimited" understanding of its audience aligns, in a way, with common understandings of evangelicalism. It even accords with definitions of evangelicalism that emphasize such characteristics as "conversionism" and "activism," which together gesture toward an active pursuit of unlimited conversions to Christianity.[64] Citing Jesus's injunction in Matthew 28:19 to "make disciples of all nations," an employee in the book sales department remarked, "Our customers are the entire world—if we believe the *Great Commission*." Seemingly enacting this Commission, the company even reached beyond

Christian readers. Discussing the company's turn toward "modern packaging and marketing techniques," for example, one profile from 1980 explains how Zondervan planned to capitalize on the Jewish festival of Purim to market one of its lead books for that fall, a fictional story based on the Hebrew Bible book of Esther by the author Gini Andrews, entitled *Esther: The Star and Sceptre*. "Zondervan will market the book heavily in New York," the *Grand Rapids Press* reported, "in search of strong sales in the large Jewish population."[65] Although this plan to transform Jewish readers into customers arguably expressed the soteriological objective of leading Jews to accept the Christian messiah, the plan also reflected an effort to shift away from more bounded conceptions of its market.

Had Zondervan's business model and stock revenue enabled the company to heed the Great Commission on a scale it had not previously? Or, by contrast, had conversionist ideology and rhetoric allowed the company to justify its desire to raise revenue and secure the price of its stock, as public shareholders expect? The question is impossible to answer, since Zondervan executives themselves likely would have answered both parts of the question affirmatively. More to the point, the impulse to reduce Zondervan's motivation to principle or profit obscures the company's fundamental elision of tradition and results. The business form of the public corporation, and the market logic it demanded, had encapsulated that financial faith. But more than a century of belief within business had made that faith possible.

Conclusion

Why are you reading this book? You could answer this question in at least two ways. On the one hand, you could emphasize the book's content, citing its roster of authors, its title, its topic, its historiographic timing, and more. On the other hand, you could focus less on the content of the book itself than on the modes of production, distribution, and consumption that created the book and delivered it to you. Like this second answer, recent scholarship about religion and media often has focused less on the content of media than on its modes of circulation. "Religions are constituted through an architecture of circulation and representation," Charles Hirschkind and Brian Larkin explain, "that in turn creates the pragmatic contexts for modes of practice and worship."[66] As Hirschkind, Larkin, and other theorists of media and religion emphasize, the social phenomena that we recognize in the past and present as "religion" or particular "religions" neither exist naturally nor remain static across time and space. Those phenomena take shape and persist only through continual creation. Insofar as varied forms of media allow ideas, practices, scripts, and sensibilities to circulate socially, media constitutes religions. As a social phenomenon constituted entirely through networks of churches, teachers, teachings, and material objects, "evangelicalism" provides a paradigmatic example of mediated religion. But the question remains: what enables and orients the circulation and representation that Hirschkind and Larkin identify? Both this chapter and this volume point toward the authority of business. That authority ultimately shapes religions' architecture, just as religions enable that authority.

The business turn in the study of American religion is, in part, an attempt to recognize and reckon with authority. To be clear, in its colloquial sense, the notion of "authority" not only tends to overemphasize coercion or constraint on human activity but also tends to underemphasize the way that people make meaning for themselves within and through systems of power.[67] As historians of communication and reading have emphasized, texts do not determine meaning; readers make it.[68] This is an important point, for authority is not hegemony. Instead of merely reifying obligation or coercion, however, the concept of authority highlights the social processes that shape our preferences and behaviors. As a social field that manifests market orientations, business has effected authority by cultivating complementary orientations. "Evangelicalism" names just one.

Such a conception of evangelicalism invites reflection upon its social composition, especially with regard to race and ethnicity. Why, the historian Jonathan Walton asks, do histories of evangelicalism and evangelical media perpetuate a "crude historical and theoretical reductionism that equates evangelical media with the Religious Right and cuts out a host of African American participants"? He insists that "American evangelicalism . . . is not ecclesiastically, theologically, or racially homogeneous."[69] As Walton suggests, one explanation for evangelicalism's homogeneous historiography lies in a reductionism that portrays a "denomination" populated primarily by white people. Undeniably, historians have underrepresented African Americans in their accounts of evangelicalism's history. But another answer to Walton's question recognizes that evangelicalisms take shape through mediation. As the activities of companies such as Zondervan illustrate, that mediation has occurred largely through the activity of businesses that have solicited evangelical constituencies as consumer markets. Insofar as businesses typically have pursued those markets in white, middle-class suburbs and sought to capitalize upon suburban socioeconomic orientations, they have cultivated white evangelicalisms.[70] And yet, as Walton's study of "black televangelism" evidences, scholars can seek to understand the social fields that produce homogeneous constituencies and categories without accepting those categories as analytically or historically definitive.

Attention to evangelicalism's financial faith also helps explain why, as Colleen McDannell noted in the 1990s, "Christian retailing, American-style, . . . is being exported."[71] Evangelical merchandise markets went abroad, along with their evangelical orientations, because the markets that they complemented have expanded globally. As a tide of critical scholarship on the theme of "neoliberalism" has argued since the 1990s, markets have come to dominate social life around the world. Neoliberalism might be understood, Kathryn Lofton explains, as "the summary term for that drift toward a society determined by markets." In such a society, "the agent of the better world is conceived always as *consumer*."[72] As Bethany Moreton evidences through her study of Walmart, evangelicals have contributed to the rise of neoliberal logic by helping to "keep the free market holy."[73]

But evangelicals are not alone. The ideal of the free market and the businesses that manifest that ideal find support not just from evangelicals in the United States but also from such socially and geographically distant groups as Indonesian Muslims. Exploring what he describes as "market Islam," for example, Daromir Rudnyckyj illustrates how "self-styled spiritual reformers and corporate managers" have developed "a set of discursive practices intended to make Indonesian Muslims amenable to what they term the 'free market.' "[74] And yet, if evangelicals are not alone, they are special. As the U.S. Supreme Court's 2014 decision in *Burwell v. Hobby Lobby, Inc.* illustrates, evangelicals have proven preeminent not only in their dedication to cultivating faith within the market but also in the level of social power that they have acquired through business.

To be sure, narratives of neoliberalism's rise and evangelicalism's relationship with business can appear as declension narratives. By highlighting business authority, however, I do not mean to idealize a utopian society before business or beyond markets. Nor do I desire to color all business decisions and activities with cupidity. As Catherine Brekus notes, American Christians recurrently "have struggled to nurture a different model of selfhood than one sanctified in the market."[75] To ask why you are reading this book, however, is to ask less about the struggle that markets provoke than about the taken-for-granted ease with which we come to embrace some authorities over others.

Notes

1. "A Religious Publisher Gets More Worldly About Management," *Businessweek*, June 18, 1984.

2. Ed Kotlar, "Zondervan Modernizes in Search of Christian-Oriented Readers," *Grand Rapids Press*, July 30, 1980.

3. "A Religious Publisher Gets More Worldly About Management."

4: Although city-center "marketplaces" and even "markets" of commercial exchange existed before modern forms of capitalism, Craig Greenman notes that the abstract notion of "the market" carries "belief in the metaphysical position of the market, as abstract and value-neutral." To recognize Greenman's point, I link "the market" to capitalism here, even as I recognize that other scholars might find the concept useful for describing ancient or alternative economies. Craig Greenman, "What Is the Market?," *Journal of Social Philosophy* 33, no. 1 (January 2002): 97–116, esp. 108.

5. On the ATS and slavery, see David Paul Nord, *Faith in Reading: Religious Publishing and the Birth of Mass Media in America* (New York: Oxford University Press, 2004), 152–154.

6. "A Measure of Economy," *The Independent* 13, no. 673 (October 24, 1861): 4.

7. On contested uses of the term *evangelical*, see Linford D. Fisher, "Evangelicals and Unevangelicals: The Contested History of a Word, 1500–1950," *Religion and American Culture: A Journal of Interpretation* 26, no. 2 (July 2016): 184–226.

8. See John Patrick Daly, *When Slavery Was Called Freedom: Evangelicalism, Proslavery, and the Causes of the Civil War*, Religion in the South (Lexington: University Press of Kentucky, 2002).

9. On the fundamentalist Protestant shift toward "evangelical" language as a means of describing their ideal conservative Protestant constituency, see Joel A. Carpenter, *Revive Us Again: The Reawakening of American Fundamentalism* (New York: Oxford University Press, 1997). See also George M. Marsden, *Reforming Fundamentalism: Fuller Seminary and the New Evangelicalism* (Grand Rapids, MI: William B. Eerdmans, 1987).

10. George M. Marsden, "The Evangelical Denomination," in *Evangelicalism and Modern America*, ed. George M. Marsden (Grand Rapids, MI: William B. Eerdmans, 1984), vii–xix, quote on viii.

11. David F. Wells and John D. Woodbridge, *The Evangelicals: What They Believe, Who They Are, Where They Are Changing* (Nashville, TN: Abingdon Press, 1975); Mark A. Noll, David W. Bebbington, and George A. Rawlyk, eds., *Evangelicalism: Comparative Studies of Popular Protestantism in North America, the British Isles, and Beyond 1700–1900* (New York: Oxford University Press, 1994); Donald W. Dayton and Robert K. Johnston, eds., *The Variety of American Evangelicalism* (Pasadena, CA: Wipf and Stock, 1998). On the project of defining evangelicalism's boundaries, see Leonard I. Sweet, "Wise as Serpents, Innocent as Doves: The New Evangelical Historiography," *Journal of the American Academy of*

Religion 56, no. 3 (Autumn 1988): 397–416; Jon R. Stone, *On the Boundaries of American Evangelicalism: The Postwar Evangelical Coalition* (New York: St. Martin's Press, 1997).

12. David W. Bebbington, *Evangelicalism in Modern Britain: A History from the 1730s to the 1980s* (London: Unwin Hyman, 1989), 2.

13. Marsden, "The Evangelical Denomination," ix.

14. See Jason C. Bivins, *Religion of Fear: The Politics of Horror in Conservative Evangelicalism* (New York: Oxford University Press, 2008); Molly Worthen, *Apostles of Reason: The Crisis of Authority in American Evangelicalism* (New York: Oxford University Press, 2013); Matthew Burton Bowman, *The Urban Pulpit: New York City and the Fate of Liberal Evangelicalism* (New York: Oxford University Press, 2014).

15. Kathryn Lofton, *Oprah: The Gospel of an Icon* (Berkeley: University of California Press, 2011), 73.

16. Timothy Gloege, *Guaranteed Pure: The Moody Bible Institute, Business, and the Making of Modern Evangelicalism* (Chapel Hill: University of North Carolina Press, 2015), 6.

17. For the classic theorization of mediated "imagined communities," see Benedict R. Anderson, *Imagined Communities: Reflections on the Origin and Spread of Nationalism*, 2nd ed. (London: Verso, 1991). More recent media theory has developed Anderson's insights by positing broader conceptions of religious sociality. Birgit Meyer, for example, suggests that scholars of religion and media conceive of social groups not as "communities" premised upon "vertical, hierarchical relations" but rather as "formations" that take shape processually. Birgit Meyer, "Introduction: From Imagined Communities to Aesthetic Formations: Religious Mediations, Sensational Forms, and Styles of Binding," in *Aesthetic Formations: Media, Religion, and the Senses*, ed. Birgit Meyer (New York: Palgrave Macmillan, 2009), 1–30.

18. Candy Gunther Brown, *The Word in the World: Evangelical Writing, Publishing, and Reading in America, 1789–1880* (Chapel Hill: University of North Carolina Press, 2004), 10.

19. John Lardas Modern, *Secularism in Antebellum America: With Reference to Ghosts, Protestant Subcultures, Machines, and Their Metaphors; Featuring Discussions of Mass Media, Moby-Dick, Spirituality, Phrenology, Anthropology, Sing Sing State Penitentiary, and Sex with the New Motive Power*, Religion and Postmodernism (Chicago: University of Chicago Press, 2011), 53, 75.

20. "A Measure of Economy."

21. Douglas Carl Abrams, *Selling the Old-Time Religion: American Fundamentalists and Mass Culture, 1920–1940* (Athens: University of Georgia Press, 2001), 123–129; Carpenter, *Revive Us Again*, 132; R. Laurence Moore, *Selling God: American Religion in the Marketplace of Culture* (New York: Oxford University Press, 1994), 5.

22. On field theory in religious studies, see Courtney Bender, "Practicing Religion," in *The Cambridge Companion to Religious Studies*, ed. Robert A. Orsi, Cambridge Companions to Religion (New York: Cambridge University Press, 2012), 273–295, esp. 280–281; see also John Levi Martin, "What Is Field Theory?," *American Journal of Sociology* 109, no. 1 (July 1, 2003): 1–49, esp. 42. The notion of a "field" as a network of forces that orient strategies and actions is most commonly associated with Pierre Bourdieu, who expressed the idea in such works as *The Field of Cultural Production: Essays on Art and Literature* (New York: Columbia University Press, 1993), 30.

23. On the promise of the market, see Daniel Walker Howe, "Charles Sellers, the Market Revolution, and the Shaping of Identity in Whig-Jacksonian America," in *God and Mammon: Protestants, Money, and the Market, 1790–1860*, ed. Mark A. Noll (Oxford: Oxford University Press, 2002), 54–74.

24. Philip Schaff, *America* (New York: Charles Scribner, 1855), 236.

25. Ibid., 33–34.

26. For a survey of these and other industrial developments, see John Lauritz Larson, *The Market Revolution in America: Liberty, Ambition, and the Eclipse of the Common Good* (New York: Cambridge University Press, 2010).

27. Daly, *When Slavery Was Called Freedom*, esp. ch. 5.

28. See Nord, *Faith in Reading*.

29. Nord, *Faith in Reading*, 39. Peter Dobkin Hall notes that "by the 1840s, certain major evangelical associations had become the largest eleemosynary organizations in the United States." Peter Dobkin Hall, "Religion and the Organizational Revolution in the United States," in *Sacred Companies: Organizational Aspects of Religion and Religious Aspects of Organizations* (New York: Oxford University Press, 1998), 99–115, quote on 102.

30. "Increasing Demand for Religious Books," *New York Evangelist* 23, no. 23 (June 3, 1852): 92.

31. Alfred D. Chandler, *The Visible Hand: The Managerial Revolution in American Business* (Cambridge, MA: Belknap Press of Harvard University Press, 1977), 285.

32. Throughout the tracts that it produced, the ATS regularly encouraged readers to look nostalgically on an imagined preindustrial economy characterized by what Mark Schantz describes as "community obligations, benevolence, and charity." Insofar as the ATS and its wealthy patrons "insisted on a world in which spiritual values triumphed over the temporal," Schantz explains, they seem to have viewed their own "rise to affluence with profound uneasiness, perhaps sensing that their very prosperity undercut the religious values they professed to hold dear." Mark S. Schantz, "Religious Tracts, Evangelical Reform, and the Market Revolution in Antebellum America," *Journal of the Early Republic* 17, no. 3 (Autumn 1997): 425–466, quote on 465.

33. David Paul Nord, "Benevolent Capital: Financing Evangelical Book Publishing in Early Nineteenth-Century America," in *God and Mammon: Protestants, Money,*

and the Market, 1790–1860, ed. Mark A. Noll (Oxford: Oxford University Press, 2002), 147–170, esp. 164.

34. W. S., "The Moral Influence of 'Money-Making,'" *New York Evangelist*, March 12, 1836.

35. Katherine Carté Engel, *Religion and Profit: Moravians in Early America* (Philadelphia: University of Pennsylvania Press, 2009), e.g., 134.

36. See John Corrigan, *Business of the Heart: Religion and Emotion in the Nineteenth Century* (Berkeley: University of California Press, 2002), quote on 165; see also Kathryn Long, *The Revival of 1857–58: Interpreting an American Religious Awakening* (New York: Oxford University Press, 1998)

37. William R. Moody, *The Life of Dwight L. Moody* (New York: Fleming H. Revell, 1900), 49.

38. George John Stevenson, *Historical Records of the Young Men's Christian Association, from 1844 to 1884* (London: Christian Commonwealth Office, 1884), 23.

39. For more on Moody, see Bruce J. Evensen, *God's Man for the Gilded Age: D. L. Moody and the Rise of Modern Mass Evangelism* (Oxford: Oxford University Press, 2003).

40. Heath W. Carter, *Union Made: Working People and the Rise of Social Christianity in Chicago* (New York: Oxford University Press, 2015), 23; Gloege, *Guaranteed Pure*, 141.

41. "Religion and Business: There Is No War Between Churches and Counting Houses," *Nashville Tennessean*, December 21, 1891, 6.

42. Dwight L. Moody, *Twelve Select Sermons* (Chicago: F. H. Revell, 1881), 141.

43. Carter, *Union Made*, 82.

44. See Stewart Davenport, *Friends of the Unrighteous Mammon: Northern Christians and Market Capitalism, 1815–1860* (Chicago: University of Chicago Press, 2008), 59, 205.

45. J. H. Gilmore, "The Literary Possibilities of the Pastorate," *Baptist Quarterly Review* 10, no. 37 (January 1888): 119.

46. Gloege, *Guaranteed Pure*, 7–8, 36.

47. George Henry Doran, *Chronicles of Barabbas, 1884–1934* (New York: Harcourt, Brace, 1935), 21

48. Quoted in Sarah R. Hammond, "'God Is My Partner': An Evangelical Business Man Confronts Depression and War," *Church History: Studies in Christianity and Culture* 80, no. 3 (2011): 498–519, quote on 508. See also Darren Dochuk, "Moving Mountains: The Business of Evangelicalism and Extraction in a Liberal Age," in *What's Good for Business: Business and American Politics Since World War II*, ed. Kim Phillips-Fein and Julian E. Zelizer (New York: Oxford University Press, 2012), 72–90.

49. Gideons International, *Twenty-Two Years' History of the Gideons: The Christian Commercial Travelers' Association of America, 1899–1921* (Chicago: Gideons, 1921), 15.

50. Albert W. Lorimer, *God Runs My Business: The Story of R. G. LeTourneau, Farmhand, Foundry Apprentice, Master Molder, Garage Mechanic, Laborer, Inventor, Manufacturer, Industrialist, Christian Business Man, and Lay Evangelist* (New York: Fleming H. Revell, 1941), 155, 158.

51. See Darren E. Grem, "*Christianity Today*, J. Howard Pew, and the Business of Conservative Evangelicalism," *Enterprise and Society* 15, no. 2 (June 1, 2014): 337–379, esp. 351, 361. For an excellent study of the oil economy's debt to evangelical entrepreneurs and ideas, see Darren Dochuk, "Blessed by Oil, Cursed with Crude: God and Black Gold in the American Southwest," *Journal of American History* 99, no. 1 (June 2012): 51–61.

52. James E. Ruark, *The House of Zondervan*, 2nd ed. (Grand Rapids, MI: Zondervan, 2006), 142.

53. Ron Harris, "Spread of Legal Innovations Defining Private and Public Domains," in *The Cambridge History of Capitalism*, ed. Larry Neal and Jeffrey G. Williamson (Cambridge, UK: Cambridge University Press, 2013), 2:127–168, esp. 143.

54. Julia C. Ott, *When Wall Street Met Main Street: The Quest for an Investors' Democracy* (Cambridge, MA: Harvard University Press, 2011), 2, 16.

55. Harris, "Spread of Legal Innovations Defining Private and Public Domains," 143.

56. Ott, *When Wall Street Met Main Street*, 216.

57. Adam Smith, *An Inquiry into the Nature and Causes of the Wealth of Nations* (1776), book IV, ch. 2, para. 9.

58. Ibid., book IV, ch. 2, para. 10.

59. Quoted in Ruark, *The House of Zondervan*, 140–141.

60. *The Zondervan Corporation: 1982 Annual Report*, Zondervan Publishing House, Grand Rapids, Michigan, 7.

61. "Zondervan Registers Offering," *Wall Street Journal*, September 28, 1973.

62. "Dividend News: Zondervan Votes Split; Public Offering Planned," *Wall Street Journal*, May 30, 1979.

63. "Who Are Our Customers?" *Zondervan Corporation News*, November 1984, 2. Zondervan Publishing House archives, Grand Rapids, Michigan.

64. Bebbington, *Evangelicalism in Modern Britain*, 2–17.

65. Ed Kotlar, "Zondervan Modernizes in Search of Christian-Oriented Readers," *Grand Rapids Press*, July 30, 1980.

66. Charles Hirschkind and Brian Larkin, "Introduction: Media and the Political Forms of Religion," *Social Text* 26, no. 3 (September 2008): 1–9, quote on 2.

67. These contrasting conceptions of authority draw much greater treatment from a wide variety of theorists who make analogous comparisons, including Michel de Certeau's distinction between the "strategies" of producers and the "tactics" of ordinary individuals and Michel Foucault's distinction between "technologies of power, which determine the conduct of individuals and submit them to certain ends or domination" and "technologies of the self, which permit individuals to effect by their own means or with the help of others a certain number of operations

on their own bodies and souls, thoughts, conduct, and way of being." Both kinds of technologies represent modes of authority. Michel Foucault, *Technologies of the Self: A Seminar with Michel Foucault*, ed. Luther H. Martin, Huck Gutman, and Patrick H. Hutton (Amherst: University of Massachusetts Press, 1988), 17; Michel de Certeau, *The Practice of Everyday Life* (Berkeley: University of California Press, 1984).

68. On readers' ability to contest "the way the culture structures their lives," see Janice A. Radway, *Reading the Romance: Women, Patriarchy, and Popular Literature* (Chapel Hill: University of North Carolina Press, 1984).

69. Jonathan L. Walton, *Watch This! The Ethics and Aesthetics of Black Televangelism* (New York: New York University Press, 2009), 26.

70. See Eileen Luhr, *Witnessing Suburbia: Conservatives and Christian Youth Culture* (Berkeley: University of California Press, 2009).

71. Colleen McDannell, *Material Christianity: Religion and Popular Culture in America* (New Haven: Yale University Press, 1995), 268.

72. Kathryn Lofton, "Considering the Neoliberal in American Religion," in *Religion and the Marketplace in the United States*, ed. Jan Stievermann, Philip Goff, and Detlef Junker (New York: Oxford University Press, 2015), 269–288, esp. 275, 285; on neoliberalism's characteristics and its conceptual vagueness, see Catherine Kingfisher and Jeff Maskovsky, "The Limits of Neoliberalism," *Critique of Anthropology* 28, no. 2 (June 1, 2008): 115–126, esp. 116–117.

73. Bethany Moreton, *To Serve God and Wal-Mart: The Making of Christian Free Enterprise* (Cambridge, MA: Harvard University Press, 2009), 271.

74. Daromir Rudnyckyj, "Market Islam in Indonesia," *Journal of the Royal Anthropological Institute* 15 (January 1, 2009): S183–S201, esp. S186; see also Daromir Rudnyckyj, "Spiritual Economies: Islam and Neoliberalism in Contemporary Indonesia," *Cultural Anthropology* 24, no. 1 (February 1, 2009): 104–141.

75. Catherine A. Brekus, "The Perils of Prosperity: Some Historical Reflections on Christianity, Capitalism, and Consumerism in America," in *American Christianities: A History of Dominance and Diversity*, ed. Catherine A. Brekus and W. Clark Gilpin (Chapel Hill: University of North Carolina Press, 2011), 279–306, quote on 302.

2

Fundamentalism and the Business Turn

Timothy E. W. Gloege

HUMANS HAVE LONG extracted resources from the environment. We have created and constructed, planted and improved. We have provided services for others—both for payment and under threat. We traded for things we did not have and then consumed the goods we acquired. We offered loans and expected compensation in return. We invested resources into expanding production and advertised what we had in excess. These basic economic activities—production, labor, trade, lending, investment, promotion, and consumption—are found throughout time and across cultures.

In contrast, economic *systems*, the ways that societies organize and justify those economic activities, have varied dramatically. They structure the roles we embody—proprietor, apprentice, consumer, slave—and determine the range of "rational" and "moral" economic choices. Those roles and rules may presume a natural order, but that order is based upon cultural understandings of self, society, and our obligations to each other. Is it fair to take the labor of others? Do gifts come with strings attached? Can the wealthy ignore the needs of their communities, their extended families, their own children? These questions are answered differently depending on the system, and they change over time. The neoclassical economics of our present moment may presume a timeless capitalist logic, akin to the laws of physics,[1] but it is impossible to separate it, or any economic system, from its legitimizing social, political, and moral ideologies.

Economic systems, in other words, are the rules of a sprawling game, but it is only one of several that we play simultaneously, each with distinct rules. We do not expect strict uniformity across games; it is not hypocrisy that a judge does not operate her home by the rules of the courtroom. Yet their boundaries are permeable. Though any cross-fertilization is contingent, the rules of one sphere can influence another.

The underlying logic of a religious tradition is no different from any other cultural system. It has its own rules, but it both shapes and is shaped by the other systems it intersects. Thus, even the most moribund guardian of a tradition will inevitably alter its rules to accommodate new circumstances.[2]

By this account, then, the "business turn" in the study of religion is simply an examination of the overlap between a particular economic system and a religious tradition. Any novelty in this approach stems from unwarranted assumptions that religion and economy reside in hermetically sealed spheres. Such framing has weighed especially heavy on the historiography of fundamentalism. Its earliest interpreters depicted fundamentalism as a hysterical reaction to, and rejection of, all forms of "modernity" (economy included).[3] Seminal works by Ernest Sandeen, George Marsden, Joel Carpenter, and many others offered greater nuance, but the idea that fundamentalism existed independent of the modern world persisted. It was "old-time religion" statically rooted in an eighteenth-century cultural framework.[4] The social scientific category of "fundamentalism," understood as a transreligious, antimodern tendency, reinforced this perception.[5] These older theories have become increasingly untenable under the accumulation of evidence suggesting that fundamentalists shop at the mall and adeptly use mass media just like everyone else. They are maintained only by the dubious assumption that religious belief and practice can exist independent of their broader cultural context.[6]

Historical accounts of the Religious Right started the process of reevaluating fundamentalism's antimodernity. Although these narratives typically began after the 1930s and focused primarily on southern "plainfolk" evangelicals, they raised important new questions about the northern beginnings of the movement.[7] Why would the same "old-time religion" suddenly engage the wider world in the mid-twentieth century when it could not in 1920? Was ten or twenty years of "cultural withdrawal" really long enough to effect a substantial change, or had the movement always been modern?

Following the entwined historical developments of fundamentalism and modern business from their beginnings in the 1870s provides a new framework for understanding this religious movement and its relationship to the modern world.

Who were these fundamentalists? First and foremost, they were evangelicals—which is to say they believed an authentic faith consisted in a "personal relationship with God" facilitated by prayer and Bible reading and yielding empirically measurable results.[8] But they add to this the assertion that anyone who has a real relationship with God adheres to a set of basic doctrinal propositions that cut across denominational lines. Formulating and promoting these essential doctrines was the intent of the publication *The Fundamentals*, out of which the movement was born.

What are these "fundamentals?" Herein lies the rub, since there has been no agreement on specifics. *The Fundamentals* were unsystematic and left out doctrines that even its organizers deemed "essential." No other creed or doctrinal system has been embraced by everyone in the movement. Thus, I argue that fundamentalism is defined not by an actual creed, but by the *conviction* that a doctrinal base exists and that it is essential to one's faith. And that conviction, that dream of a doctrinal foundation is maintained through the practices of consumer capitalism. Fundamentalism owes its existence to modern business.

BOTH CAPITALISM AND evangelicalism rest on three key features of the British Enlightenment. First, society was conceptualized as a group of autonomous rational individuals who had a natural right to self-determination. Thus, they rejected eternal, God-ordained social hierarchies. Second, they believed that societies operated by mechanisms similar to the "natural laws" postulated for the universe. Discovering and applying these principles brought social order. Finally, they insisted that all truth claims, including tradition and holy writ, must be evaluated by reason and be confirmed with empirical, quantifiable evidence.

Smith's individualistic economic theory, set out in *The Wealth of Nations*, mirrored Enlightenment principles. In striking contrast to earlier organic conceptions of society, he began with individual rational economic actors. But then he went further, rejecting the idea that "moral" economic actors always must consider the collective good of society. Instead, he postulated that individuals acting out of their own economic self-interest would bring about the greatest good for society. Thus, the market would correct itself, holding bad actors to account and rewarding the good, to the betterment of everyone. In this revolutionary idea, modern capitalism was born.[9]

Enlightenment assumptions were also embedded in evangelicalism. Convinced that human institutions only stifled authenticity and that hierarchies benefited corruption, evangelicalism reconceptualized Christianity as consisting of individual believers who had personal relationships with God. Just as the world should be investigated empirically on its own terms, so too the Bible should be interpreted free of the prejudicial accretions embedded in theological systems. They also asserted with mechanistic optimism that God would guide this individualistic faith without human intervention the same way gravity controlled the planets and free markets corrected themselves. Authentic faith produced empirically measurable "fruit": good works, conversions, answered prayers, even miracles. Mistakes were possible, but human interventions only made things worse, impeding God's invisible hand.

Claims to empiricism notwithstanding, both capitalism and evangelicalism were rooted in unproven assertions. Those with eyes to see noted that the very foundations of self-interested capitalism in America—the "open land" of its agricultural economy and the slave labor responsible for most commodity production—came at the expense of other people's rights to property and liberty. The claim that self-interest produced social good was plausible only by imposing a racist logic that considered Europe the apex of human civilization and nonwhite people subhuman.[10] Neither did antebellum Americans find evidence that capitalism was a self-correcting system. Smith's economic theories presumed compact populations in stable communities closely superintended by nation-states. America's attenuated frontier of isolated communities and mobile populations proved impossible for the invisible hand to govern. The roving peddler could leave before the consequences of selling shady wares became evident.[11]

The fruits of evangelicalism revealed a similar paucity of evidence that one God communicated directly to individuals. During the Great Awakening in the 1730s and 1740s, an evangelical orientation stirred up social disorder. Lay preachers claimed miraculous power, women claimed positions of spiritual authority, and slaves rebelled. Iconoclasts challenged tradition and social elites by stoking bonfires with venerated Puritan texts and luxury items. Self-regulating religious systems, it seemed, shared the same shortcomings as self-regulating markets. No miracle worker would try dividing a river twice, but there was nothing to keep him from drowning the first time around.[12]

Thus, whatever the appeal of Enlightenment ideas, both economy and religion relied on institutions to maintain social order in antebellum America. Conventional republican social theory asserted that a virtuous citizenry capable of capitalism and democracy was developed within a "private sphere." But it was the institutions themselves—the regulation they imposed and the social relations they facilitated—that maintained order. Schools, reform groups, political parties, guilds, lodges, and churches created an overlapping set of compact social networks. Churches that were part of denominations helped extend these networks on regional and national levels. Thus, membership gave entrance into a circle of trust that offered benefits both for eternity and for the here and now.[13]

Informal methods of market accountability had limits. There was no shortage of forged currency, dishonest peddlers, insider trading, repossessed farms, broken contracts, and failed promises. Some people were hoodwinked into investing in real estate at inflated prices or in yet another unneeded canal.[14] But in the aggregate, white men believed the free market worked well enough, blissfully unaware that this faith survived by a parasitic dependence on the labor and land of the oppressed and on other systems of accountability.

America's Protestant denominational system worked remarkably well, especially since the nation lacked a key ingredient of other European nation-states: an established national church. Without a literal institutional foundation for public morality, elite Protestants used a clever sleight of hand. They asserted that there existed a "religion of the Old and New Testaments" held by all virtuous Americans. Because it was never defined, local elites in relatively homogeneous communities negotiated the details among themselves. (Religious minorities acceded to this "orthodoxy" or paid the price of ostracization—even outright persecution.) This produced a welter of incommensurate local "orthodoxies," but since antebellum America was made up of "island communities," the fiction held.[15]

Thus, regardless of the claims of self-regulating markets or an evangelical faith, antebellum America's social order was rooted in traditional institutions. A minister might use imagery of a personal relationship with God or encourage devotional Bible reading, but neither trumped clerical authority or theological tradition. Authentic evangelical religion, with all its associated disorder, existed only on the periphery. To be a respectable Protestant was to partake of a community, superintended by a tradition and institutions that preceded you and extended beyond your lifetime. It was this informal establishment of denominational Protestantism—networks of churches that were formally, organically, and legally connected to one another and controlled by elites—that justified the moral order.

The dreams of self-correcting markets and evangelical religion were ideological twins at cross purposes. For a distended market economy to work, it needed institutional religion to help bring social stability, not roiling religious individualism. Society required religion that, like other "private" spaces, was ordered by structured hierarchies—parents over children, teachers over students, ministers over laity. Church was not the sphere of choice or self-actualization. It was where discipline and drilling forged strong, virtuous souls capable of choosing rightly at the poll or in the market. Church was a counterbalance to the market and thus, like family, was impervious to its logic.[16]

IN THE 1870S, America's market economy began a rapid transformation to corporate capitalism. New transportation and communication systems created a truly national marketplace for the first time. Meanwhile, new industrial technology, work processes, and reliable sources of power transformed human labor into a fungible commodity. More workers earned wages and purchased more goods than they produced. Increasingly, these purchases were made in mass retail operations—by mail order or at lower-cost chain or department stores. These businesses required capital that only an investor pool could provide. With too many "owners" to offer unified leadership—indeed, as production became too complex for a single person to direct effectively—a new professional class was hired to manage complex bureaucratic structures and direct day-to-day operations.[17]

Modern business created new opportunities but also new problems. The mass scale outstripped the ability of personal relations to maintain economic order. Who should be held responsible for a defective shoe when investors demanded profitability, managers demanded greater efficiency, and multiple workers performed only one step of a complex manufacturing process?

By the 1880s most elites agreed that the corporation was the answer. Corporations could own real estate, engage in legally binding contracts, accumulate wealth, and reinvest it. Their potential to amass immense power and insulate individuals from direct responsibility made antebellum Americans wary; thus corporate charters were granted cautiously, usually to public works projects with limited life spans. But the needs of modern business convinced the Supreme Court that granting corporations independent and perpetual legal personhood was a social benefit. A series of decisions transformed the corporation into a mundane feature of everyday capitalism.[18]

Corporate personhood seemed to solve the problem of trust. By granting a corporation existence independent of any owner or employee, it could embody its reputation in a trademark. This had the potential to be a valuable asset, since it effectively granted a legal monopoly to the trademarked good, with all the market power that entailed. This fiscal motivation, they believed, would ensure that a corporation remained honest.[19]

Thus, modern corporations resurrected the old faith that "natural" mechanisms could create self-regulating markets, but the truth of the matter was much messier. Almost every new technique of corporate capitalism was rooted in elaborate legal fictions that "existed" only through a massive regulatory regime: from the corporation itself to its trademark and to the idea that labor is a commodity distinct from a worker. Government bureaucracy created and tracked these entities; legal bureaucracy provided avenues for corporations to protect their intangible assets. Commodifying capital and labor provided corporations with the mechanism to create an independent identity. The roles of owner, manager, and worker were temporary and fluid, with no permanent legal bearing on a corporate identity. Anyone who threatened that reputation could be dismissed or bought out.

Created by business and blessed by the courts, a new corporate order was largely in place at the turn of the twentieth century, impacting nearly every other arena of experience in the process. The need for large workforces spurred rapid urbanization. New metropolises such as Chicago were sprawling masses of disconnected migrants from the hinterlands and overseas. Immediate emergencies of sanitation, housing, and transportation overwhelmed the Protestant elite, leaving no time to address the moral contagions cultivated by urban anonymity—the tavern, the card table, and the brothel.[20]

At a time when social stability was needed more than ever, the old denominational order faltered. Its moral authority, already severely compromised by the Civil War, suffered further as increased connectivity revealed old orthodoxies to be deeply idiosyncratic. Then there were the logistics of urban Christianity, where unsaved souls exceeded pew space many times over. The gossamer threads of the old social order, spun by shared church membership and kinship, simply could not scale up to the modern urban context.[21]

With denominational establishments foundering in the city, evangelicalism's individualism was an appealing alternative. A personal relationship with God, nurtured by a private reading of the Bible, required no stately buildings or denominational sanction. And so a generation of pragmatic evangelicals pushed a new reform agenda. They formed Sunday schools, religious clubs such as the YMCA, and independent missions that focused on evangelism and creating ad hoc Christian community.

Since cities were centers of commerce, many evangelical reformers were men of business. It permeated their identity and modes of thinking. In fact, they self-consciously applied new business ideas to what they called "Christian work." The result was a new evangelicalism freed from the constraints of traditional Protestantism. Gilded Age "corporate evangelicals" resurrected the hope of self-regulating religion, this time bolstered by modern business.

No one exemplified this business-infused evangelicalism better than the celebrity revivalist Dwight L. Moody. A successful salesman without any theological training, Moody understood his faith primarily in business terms. A sincere believer was a "Christian worker," taking God's direction the way an employee followed management. The Bible, like ordinary business correspondence, contained God's personal message to the reader. Moody promised that his Christian work would produce a chain reaction of conversions that would ultimately restore the social order with utmost efficiency. And he believed it. His message was especially popular among the urban middle classes. But his lasting legacy was the Moody Bible Institute in Chicago (MBI), founded in 1889 to train the army of Christian workers he promised would convert the city's working-class "masses."[22]

But by the mid-1890s, it was clear that even a business-infused evangelicalism had the same potential for "disorder" that had led its forebears to install churchly guardrails. Bands of working-class Christians, sometimes nonwhite, sometimes women, gathered in their own missions and storefront churches and claimed the right to interpret the Bible for themselves. They claimed that God made ironclad contractual promises to intervene miraculously in the natural world. Attempts at faith healing or financial support by prayer alone produced want, starvation, and even preventable deaths. Meanwhile, "plainfolk" evangelicals in the rural South and West lent support to the populist movement. They treated the communal relations of the Bible as templates for living and Jesus's Sermon on the Mount as a condemnation of modern capitalism. Among both groups, Moody's distinctive evangelical orientation seemed to serve revolutionary ends.[23]

In a world of supersized corporations and complex heterogeneous societies, the informal, church-based social order would no longer hold. They needed the power of a nation-state. And so secular reform movements stepped in to do what the old Protestant order and evangelical religion could not. Progressives from various religious persuasions (and some with no religion at all) united on a pragmatic basis to advocate various reforms, including new regulations for the economy. The Pure Food and Drug Act introduced basic consumer protections, and the Supreme Court accepted the constitutionality of state-imposed work protections. The social and economic order was now maintained by a burgeoning complex of governmental and legal bureaucracies, whether acknowledged or not.[24]

Thus the twentieth century ushered in a new consumer capitalist order both created and regulated by government. Some see this shift representing a religious declension as the secular state displaced informal religious oversight. But that assessment is too stark. State and quasi-governmental projects such as professionalization still relied on a public morality to justify their regulatory incursion. There was plenty of space for religion to guide and direct these ostensibly "secular" projects. And in the early twentieth century, it was white middle-class Protestantism that held that authority.[25]

The question of the moment was who would speak for Protestantism now that the local, patchwork "orthodoxy" of antebellum America had disintegrated. It would fuel the battle between fundamentalists and modernists in the 1920s.

CORPORATE EVANGELICALS BELIEVED that speaking for the Protestant establishment was their birthright. But they acknowledged that their business-infused evangelicalism needed refinement to prevent disorder. The solution was a new method of biblical interpretation called dispensationalism. Rooted in modern engineering and legal techniques,[26] it produced a careful, legalistic reading that effectively quarantined disruptive critiques and practices by claiming different parts of scripture were intended for different times, or "dispensations." Thus, Jesus's anticapitalist ethics were written for a future age, and faith healing was promised primarily to those without access to modern medicine. Dispensational guardrails kept evangelical practice aligned with middle-class propriety. But there was ample space within those boundaries to communicate with a personal God who quietly guided believers and even discreetly altered the course of events.

The Scofield Reference Bible facilitated the perception that dispensationalism was an intrinsically "biblical" methodology. The culminating work of the lawyer turned Bible teacher Cyrus Scofield, it had the dispensational framework baked into each page through study notes and cross-references. Published by Oxford University Press in 1909, it drafted off the ancient associations of that venerable educational institution. The Scofield Bible became standard equipment for conservative evangelicals who wanted to "just read the Bible," but it also introduced the methodology to readers in ethnic and mainline denominations.

Corporate evangelicals realized as well that institutions were essential for promoting and validating dispensational evangelicalism. They modeled their organizations on the same corporate structures that brought order to the modern marketplace. The most important of these was a completely restructured Moody Bible Institute. Henry Parsons Crowell, the forward-looking president of Quaker Oats, became its new president in 1904 and introduced corporate bureaucratic governance to a religious context. It became a template for countless other fundamentalist institutions.

Meanwhile, corporate evangelicals' new concern for "pure religion" shifted the primary identity of authentic believers. No longer "Christian workers" judged on their productivity, they became Christian consumers, judged on their ability to recognize and choose correctly among an array of theological offerings. The relationship between God and the individual mirrored new relationships that consumers were developing with faceless corporations, rooted in emotional appeals and promises of fulfillment and guaranteed satisfaction.

Choosing religion rightly was important because dispensational evangelicalism had competition. Protestant modernism maintained many aspects of the traditional communal faith. Church mattered, and ordinary believers were encouraged to take their cues from trained theologians and ministers. But the content of that teaching could depart dramatically from traditional theology. Modernists took modern science seriously and sought to square belief and practice accordingly. Their methodological approach to biblical interpretation, higher criticism, used sophisticated layers of textual and historical analysis to produce sleek ethical precepts. Modernists were also driven by practical concerns. Ecumenical projects such as the Federal Council of Churches brokered unity across denominations by focusing on social reform instead of doctrine.[27] Though often producing opposite results, both dispensational evangelicalism and modernism were modern, emphasizing process above content.[28]

Modernism's home in denominational bureaucracies and universities was an advantage, but corporate evangelicals would not concede without a fight. They fired the first shot with a publication from which they would eventually take their name. *The Fundamentals* was originally conceived by the Los Angeles oilman Lyman Stewart, but MBI leadership joined in and transformed the project. It was designed to outline the "fundamentals" of conservative Protestantism while attacking the modernist alternative. They would rally conservatives around the country by sending a high-quality publication free of charge to ministers, seminarians, and other types of religious workers throughout the English-speaking world.

Like any savvy marketer, the organizers knew they had to gain their audience's trust, especially denominational conservatives who were intrinsically suspicious of evangelicals. Their solution was to convince leading conservative scholars from every major denomination to contribute essays, appealing to their common enemy. Organizers were fully aware that they had significant theological disagreements, but they believed it was more important to leverage their reputations. Thus, prominent academics such as Benjamin B. Warfield were not trusted collaborators but celebrity spokes-scholars. Like artists composing a mosaic, corporate evangelicals took small pieces of each author's oeuvre, decontextualized it, and placed it alongside the work of dispensational Bible teachers more to their liking. In another era, these tactics might have seemed dishonest. But this subtle manipulation was standard practice among marketers, who used Quakers to stand in for complex faceless conglomerates.[29]

Their tactics worked, and *The Fundamentals* united conservatives, once divided by denomination, into a nationwide movement. But they never managed to formulate the conservative Protestant baseline they intended. Instead, conservatives rallied against the enemies of "orthodoxy." They were united by a commitment to the *idea* of conservative Protestantism, which was never defined. Different groups filled in the blanks for themselves without reference to others in the coalition. It effectively united an impossibly diverse group under the label "fundamentalist."

So long as "fundamentalism" remained in the abstract, it was an effective rallying cry, but when corporate evangelicals attempted to formally organize the movement in 1919 through the World's Christian Fundamentals Association (WCFA), they realized it was beyond their ability to control. Corporate evangelicals failed to persuade most conservative denominationalists to join in the effort. They were never entirely comfortable with dispensationalism, and their suspicions only grew during World War I. Current events convinced the most ardent dispensational advocates that they were witnessing the "signs of the times." Thus, they brashly trumpeted the apocalyptic implications of their method: prophecies filled with raptured believers, epic battles with the forces of evil, and an Antichrist destined to rule the world through a false church and one-world government. The overweening confidence in the ability of dispensationalism to provide certain knowledge only pushed careful denominational conservatives further away.

Neither could the WCFA bridge a growing divide within the dispensational camp. "Plainfolk" evangelicals who adopted the dispensational method exhibited striking differences with corporate evangelicals in class identity and politics. Suspicious of modern capitalism, plainfolk evangelicals understood their faith in a political and legal register, rather than through the economic metaphors that corporate evangelicals favored. There was overlap between the political/legal and economic models; the Bible could support both. But these different emphases mattered.

While corporate evangelicals understood salvation primarily as an act of free exchange between God and the individual believer, plainfolk fundamentalists focused on obligation. God expected obedience and promised protection. Corporate evangelicals tended to see the unsaved as potential clients and themselves as part of God's salesforce. Plainfolk fundamentalists, in contrast, understood themselves to be God's political operatives. The unsaved were lawbreakers needing discipline; God was a celestial police officer, knocking heads to maintain order. An economic model treated salvation as an opportunity; the political model saw it as protection from divine judgment and the devil. While sectarians attacked and legislated, corporate evangelicals warned and persuaded.

Numerically superior, plainfolk evangelicals made the WCFA their base of operations for a militant crusade against liberalism. Corporate evangelicals bitterly complained about this, then quietly extricated themselves from the WCFA and even distanced themselves from the "fundamentalist" label they helped create. When plainfolk fundamentalists launched their national campaign against evolution, culminating in the Scopes trial in 1925, corporate evangelicals were nowhere to be found. They were no fans of Darwin, but they knew a promotional boondoggle when they saw it.[30]

Even more damage came by the plainfolk-led heresy hunting within the major denominations. Their unflagging belligerence, often in a dispensational key, alienated many more denominational conservatives than it attracted. Moderate modernists, in contrast, offered concessions to traditionalists. They agreed to share denominational governance, backed off critiques of traditional doctrine, and focused instead on practical social reform and facilitating ecumenical cooperation. Forced to choose, traditionalists saw moderate modernists as less of a departure from their traditional faith than fundamentalist radicals. Plainfolk fundamentalists left to form their own independent denominations and churches. By their accounting, the furtherance of "pure religion" came through homogeneity and legalistic prescriptions. They assumed all right-thinking people saw the world as they did and demanded near-identical theological alignment from allies. Although many corporate evangelicals remained in mainline denominations, they were a silent minority. Thus the battle for the Protestant establishment was settled and the fundamentalists lost. Modernists in the Federal Council of Churches would represent Protestantism to the secular world.[31]

Having lost the ability to speak for respectable Protestantism, corporate evangelicals could only try to influence it from the outside. Purity was still important to them, so they invested most of their religious energy in parachurch organizations where they could control theological production without interference. But they were suppliers, not litigators, and thus happy to distribute their theological product to any takers. By their accounting, dispensational evangelicalism was a single ingredient in a larger recipe, like yeast supplied to denominational bakeries. Pure religion could take many forms and flavors so long as it was properly leavened. Institutions such as MBI (now "the virtual Vatican of Fundamentalism")[32] churned out a growing catalog of books, periodicals, and radio programs starting in the mid-1920s. They serviced denominational traditionalists, plainfolk fundamentalists, and some Pentecostals as well. But the low cost of entering into independent home-grown ministry created a crowded marketplace. The cornucopia of plainfolk and Pentecostal competitors served only to remind mainline Protestants anew of the dangers of evangelical assumptions to social stability.[33]

The problem of sectarian fundamentalists and Pentecostals revealed the limits of branding techniques for engendering and enforcing "orthodoxy." Secular brands worked in the marketplace only because of hidden regulation that was impossible in a religious context. There was simply no way for corporate evangelicals to prevent anyone from claiming the "fundamentalist" label. They could protect a particular institution, but to equate it and it alone with "orthodoxy" was a sectarian move; it could not be the basis for a broad-based public morality.

Corporate evangelicals had envisioned a new way of being a respectable conservative Protestant: one in which every action was consciously, freely, and sincerely chosen and doctrinal compromises were unnecessary. But the religious infrastructure in which they resided was structured to facilitate stability and continuity, not variety and choice. Respectable Protestantism could not live on books and radio alone; it also needed churches. A handful of large, respectable fundamentalist churches were available in Chicago, Boston, Los Angeles, and other cities with dense populations and transit capable of supporting them. But most middle-class Americans in smaller towns had little if any choice outside of the major denominations. There were also social and psychological barriers to the corporate evangelical vision. Consumer practices were relatively novel for all but a small subset of Americans in the elite and professional classes. For most people, these practices did not yet feel natural. It seems, then, that a corporate-inspired fundamentalism faltered not because it was antimodern, but because it was too far ahead of its time.

FOR MANY CONTEMPORANEOUS observers, the Great Depression was a crisis of modern capitalism. Massive economic hardship hit millions of ordinary citizens; most suffered through no fault of their own. Faith in self-regulating markets was hard to find, and with private benevolence overwhelmed, citizens turned to government for assistance. There was a resurgence of an old communal spirit.[34]

Despite these appearances, the Great Depression actually facilitated the further dominance of modern consumer capitalism. Economic hardship decimated the once-thick networks of small retailers, producers, and entertainers. It caused sharp drops in immigration that loosened ethnic ties and ushered once-isolated enclaves into the larger mass culture. With fewer competitors, corporate producers, retailers, and mass media quickly filled the void. A proliferation of commercial radio and film then further reinforced and naturalized the new habits of identity creation through consumption while further promoting branded products.[35]

A similar dynamic was at play with consumer capitalism's religious analogue. Hard economic times pruned the luxuriant overgrowth of independent sectarian religious organizations—especially radical evangelical groups in the working classes. When margins became razor thin, those unable or unwilling to implement corporate efficiencies were typically the first to fail. The Pentecostal groups that survived looked increasingly like the corporate evangelicals that early leaders had once critiqued. Thus, surviving remnants of the ragtag faith-healing networks ultimately begat Oral Roberts, the modern prosperity gospel, and much of modern televangelism. Other Pentecostal groups formed denominations. In short order, a middle-class Assemblies of God congregation became barely distinguishable from a garden-variety Baptist church.[36]

A similar consolidation among sectarian fundamentalists gave rise to figures including Bob Jones, John Rice, and Carl McIntire. They commanded an extensive national following through publications, radio broadcasts, and educational institutions. They remained strongest in the South, but adherents migrated to California and to the urban North. Political frameworks continued to structure their belief and practice. They were defenders of the faith, and theirs was a politics of purity, often entwined in the racist assumptions and sexist hierarchies of America's majority culture. Free market ideology animated their anticommunist politics, but not their understanding of the religious world; it was powers and principalities, authority and spiritual warfare at work, not market principles.[37]

Though denominations were ascendant at this time, there were forces at work that were slowly loosening this dominance. Internal migration weakened denominational ties and further increased local heterogeneity, especially on the West Coast.[38] In a new social environment, conservatives seeking alternatives to liberalism were more likely to migrate into evangelical networks rather than a strange churchly conservativism of another denomination. Limits on new immigration accelerated the Americanization of ethnic

Protestant denominations. For the more conservative-leaning of these, especially those with large middle-class populations involved in technical professions, evangelicalism was a natural path to make their faith more American.

Corporately structured institutions such as MBI had a distinct advantage in this changing landscape. They expanded their publishing and radio footprints (regularly absorbing struggling concerns), bolstered their educational offerings, and sent representatives around the country to simultaneously evangelize and cultivate new financial supporters. They trained thousands of missionaries, most of whom were funneled into new independent missionary boards. Corporate evangelical broadcasting also flourished. Millions of Americans tuned into Charles Fuller's *Old Time Revival Hour* on the Mutual Broadcasting Network. There they heard the individualistic dispensationalist-oriented gospel that Fuller had learned at the corporate evangelical stronghold of Biola, the Los Angeles-based Bible Institute founded by the financial backer of *The Fundamentals*, Lyman Stewart.[39]

Cracks in the liberal establishment edifice began appearing in the 1940s. Politically conservative business interests had grown frustrated with liberal Protestantism's critiques of capitalism and promotion of New Deal policies. These conservatives, like corporate evangelicals, embraced a vague Christian libertarianism that understood free-market capitalism as a natural system and salvation as an individualistic rather than communal endeavor. If corporate America was not intrinsically sympathetic to fundamentalist apocalyptic theology, the suggestion that Franklin D. Roosevelt might be the Antichrist reflected their growing fear of New Deal totalitarianism.[40]

To maintain their influence, liberals began using their political and commercial connections to undermine their evangelical competitors. The Federal Council of Churches especially had been the organization that government officials or secular media called when they needed "Protestant" input on movie censorship, military chaplaincy, or the selection of radio preachers for free religious programming. Amid fears that the potent combination of radical religion and populist politics might stir insurrection, the Federal Council convinced radio networks to cease selling airtime to religious programmers. Though ostensibly aimed at men such as Gerald Winrod and Catholic priest Charles Coughlin, it threatened even respectable radio preachers such as Charles Fuller. In any event, the policy would have given liberals an effective monopoly over Protestant religion on the national airwaves.[41] It was a wake-up call, signaling how much the reputation of even moderate, business-oriented fundamentalists had decayed.[42] Whatever the respectability of individuals like Fuller, the movement as a whole needed rehabilitation.

Corporate evangelicals responded by starting the National Association of Evangelicals (NAE) in 1942 to lobby for their interests in Washington. It was intended to be a respectable but conservative counterbalance to the Federal Council of Churches. Yet drawing a line between the principled conservative and an aberrant extremist could be a messy affair. There were major complications for MBI, for example, which now serviced a large sectarian fundamentalist clientele. MBI leadership had been integral to starting the NAE, but when the powerful fundamentalist Carl McIntire started actively opposing it, they were forced to distance themselves publicly (though they continued to coordinate by back channels).[43]

For neo-evangelicals at the NAE, sectarian opposition was a blessing. It became the negative referent they needed to claim the conservative but respectable "center," even though their differences with fundamentalists were matters of style. Neo-evangelicals held to the same dispensational evangelicalism that MBI had been promoting for the previous half century; they were simply careful not to mention this to outsiders. The tactic worked. A new "evangelical" movement could claim, at last, to represent a nondenominational "conservative" Protestantism. Although it could not speak as *the* voice of respectable middle-class Protestantism, neither could liberals.

Throughout the 1940s and 1950s, neo-evangelicals consolidated their new identity in several new institutions. Nearly all of these had direct connections to older corporate evangelical institutions such as MBI. The National Religious Broadcasters was founded at a meeting held at Moody Church in 1944; MBI graduate William Ward Ayer served as its first chair. Despite its claim to represent all "religious" broadcasters, within three years it became the "official radio arm" of the NAE.[44] Fuller Seminary was founded in Pasadena, California, in 1947 with the promise to offer a rigorous intellectual defense of dispensationally infused evangelicalism. It was supported financially by Charles Fuller and organized by a small coterie of men including Wilbur Smith, a former professor at MBI. Smith's father, a wealthy fruit wholesaler in Chicago, had been an MBI trustee and also served on the organizing committee for *The Fundamentals*.[45]

The ways that neo-evangelicals defended their faith were identical to their corporate evangelical forebears: rooted in practices of engineers and lawyers rather than academics. Their task was not an open-ended search for truth; rather, they worked backward to justify the dispensational beliefs they considered non-negotiable. Fuller's approach was no different from MBI's award-winning film series from the mid-1940s, Sermons from Science. Using sophisticated filming techniques and compelling, if simplistic, analogies from

nature, the films subtly suggested evidence of God's intelligent design in creation. Their broad positive messages led to their use by the U.S. Air Force in
a character-building program. Yet these were works of public relations, not
science.[46]

Bolstering neo-evangelical institutions was the emergence of a celebrity
spokesperson, the revivalist Billy Graham. After a highly-publicized Los
Angeles revival in 1949, promoted by William Randolph Hearst, Graham
became the heir to the corporate evangelical mantle once worn by Dwight
L. Moody. Though Graham was a southerner, his ministry was based in
Minneapolis and influenced at every turn by northern corporate evangelical
strongholds like Wheaton College and Youth for Christ. Graham was also
admired by many of the business elites in his generation. He carefully cali-
brated his evangelical gospel with dispensational instruments to insure easy
middle-class consumption. A master of mass media, Graham quickly rock-
eted to celebrity status. In 1950 he was meeting with Harry Truman, and a
year later he was featured on the cover of *Look* magazine. His claim to an
evangelical identity combined with his willingness to cooperate with mainline churches made it difficult for liberals to argue that the movement he represented was "sectarian."[47]

The fitting culmination of the neo-evangelical project was the establishment of *Christianity Today*. The unofficial mouthpiece of evangelicalism, the
magazine's creation had striking parallels to the corporate evangelical project
that gave birth to fundamentalism. They too relied on the contributions of an
oilman, J. Howard Pew, who was distressed by the liberalism of his denomination. They too sent the magazine free of charge to every pastor in the United
States for a year. Its first editor, Carl Henry, had written a thesis on church
publicity and saw the magazine as the capstone to evangelicalism's rehabilitation. Early issues were designed "to secure . . . theological respect and intellectual dignity." But after that, he promised, it would "become theologically
and ecclesiastically more aggressive."[48] The word *Christianity* in the title is
noteworthy—suggesting that they had learned from their forebears to avoid
neologisms that could take on sectarian associations. The title also spoke to
its totalizing designs: to speak not simply for evangelicals nor for conservative
Protestants but for the "orthodox" Christian faith.

AFTER 1960, neo-evangelicals finally succeeded in creating a "conservative
Protestantism" independent of denominations and rooted in a consumer-
oriented religious identity. Its success was ensured by a new social and cultural environment capable of sustaining it. Consumer capitalism had been

fully naturalized—indeed, there were few alive who remembered a time before branded consumer goods, national markets, and a mass media. The resulting dominance of consumer identities bled into nearly every arena of experience—from politics to ethnic identity to education.[49]

The resonances between the assumptions of evangelicalism and consumer capitalism helped to further naturalize each other. The religious ecosystem of evangelicalism was structured by a set of unquestioned tenets: individualism, the necessity of individual choice in signaling a sincere faith, the expectation that an authentic faith would produce empirically measurable results, and a dispensational method of biblical interpretation (often called a "literal" inter-pretation)[50] that separated individual morality from "natural" social systems like consumer capitalism.

By the 1980s, the evangelical marketplace—the literal products, broad-casts, and institutions—had expanded to the point that anyone could cre-ate a middle-class Protestant identity without recourse to denominations. With the atomistic mobility of automobile-centric households and suburban freeways, American Protestantism was at last freed from the geographic con-straints of the neighborhood church. Massive nondenominational churches have become as common as corporations, dwarfing their denominational competitors. An evangelical infrastructure was finally in place, and as it became dominant, it occluded churchly denominationalism—once the staple of Protestant conservativism—from the public imagination.

A final revolutionary shift in business ensured that evangelicalism would become the dominant form of American Protestantism in the late twenti-eth century. It was in the 1960s that American business perfected the pro-cess of market segmentation. Before this, manufacturers of consumer goods chased a mass market. They produced a single product and competed with each other for the loyalty of the "mass," which typically was equated with the white middle classes. Segmented marketing used demographic information and psychoanalytic techniques to discover and target smaller groups with spe-cially tailored ads. Product lines were tweaked occasionally to accommodate a group's unique tastes. If the mass market was like filling a vase with large stones, market segments were the pebbles and sand filling that space more efficiently. It began with previously ignored groups such as African Americans and Latinos. But as Thomas Frank explains, marketers eventually realized that this information could be used to *create* new market segments—"to call group identities into existence where before there had been nothing but inchoate feelings and common responses to pollsters' questions." In all cases, the result of market segmentation was the deeper penetration of corporate capitalism.[51]

Techniques associated with market segmentation offered solutions to two problems that seemed intractable to corporate evangelicals in the 1910s. First, they made any need to formulate an all-encompassing evangelical "orthodoxy" unnecessary. Instead, market segments (usually anchored by a corporately structured institution) essentially functioned like nineteenth-century "island communities." Each church, parachurch organization, or short-term project created its own contingent standard of "orthodox" belief and practice. It then enforced strict internal conformity, dismissing disagreements with other groups as matters of style. Religious mobility allow individual believers to join those communities that best align with their convictions and to leave when they drift apart. It is not sectarian because any institutional connection is episodic.

Second, market segments efficiently contained failure. The radical subjectivity, oversized personalities, insistent certainty, and bias toward empirical measurability were no less prevalent in evangelicalism after 1960 than before and created no less "disorder" as measured by middle-class standards. But market segmentation ensures that the closeted sexual peccadillos of evangelical celebrities or extravagant lifestyle choices of its ministers remain individual failures. They do not raise doubts about the evangelical ecosystem any more than an unscrupulous local business or an *E. coli*-tainted fast food restaurant threatens capitalism. In fact, revealing such failures ironically becomes evidence that the system roots out misbehavior. The overabundance of American evangelical ministries ensures there are numerous alternatives ready to service any recently orphaned customers.

As ideas of citizenship became more consumer-like and practices of market segmentation were introduced into politics, the way was opened for the formation of an evangelical political bloc. Judicious lobbying by the NAE, early efforts by Carl McIntire, and indispensable grassroots organizing created the foundation. This was then leveraged in the 1980s by resurgent sectarian leaders. Jerry Falwell, Pat Robertson, and southern transplants in the West understood religious identity in terms of citizenship and easily found a place within the new religious right. Taking a page from the NAE, both Falwell and Robertson used the unseemly televangelist scandals in the mid-1980s as their own negative referents, bolstering their respectability. Since at least the mid-1990s conservative evangelicals have dominated Republican Party politics, and for most of this time it has been difficult to tell one evangelical group from another.[52] And the cross-fertilization of political, economic, and religious identities produced such a powerful, mutually reinforcing combination that many of the late twentieth-century faithful have conflated conservative politics and religious orthodoxy. It created for conservative evangelicals a new moral order, rooted in the rhetoric of family values. For them, the prevailing brand of free market ideology in the Republican Party seems like the only conservative option.[53]

Protestants who wholeheartedly embrace evangelical assumptions are content to spend their lives in the system, either as faithful customers of a particular set of institutions or freely flitting from one to another in a quest for self-improvement. Others try, with varying levels of success, to migrate to a different ecosystem—embracing "mainline" Protestantism, or seeking remnants of a churchly tradition in more conservative Anglican, Catholic, or Eastern Orthodox communions. Others leave Christianity altogether. Yet in the end, it may be impossible for those born into evangelicalism to ever escape it. Given the fact that sincere choosing is central to an evangelical orientation, perhaps the decision to leave, rather than to mindlessly remain, is itself the apex of faithfulness to this ethos. Perhaps that convert is merely shopping in a more exotic locale, bringing his or her evangelicalism in tow. Whatever the case, odds are that if they settle in a Christian congregation, it too will have been touched, however lightly, by evangelicalism's orientation and products.

IN SEEKING TO puzzle out the persistence of "old-time religion" in a modern age, sociologist Christian Smith posited that conservative evangelicalism thrives because it is embattled.[54] To be sure, evangelicals believe this. Neither a two-term evangelical president nor the evangelical voting bloc's veto power over the platform of a major political party has mollified their sense that they are cultural outsiders under constant threat of persecution.

But the truth is that evangelicalism thrives precisely because it is so in step with our present moment. Drafting off the hegemonic influence of consumer capitalism in the United States, evangelicalism just feels natural. For many Americans, accepting or rejecting Christianity is done on evangelical terms. If evangelicalism is unappealing, so is the Christian faith.

Of course, a society dominated by evangelical categories is only one of many possible worlds we could be inhabiting, and it may be that it is already in decline.[55] But whatever the fate of evangelicalism, it is certain that this "old-time religion" is one that was only recently invented.

Notes

1. Philip Mirowski, *More Heat than Light: Economics as Social Physics, Physics as Nature's Economics* (New York: Cambridge University Press, 1991).

2. The idea of a religious tradition functioning like a game is taken from Alasdair MacIntyre, *After Virtue: A Study in Moral Theory*, 2nd ed. (Notre Dame, IN: University of Notre Dame Press, 1984).

3. Stewart G. Cole, *The History of Fundamentalism* (Westport, CT: Greenwood Press, 1971).

4. Ernest R. Sandeen, *The Roots of Fundamentalism: British and American Millenarianism, 1800–1930* (Chicago: University of Chicago Press, 1970); George M. Marsden, *Fundamentalism and American Culture: The Shaping of Twentieth-Century Evangelism, 1870–1925* (New York: Oxford University Press, 1980); Joel Carpenter, *Revive Us Again: The Reawakening of American Fundamentalism* (New York: Oxford University Press, 1997); Ferenc Szasz, *Divided Mind of Protestant America, 1880–1930* (Tuscaloosa: University of Alabama Press, 1982); Martin E. Marty, *Modern American Religion*, vol. 1, *The Irony of It All, 1893–1919* (Chicago: University of Chicago Press, 1987).

5. Martin E. Marty and R. Scott Appleby, eds., *The Fundamentalism Project*, 5 vols. (Chicago: University of Chicago Press, 1991).

6. James Gilbert, *Redeeming Culture: American Religion in an Age of Science* (Chicago: University of Chicago Press, 1997); Diane Winston, *Red-Hot and Righteous: The Urban Religion of the Salvation Army* (Cambridge, MA: Harvard University Press, 1999); Douglas Abrams, *Selling the Old-Time Religion: American Fundamentalists and Mass Culture, 1920–1940* (Athens: University of Georgia Press, 2001).

7. Elizabeth A. Fones-Wolf, *Selling Free Enterprise: The Business Assault on Labor and Liberalism, 1945–60* (Urbana: University of Illinois Press, 1995); Darren Dochuk, *From Bible Belt to Sunbelt: Plain-Folk Religion, Grassroots Politics, and the Rise of Evangelical Conservatism* (New York: W. W. Norton, 2010); Daniel K. Williams, *God's Own Party: The Making of the Christian Right* (New York: Oxford University Press, 2012); Bethany Moreton, *To Serve God and Wal-Mart: The Making of Christian Free Enterprise* (Cambridge, MA: Harvard University Press, 2009); Kevin M. Kruse, *One Nation Under God: How Corporate America Invented Christian America* (New York: Basic Books, 2015).

8. This definition is my own and explained more fully in Timothy Gloege, *Guaranteed Pure: The Moody Bible Institute, Business, and the Making of Modern Evangelicalism* (Chapel Hill: University of North Carolina Press, 2015). The meaning of this term has shifted over time. In the nineteenth century, it referred to denominations that elites considered to be mainstream—differentiated from Catholics, Unitarians and Universalists, and a welter of "sects" deemed disreputable for one reason or another by the white middle classes. For the typical nineteenth-century usage, see Robert Baird, *Religion in America: Or an Account of the Origin, Relation to the State, and Present Condition of the Evangelical Churches in the United States: With Notices of the Unevangelical Denominations* (New York: Harper and Brothers, 1844). Studies of nineteenth-century Protestantism often adopt this definition. See, for example,

John Lardas Modern, *Secularism in Antebellum America: With Reference to Ghosts, Protestant Subcultures, Machines, and Their Metaphors: Featuring Discussions of Mass Media, Moby-Dick, Spirituality, Phrenology, Anthropology, Sing Sing State Penitentiary, and Sex with the New Motive Power* (Chicago: University of Chicago Press, 2011).

9. Adam Smith, *An Inquiry into the Nature and Causes of the Wealth of Nations* (London: N. Kelly, 1801); Joyce Appleby, *The Relentless Revolution: A History of Capitalism* (New York: W. W. Norton, 2010), 14–15; Stewart Davenport, *Friends of the Unrighteous Mammon: Northern Christians and Market Capitalism, 1815–1860* (Chicago: University of Chicago Press, 2008); Daniel Walker Howe, *Making the American Self: Jonathan Edwards to Abraham Lincoln* (New York: Oxford University Press, 2009).

10. See Sylvester A. Johnson, *African American Religions, 1500–2000* (New York: Cambridge University Press, 2015), 13–55 on the role of "self-interest" (including among African participants) in the slave trade and the complex interrelationship between religion and capitalism in it. See also William Cronon, *Changes in the Land: Indians, Colonists, and the Ecology of New England* (New York: Hill and Wang, 1983). Uncompensated work of married women also supported market capitalism. See Jeanne Boydston, *Home and Work: Housework, Wages, and the Ideology of Labor in the Early Republic* (New York: Oxford University Press, 1994).

11. Walter A. Friedman, *Birth of a Salesman: The Transformation of Selling in America* (Cambridge, MA: Harvard University Press, 2004), 14–33; Stephen Mihm, *A Nation of Counterfeiters: Capitalists, Con Men, and the Making of the United States* (Cambridge, MA: Harvard University Press, 2009).

12. My full account is in "The Trouble with Christian History: Thomas Prince's Failed 'Great Awakening,'" *Church History* 82, no. 1 (March 2013): 125–165.

13. Karen Halttunen, *Confidence Men and Painted Women: A Study of Middle Class Culture in America, 1830–70* (New Haven: Yale University Press, 1986); Stuart Mack Blumin, *The Emergence of the Middle Class: Social Experience in the American City, 1760–1900* (New York: Cambridge University Press, 1989); Mary P. Ryan, *Cradle of the Middle Class: The Family in Oneida County, New York, 1790–1865* (New York: Cambridge University Press, 1983).

14. Scott A. Sandage, *Born Losers: A History of Failure in America* (Cambridge, MA: Harvard University Press, 2005); John Lauritz Larson, *Internal Improvement: National Public Works and the Promise of Popular Government in the Early United States* (Chapel Hill: University of North Carolina Press, 2001).

15. Robert H. Wiebe, *The Search for Order, 1877–1920* (New York: Hill and Wang, 1967); Robert T. Handy, *A Christian America: Protestant Hopes and Historical Realities* (New York: Oxford University Press, 1984); David Sehat, *The Myth of American Religious Freedom* (New York: Oxford University Press, 2011).

16. This, in contrast to Roger Finke, *The Churching of America, 1776–2005: Winners and Losers in Our Religious Economy* (New Brunswick, NJ: Rutgers University Press, 2005).

17. Alfred D. Chandler, *The Visible Hand: The Managerial Revolution in American Business* (Cambridge, MA: Belknap Press, 1993); David Montgomery, *The Fall of the House of Labor: The Workplace, the State, and American Labor Activism, 1865–1925* (Cambridge: Cambridge University Press, 1987); Susan Strasser, *Satisfaction Guaranteed: The Making of the American Mass Market* (Washington, DC: Smithsonian Books, 2004).

18. Martin J. Sklar, *The Corporate Reconstruction of American Capitalism, 1890–1916: The Market, the Law, and Politics* (New York: Cambridge University Press, 1988), esp. 43–53; Naomi R. Lamoreaux, *The Great Merger Movement in American Business, 1895–1904* (Cambridge University Press, 1988); Chandler, *The Visible Hand.*

19. Strasser, *Satisfaction Guaranteed.*

20. Paul S. Boyer, *Urban Masses and Moral Order in America, 1820–1920* (Cambridge, MA: Harvard University Press, 1978).

21. Paul Allen Carter, *The Spiritual Crisis of the Gilded Age* (DeKalb: Northern Illinois University Press, 1971); James Turner, *Without God, Without Creed: The Origins of Unbelief in America* (Baltimore: Johns Hopkins University Press, 1985); Mark A. Noll, *The Civil War as a Theological Crisis* (Chapel Hill: University of North Carolina Press, 2006).

22. This and following material on the Moody Bible Institute are based on Gloege, *Guaranteed Pure.*

23. Joe Creech, *Righteous Indignation: Religion and the Populist Revolution* (Urbana: University of Illinois Press, 2006); Jarod Roll, *Spirit of Rebellion: Labor and Religion in the New Cotton South* (Urbana: University of Illinois Press, 2010); Gloege, *Guaranteed Pure,* 90–113.

24. Michael E. McGerr, *A Fierce Discontent: The Rise and Fall of the Progressive Movement in America, 1870–1920* (New York: Oxford University Press, 2005), 147–181; James Harvey Young, *Pure Food: Securing the Federal Food and Drugs Act of 1906* (Princeton: Princeton University Press, 1989); Nancy Woloch, *Muller v. Oregon: A Brief History with Documents* (Boston: Bedford/St. Martin's, 1996).

25. Tracy Fessenden, *Culture and Redemption: Religion, the Secular, and American Literature* (Princeton: Princeton University Press, 2006); Talal Asad, *Formations of the Secular: Christianity, Islam, Modernity* (Stanford: Stanford University Press, 2003).

26. B. M. Pietsch, *Dispensational Modernism* (New York: Oxford University Press, 2015).

27. Charles Howard Hopkins, *The Rise of the Social Gospel in American Protestantism, 1865–1915* (New Haven: Yale University Press, 1940); R. Laurence Moore, "Secularization: Religion and the Social Sciences," in *Between the Times: The Travail of the Protestant Establishment in America, 1900–1960,* ed. William R. Hutchison (Cambridge: Cambridge University Press, 1989), 233–251; Mark A. Noll, *Between Faith and Criticism: Evangelicals, Scholarship, and the Bible in*

America (Grand Rapids, MI: Baker, 1991); Susan Curtis, *A Consuming Faith: The Social Gospel and Modern American Culture* (Columbia: University of Missouri Press, 2001); Heath W. Carter, *Union Made: Working People and the Rise of Social Christianity in Chicago* (New York: Oxford University Press, 2015).

28. Kathryn Lofton, "The Methodology of the Modernists: Process in American Protestantism.," *Church History* 75, no. 2 (June 2006): 374–402; Kathryn Lofton, "Commonly Modern: Rethinking the Modernist-Fundamentalist Controversies," *Church History* 83, no. 1 (2014): 137–144.

29. I explore *The Fundamentals* in greater detail in *Guaranteed Pure*, 162–192. On the development of modern advertising, see Daniel Pope, *The Making of Modern Advertising* (New York: Basic Books, 1983); Pamela Walker Laird, *Advertising Progress: American Business and the Rise of Consumer Marketing* (Baltimore: Johns Hopkins University Press, 2001); Roland Marchand, *Advertising the American Dream: Making Way for Modernity, 1920–1940* (Berkeley: University of California Press, 1986).

30. Edward J. Larson, *Summer for the Gods: The Scopes Trial and America's Continuing Debate over Science and Religion* (New York: Basic Books, 1997).

31. For an important but slightly different take on these developments, see J. Michael Utzinger, *Yet Saints Their Watch Are Keeping: Fundamentalists, Modernists, and the Development of Evangelical Ecclesiology, 1887–1937* (Macon, GA: Mercer University Press, 2006). On the mainline and its representation of Protestantism, see William R. Hutchison, ed., *Between the Times: The Travail of the Protestant Establishment in America, 1900–1960* (Cambridge: Cambridge University Press, 1989); Tona J. Hangen, *Redeeming the Dial: Radio, Religion and Popular Culture in America* (Chapel Hill: University of North Carolina Press, 2002); Andrew Preston, *Sword of the Spirit, Shield of Faith: Religion in American War and Diplomacy* (New York: Anchor, 2012); Matthew S. Hedstrom, *The Rise of Liberal Religion: Book Culture and American Spirituality in the Twentieth Century* (New York: Oxford University Press, 2012).

32. Joel Carpenter, ed., *Enterprising Fundamentalism: Two Second-Generation Leaders*, (New York: Garland, 1988), 2.

33. Joe Creech, "Visions of Glory: The Place of the Azusa Street Revival in Pentecostal History," *Church History* 65, no. 3 (September 1996): 405–424, doi:10.2307/3169938; Carpenter, *Revive Us Again*; David Edwin Harrell, *All Things Are Possible: The Healing and Charismatic Revivals in Modern America* (Bloomington: Indiana University Press, 2000); Randall J. Stephens, *The Fire Spreads: Holiness and Pentecostalism in the American South* (Cambridge, MA: Harvard University Press, 2010).

34. Robert S. McElvaine, *The Great Depression: America 1929–1941* (New York: Three Rivers Press, 1993); Alison Collis Greene, *No Depression in Heaven: The Great Depression, the New Deal, and the Transformation of Religion in the Delta* (New York: Oxford University Press, 2015).

35. Lizabeth Cohen, *Making a New Deal: Industrial Workers in Chicago, 1919–1939* (Cambridge: Cambridge University Press, 2008), esp. 215–249.

36. Edith Waldvogel Blumhofer, *Restoring the Faith: The Assemblies of God, Pentecostalism, and American Culture* (Urbana: University of Illinois Press, 1993); Harrell, *All Things Are Possible*; Matthew Avery Sutton, *Aimee Semple McPherson and the Resurrection of Christian America* (Cambridge, MA: Harvard University Press, 2007); Shayne Lee and Phillip Luke Sinitiere, *Holy Mavericks: Evangelical Innovators and the Spiritual Marketplace* (New York: New York University Press, 2009); Kate Bowler, *Blessed: A History of the American Prosperity Gospel* (New York: Oxford University Press, 2013).

37. Markku Ruotsila, *Fighting Fundamentalist: Carl McIntire and the Politicization of American Fundamentalism* (New York: Oxford University Press, 2015); Williams, *God's Own Party*; Matthew Avery Sutton, *American Apocalypse: A History of Modern Evangelicalism* (Cambridge, MA: Belknap Press, 2014), 114–147, 262.

38. James N. Gregory, *American Exodus: The Dust Bowl Migration and Okie Culture in California* (New York: Oxford University Press, 1991); Dochuk, *From Bible Belt to Sunbelt.*

39. Gene A. Getz, *MBI: The Story of Moody Bible Institute* (Chicago: Moody Press, 1969); Philip Goff, "Fighting Like the Devil in the City of Angels: The Rise of Fundamentalist Charles E. Fuller," in *Metropolis in the Making: Los Angeles in the 1920s*, ed. Tom Sitton (Berkeley: University of California Press, 2001), 220–252.

40. Kruse, *One Nation Under God*, esp. 3–27; Sutton, *American Apocalypse*, 114–147, 262.

41. Hangen, *Redeeming the Dial*, 105; Alan Brinkley, *Voices of Protest: Huey Long, Father Coughlin, and the Great Depression* (New York: Vintage, 1983).

42. Leo P. Ribuffo, *The Old Christian Right: The Protestant Far Right from the Great Depression to the Cold War* (Philadelphia: Temple University Press, 1988), 80–127.

43. Carpenter, *Revive Us Again.*

44. Hangen, *Redeeming the Dial*, 122–124.

45. George M. Marsden, *Reforming Fundamentalism: Fuller Seminary and the New Evangelicalism* (Grand Rapids, MI: William B. Eerdmans, 1988).

46. Gilbert, *Redeeming Culture: American Religion in an Age of Science*, 121–169.

47. Grant Wacker, *America's Pastor: Billy Graham and the Shaping of a Nation* (Cambridge, MA: Belknap Press, 2014), 74–75, 98–99.

48. Molly Worthen, *Apostles of Reason: The Crisis of Authority in American Evangelicalism* (New York: Oxford University Press, 2013), 56–63, quote from 59.

49. Lizabeth Cohen, *A Consumers' Republic: The Politics of Mass Consumption in Postwar America* (New York: Vintage Books, 2003); Gary Cross, *An All-Consuming Century* (New York: Columbia University Press, 2002).

50. See, for example, Vincent Crapanzano, *Serving the Word: Literalism in America from the Pulpit to the Bench* (New York: New Press, 2000), 2–3.

51. Richard S. Tedlow, *New and Improved: The Story of Mass Marketing in America* (New York: Basic Books, 1996); Thomas Frank, *The Conquest of Cool: Business Culture, Counterculture, and the Rise of Hip Consumerism* (Chicago: University of Chicago Press, 1998), 24; Robert E. Weems Jr., "The Revolution Will Be Marketed: American Corporations and Black Consumers During the 1960s," in *Consumer Society in American History: A Reader*, ed. Lawrence B. Glickman (Ithaca, NY: Cornell University Press, 1999); Arlene Dávila, *Latinos, Inc.: The Marketing and Making of a People* (Berkeley: University of California Press, 2001).

52. Cohen, *A Consumers' Republic*; Ruotsila, *Fighting Fundamentalist*; Lisa McGirr, *Suburban Warriors: The Origins of the New American Right* (Princeton: Princeton University Press, 2002); Williams, *God's Own Party*; Susan Friend Harding, *The Book of Jerry Falwell: Fundamentalist Language and Politics* (Princeton: Princeton University Press, 2000).

53. William Connolly, *Capitalism and Christianity, American Style* (Durham, NC: Duke University Press, 2008).

54. Christian Smith, *American Evangelicalism: Embattled and Thriving* (Chicago: University of Chicago Press, 1998).

55. Steven Miller, *The Age of Evangelicalism: America's Born-Again Years* (New York: Oxford University Press, 2014).

3

Godly Work for a Global Christianity

AMERICAN CHRISTIANS' ECONOMIC IMPACT
THROUGH MISSIONS, MARKETS,
AND INTERNATIONAL DEVELOPMENT

David P. King

THE WORLD IS replete with signs of Christianity's impact on and entanglement with the global economy. In the streets of Accra, Ghana, cell phone shops on street corners abound with names such as God's Deliverance, and bus signs declare, "Jesus Is Lord!" National offices of multimillion-dollar international religious aid agencies such as World Vision, Compassion, and Samaritan's Purse line the Ghanaian capital's streets. With resources raised from Western donors and received through government contracts, these international agencies provide development aid; they also provide good salaries for young Ghanaians enabling them to enter the new middle class. On the way to the airport, you might find your cabbie blaring a local Pentecostal pastor's sermon on prosperity over the radio. As you're boarding your plane, you might run into a team of American youth in matching T-shirts arriving on a short-term mission trip to provide volunteer labor to build schools or teach Bible courses. Or you may meet Ghanaians FaceTiming with their relatives in New York, both families having attended services with other members of their Presbyterian Church of Ghana congregations on either side of the Atlantic. Initially Ghanaians sent resources to build these new churches in America. Today, these U.S.-based Ghanaian congregations are sending money back home: remittances to support families and offerings to support fellow missions around the world.[1] Examples could go on, and Ghana is by no means unique.

The institutions, networks, and markets developing around global Christian growth have continued to expand rapidly. While economic globalization has largely focused on free markets, multinational corporations, and international financial institutions such as the World Bank, this vantage point obscures the fiscal impact of other global actors. Resourcing global Christianity is big business, and while a large portion of these finances come from within local communities, American Christians have contributed significant capital as well. Sociologist Robert Wuthnow estimates that "spending by American churches on overseas ministries has risen to nearly $4 billion annually, an increase of almost 50 percent after inflation in a single decade."[2] The majority of these funds come through evolving forms of missions, international development, and social entrepreneurship.

Missions, international development, and other mediating forms of international engagement have often served as *the* place for American Christians' encounter with the world and a broader global Christianity. These institutional forms have changed rapidly alongside rapid global Christian growth, and even as they have evolved, they have continued to grow in size as American Christians have invested more of their time, attention, and money abroad. This chapter focuses on these mission and humanitarian organizations to demonstrate how their evolving institutional and financial relationships not only impact people, profits, and power dynamics overseas but also affect the global outlooks of Americans at home as they envision the world and their own role in it.

American and Global Christianity

Of course global Christianity is not new—Christianity has always been a global religion. But renewed emphasis over the past few decades has focused attention on the dramatic rise of Christianity in the non-Western world in terms of its demographics, resources, and influence.[3] At one level, this growth is simply descriptive—counting adherents and describing shifts in population centers. Scholars debate the specific numbers, but all agree that Christianity has grown dramatically in the second half of the twentieth century. In Africa, the overall Christian population is estimated to have grown from 30 million in 1945 to 380 million by 2005. A recent Pew study charted the growth of Pentecostals in Latin America from 12.6 million in 1970 to 156.9 million in 2005. The majority of Christian growth resides in the global South among evangelical, Pentecostal, and charismatic faith traditions.[4]

On another level, however, demographic descriptors point to a paradigm shift that poses deeper questions: what are the characteristics of this global

Christianity, how and why have these shifts occurred, and what do they mean for the future? For scholars of American religious history, this paradigm shift has often served as a political football for another underlying question: what does global Christian growth mean for the future of the American church?

Philip Jenkins has served as the most prominent voice promoting this paradigm shift. In his popular book *The Next Christendom*, he has claimed that by 2050 only 20 percent of the three billion Christians worldwide will be non-Hispanic whites. An average Christian is probably more likely a Pentecostal woman living in a Brazilian favela than a white male in a midwestern American suburb.[5] Jenkins's picture of global Christianity is defined by the growth of neo-Pentecostal, spirit-filled forms of faith in the global South most often contrasted to the more rationalized, modern, and perhaps secular Western forms. To make his case, Jenkins demonstrates that global Christian growth has not been tied to colonialism. In fact, only after Western imperialism receded and indigenous faith took root did Christianity blossom.[6]

Jenkins and others highlight these new centers of global Christianity largely through contrasting indigenous growth with Western Christianity's decline. For some, this shift southward is positive. Without the strictures of colonialism and undue Western influence, the global South is embracing its own style and institutional forms of faith quite distinct from Western forms. This paradigm envisions a new missiology that need not nor should not depend primarily on Western personnel and resources. When pitted against Western decline, global Christian growth has led some within American Christianity to turn to the global South as a model. Over against a secularizing society, conservative voices find common ground with their fellow brothers and sisters of the faith around the world hoping for revival at home, a shared worldview, or a link to narratives of embattlement or persecution.[7] Progressive voices find other reasons to look longingly toward the global South. They sometimes point to examples of indigenous theologies of liberation and social action working against Western economic and political structures. While Christianity in the global South continues to grow, competing visions of how the West embraces this new global Christianity have emerged.[8]

Yet for others, this dramatic growth is less positive and more worrisome. Again in contrast to Western Christian forms, the growing forms of Christianity in the global South coalesce around a theological and cultural conservatism. Their reading of scripture is often quite literal and highlights the spiritual and supernatural that may limit notions of a shared secular public sphere. With the global South's less experience with Western forms of democracy and religious pluralisms, some worry that a new clash of civilizations will pit global Christianity in the South against the West (as we have seen through the splitting of religious communions or denominations) or, even more dangerously, pitting a global Christianity against a global Islamic *ummah* on the ground outside the West (as we have seen in Sudan or Nigeria).[9]

Whether viewing the trend as positive or negative, this perspective depicts global Christianity as new, vibrant, and distinct. The resulting paradigm shift highlights how a global Christian growth outside the West is united as a "next Christendom" coalescing around common themes despite great cultural diversity, and these themes are largely are held up in contrast to the outlook and contexts of Christianity in the West.

A second perspective focuses on global Christianity not as distinct from Western forms but rather as an exemplar of a global monoculture dominated by the West. While Western colonialism may have dissipated, they would argue that American imperialism served as an equally disruptive force. Some scholars point to official political, military, and economic involvement throughout the Cold War in Southeast Asia or Latin America. Often missionaries, religious humanitarian agencies, and political voices enmeshed with an emerging Religious Right were deeply intertwined in these global engagements.[10] Yet others point to more pervasive if less official American cultural and economic influence. In *Exporting the American Gospel: Global Christian Fundamentalism*, Steve Brouwer, Paul Gifford, and Susan Rose argue that forms of American fundamentalism have been so infused in American business and media culture that it is "intertwined with the homogenizing influences of consumerism, mass communication, and production in ways that are compatible with the creation of an international market culture."[11]

As these scholars argue, if Western forms of economic globalization have taken root worldwide, so too has conservative Christianity. If the first paradigm defines global Christian growth in contrast to Western decline, this second paradigm defines it as an American export. From this perspective, the conservative forms of American Christianity growing at home are the ones growing globally as well. The defining feature may be less indigenous Christian growth and more commonalities with Western televangelists beamed overseas, free market economics, prosperity theology, and megachurches modeled after American designs.

The two paradigms outlined above turn on the question of whether global Christianity is locally diverse and distinct from Western influence through its indigenous growth or looks more like a monoculture dominated by American institutions and influence. When focusing instead on transnational connections, however, the truth is surely somewhere in between.

A third perspective highlights how global Christianity models theories of globalization more broadly.[12] Historian Mark Noll demonstrates how global Christianity has grown through indigenous agency alongside an embrace of distinctive American organizational models of voluntarism.[13] Sociologist Robert Wuthnow presents impressive empirical evidence to demonstrate America Christians' deep engagement abroad through investment of money, personnel, and other resources.[14] While there is certainly local diversity and agency as well as an imbalance of power that remains between the West and Global South, these global Christian forms are thoroughly interconnected.

This chapter explores American Christians' engagement with global Christianity through the movement of money and the institutional evolution of mission societies and faith-based humanitarianism. Of course, these global connections are never static. They evolve over time. They also are fluid, moving in real time. In fact, transnational theory's recent embrace of the concept of flows provides a perfect lens through which to explore these connected communities and the fiscal turn of a transnational American religious history.[15] Transnationalism has often studied the flow of people (through migration and immigration), information and ideologies (such as education, communication, and media culture), as well as resources (economic development or capital investment). Attending to these flows interrogates the unidirectional processes of global Christian growth highlighted by our first two paradigms. World Christianity scholar Jehu Hanciles affirms that flows, whether people or resources, undercut assessments of globalization as simply a system of Western hegemony. Instead, Hanciles declares, "the processes of globalization are multidirectional, inherently paradoxical, and incorporate movement and countermovement."[16]

A number of scholars of global Christianity have embraced the flow of people, theologies, and cultures as it has defined the interchange between the global and local, but focusing on finances has been less prevalent. Attending to the extensive flows of resources (such as social, intellectual, and financial capital) may serve as an additional lens that does not dismiss the borders of nation-states or boundaries of denominations, but in fact focuses on religion's penchant for exchange and connection. The flow of resources highlights the agency of Northern and Southern actors while not dismissing the power dynamics that larger numbers or greater economic influence brings. This fiscal turn also allows scholars to focus on the new shapes of institutions as formal and informal networks connect communities in new ways. Finances have sometimes triggered and other times trailed the evolution of missionary societies, faith-based nongovernmental organizations

(NGOs), ecumenical councils, or denominational networks. They have also demonstrated the natural overlap between what has often been delineated as three distinct sectors: government, business, and nonprofit. These overlaps are extremely important in unpacking the dynamic development of global Christianity.

Attending to the flows of resources that define the evolution of institutions, power dynamics, and international engagement also help shape the understanding of Americans' own global imaginaries. American Christians live in a global world, and they increasingly see themselves actively participating in it through ease of communication, transportation, and even the commodification of a global Christian community. The business turn in American religious history is not simply attending to the moving of money and weighing cost-benefit analyses. Economic history is also cultural history. Understanding these fiscal global flows gives insight into the way American Christians see the world and their place in it through interactions with market forces and their own global outlooks.

Religion and Globalization

The United States is deeply involved in the processes of globalization, and so is American Christianity. As Robert Wuthnow reminds us, "The globalization of American Christianity is part of the nation's wider participation in the international economic, political, and cultural community."[17] So how do globalization debates generally inform our specific focus on the economic flows of American Christians amid an increasingly global Christianity?

Globalization has most often been defined by the dual realities of (1) a growing consciousness of the world as a single place and (2) the actual compression of time and space (through phenomena such as air travel, the Internet, and the ease in movement of goods and services).[18]

Yet the predominant focus on economics has continually led scholars to define globalization most often as the expansion of Western modernity.[19] Western missionaries were often at the forefront of this work tying forms of Western capitalism to Christian culture, training a new class of non-Western elites to be future leaders in education, business, and politics. Religious studies scholars Peter Beyer and José Casanova describe globalization as connected to Western institutions and the "modern capitalist economy, nation state, and scientific rationality in the form of modern technology."[20] From this perspective, what often emerges is a shared "world culture" that appears rationalized, linked closely to science, production-oriented, and professional.[21]

The rapid growth in size and significance of international nongovernmental organizations (INGOs) on the world stage illustrates the rise of this world culture. As these INGOs come into closer contact with governments, international bodies, and one another, they exhibit a homogenization of language, practice, and organization.[22] Within international relief and development, the desire for federal funding has led many INGOs to adopt a minimum level of professionalization and regulation required by government authorities. At other times, a desire to gain cultural legitimacy among donors or a need to compete with other INGOs served as the impetus for imitation. Many of these humanitarian agencies were founded as religious, but as a recognized field of international relief and development solidified, world culture theorists argue that the leading INGOs have coalesced as a field looking remarkably similar, modern, and secular. From this perspective of a largely secularizing globalization, a humanitarian INGO might claim a religious identity, but as it operates among other international relief and development agencies, it often embodies and reflects a shared secularized world culture despite its religious mission statement or donor base.[23]

Religion has most often been linked to globalization through secularization theories. As summarized by José Casanova, we might categorize the most prevalent perspectives as (1) a differentiation of religious and secular spheres, (2) a decline of religion, and (3) a privatization of religion.[24] Following Max Weber, most have highlighted the privatization of religion as well as a transition from charismatic to bureaucratic authority.[25] If globalization is an overarching Western, rational, modern, and capitalist monoculture, then secularization makes sense. The prominent rise of new forms of global Christianity as well as global Islam outside the West, however, point to the opposite trend. Instead of the death knell of religion through the global march of a secular modernity, faith has risen in the global South both alongside as well as against modern, Western forms. And this is not only the growth of private religious practice among individuals, but it is often public religion engaging economic, political, and cultural issues. Despite these counter-trends, some scholars stick to their secularization guns. Others have reversed course, taking back their predictions of secularization and dismissing Weber's "disenchantment of the world."[26] Most find a middle ground. Globalization have led to multiple secularisms as well as to the differentiation and general bureaucratization of institutions and institutional authority.

Other scholars, however, see religion less as a barrier and more as a boon to moving global citizens into the modern economy. David Martin has made this claim through a modified Protestant ethic in his research of pentecostalism predominantly in Latin America but also Africa and Asia. He sees pentecostalism as offering an outlet from premodern social systems by promoting less hierarchical and more egalitarian relationships alongside beliefs and values that promote values of earnestness and individual choice. These religious ideals also promote family and community while prohibiting vices that often limit economic productivity. Following Martin, global pentecostalism then allows many their first entrée into modern economies with a penchant for entrepreneurism and affirmation of prosperity while giving them the values and tools to succeed. Huge percentages of Latin America's respectable poor, the new middle classes of Asian megacities, and the young and upwardly mobile in Africa are often linked through a loose global Pentecostal web and evangelical hopes of economic self-empowerment.[27]

Global pentecostalism might provide outlets to engage an increasingly modern world; it also offers a worldview that speaks to the globalization's chief existential problem, economic survival. The elasticity and utility of evangelicalism allows for what Paul Gifford names *imaginative rationality*, a set of concepts "that enable people [to] get things done in *this* world."[28] Whether people's hopes are for prosperity, health, or general well-being in a world drastically disrupted by globalization, pentecostalism claims "otherworldly assistance for this-worldly problems" to help people make sense of their current contexts.[29]

The models above presume religion in need of a response to the onslaught of a Western, modern, and largely secular globalization. Yet, as we have begun to see, religion is intricately intertwined with these global forces. Of course, globalization is not only economic but also cultural. Instead of a single globalization, Peter Berger has identified four cultural forms. First, he labels an international business culture. Defined by multinational corporations, World Economic Forums in Davos, and first-class air travelers, he describes an elite economic class. Similarly, Berger identifies a second cultural form as an intellectual elite and progressive NGO culture. Berger sees Western education, think tanks, and international development conferences in Geneva as exemplars of this second form, akin to the INGO world culture discussed above.

While the first two forms point to commonalities among a global elite, Berger's other two forms point to a more popular globalization. The third form, dominated by popular culture that is still often exported from the West, is pervaded by commodities such as McDonald's or Pepsi alongside MTV music videos or role-playing video games. Finally, the fourth form Berger identifies is the popular religious culture of global evangelicalism or pentecostalism. Networks of prosperity-preaching televangelists, parachurch agencies, or international mission agencies dominate this fourth form. Each of these cultural forms is distinct even as they overlap with one another. While global in scope, they also find diverse expressions locally. Without disputing that these faces of globalization are dominated by Western forms, Berger demonstrates that they are exhibited in both global and local, elite and popular, and secular and religious forms.[30]

Therefore, global Christianity plays a vital role in theories of globalization. When focused on economic modernization, a renewed religious vitality exhibited in neo-Pentecostal forms tests secularization narratives. When focused on the commonalties of a shared global evangelicalism, scholars debate whether this is best described as a predominantly Western-exported monoculture or the product of multiple diverse local cultures.[31] Is the rise of global evangelicalism an accommodation or affirmation of economic modernization and neoliberalism, or it is rather a reaction to Western dominance? Regardless of the conclusion, bringing cultural analysis to the study of religion and globalization allows for a broader vision and a corrective to analysis focused exclusively on economics and modernization. Global Christianity or globalization is not a single culture. Attending to how people experience these processes from multiple angles over time privileges flows and movement without ignoring Western hegemony or the local agency within the global South.

Religious Institutions

An influential paradigm among sociologists of religion has embraced market language to articulate a theory of the "religious economy." Most often linked to Laurence Iannaccone, Roger Finke, and Rodney Stark, these sociological frameworks apply categories from early sociologists such as Ernst Troeltsch and his distinctions between "church" and "sect."[32] They often analyze denominations and religious traditions through the lens of the "firm." In framing a religious marketplace, they use supply and demand as the dynamics of competition that explain the "winners" and "losers" in a religious economy. Relying on free market principles, the paradigm naturally privileges the religious vitality, diversity, and change in the American religious landscape in contrast to traditional state-church countries with increased secularization in Western Europe. The paradigm also privileges loosely affiliated denominations, voluntary societies, and less hierarchical, independent movements.[33] American religious historians have acknowledged the limits of such an overarching paradigm as explanative of American religious vitality.[34]

Despite significant critique, however, the religious marketplace metaphor has also implicitly been applied to explain America's influence abroad in global Christianity's success. As mentioned earlier, Mark Noll illustrates that it was the institutional models of voluntary agencies, parachurch groups, independent churches, and loosely affiliated denominations that set the pace for American evangelical growth in the nineteenth century and was then exported through missions alongside markets and the military.[35] Americans planted the seeds through these forms for global Christian growth. While the religious economy paradigm has significant limitations as *the* paradigm for American or global Christian growth, because of its simplicity and explanative power, it is widely cited—explicitly or implicitly—to dictate the winners and losers in a global Christian marketplace.

The new paradigm is also significant in returning attention to religious institutions. A larger fiscal turn opens a return to new forms of institutional history as well. This chapter specifically highlights the evolution of mission and faith-based development institutional networks as influenced by religious traditions, government, business, and other INGOs. Applying a modified "neo-institutional approach" taken from the field of organization studies makes it possible to identify how organizations function within a field of institutions. In an underutilized study, American religious historians Harry Stout and Scott Cormode have proposed how neo-institutionalism could redefine the place of institutions in American religious history. Noting that institutions are neither simply hierarchies nor bureaucracies, they define an institution as an "embedded social structure of rules and hierarchies created to embody and perpetuate a set of cultural norms and values among its members."[36] Institutions also represent culture, values, symbols, and ideas. Along with social relations and structural organization, institutions embody cultural logics, or assumptions and ideas that motivate people.

In examining the evolution of mission and faith-based humanitarianism, it is clear that the fields in which these organizations belong are not bereft of meaning. Debates between evangelicals and ecumenical Christians on the relationship of evangelism and social action or secular and religious approaches to mission and development are full of meaning for the organization and its constituencies. Sometimes ideas and theology help produce structural change. At other times, strategic structural decisions and market changes alter religious identity.

Often these religious institutions must be identified not as a part of one but multiple fields. For example, World Vision International, with 45,000 employees and an annual budget over $2 billion, is the largest Christian humanitarian agency in the world and has operated in multiple fields, often simultaneously: an American evangelical subculture, a collection of missionary agencies, a global evangelicalism, large-scale fund-raising nonprofit organizations, and a secular development INGO network. Understanding World Vision or any other faith-based INGO requires investigating the multiple contexts and networks in which it operates and the various audiences to which it articulates its identity. In contrast to world culture theorists, the question is not if these development organizations are religious, but often how they are religious and how the religious practices of those encountering these agencies at home and abroad shape all aspects of the organization.

Finally we must acknowledge that religious actors imbue markets with ethical and moral meaning. Attending to the moral discourse is also important and also serves as a significant site of contention between American and global Christians. While some laud free markets and limited government regulation as a divinely inspired path to nations' prosperity and economic growth, others protest these same market ideologies as desecrating the environment, promoting increased inequality between rich and poor, and dismissing global or national responsibilities for sharing resources. Whatever a business turn may mean for global Christianity, it must include the debates of international actors employing religious and moral language to argue for basic human rights or free markets as well as the overarching question: what makes for a good life?[37]

The Evolution of American Mission Institutions

Mission history has often served as a clear illustration of Western colonialism. Few would deny the connections. David Livingstone (1813–1873), nineteenth-century British explorer and missionary to Africa, famously promoted the three C's: Christianity, commerce, and civilization. While Livingstone fought to end the British slave trade, he saw no need to separate religion and empire and felt that Africans would make progress only through integrating into a modern European economy. There were objectors. Henry Venn (1796–1873), head of the Anglican Church Missionary Society (CMS) and Livingstone's contemporary, contrasted the three C's with his Three-Self formula, arguing that indigenous churches should be self-supporting, self-governing, and self-extending so that they might become independent of Western financial support, maintain local control, and grow through their own local forms.[38]

The nineteenth century was known as the great century of missions, with Western missionaries enthusiastically embracing a modernizing impulse.

Whether they succeeded in converting locals to the faith or not, countless missionary schools did succeed in training a new class of non-Western elites who embraced Western culture and economic modernization as they took roles in the leadership of education, business, and politics. At the height of imperialism, the 1910 Edinburgh Conference embodied this enthusiasm "for the immediate conquest of the world" and the "evangelization of the world in this generation."[39] Western Protestants united across theological lines to call for non-Western countries to embrace Christian conversion and civilization.

The first half of the twentieth century brought changes to the missionary enterprise as the missionary impulse was shifting from Britain to the United States. American missionaries had grown popular and powerful. U.S. presidents spoke at missionary conferences, mission leaders served as foreign diplomats, and Ivy League graduates were eager to serve the YMCA in stations around the world.[40] Yet by World War I the optimism of Edinburgh's mandate began to falter. After the Great War, many in the dominant mainline denominations adopted a broader internationalist language. Supporting Woodrow Wilson's Fourteen Points, the League of Nations, and self-determination for all peoples, they spoke more of world unity than of world conquest.[41] Influenced by modernism and the Social Gospel, some missionaries measured their success through the building of hospitals and schools rather than the counting of souls saved. Others reevaluated their view of non-Christian religions. While missions continued to grow slowly in the 1920s and 1930s, these new directions shattered the united missionary enterprise.[42]

The fundamentalists and modernists of the era exported their theological battles to the mission field. No document created greater passions than the Laymen's Foreign Missions Inquiry of 1932. Sponsored by seven mainline denominational mission boards and underwritten by liberal layman and philanthropist John D. Rockefeller Jr., the report questioned the older mission enterprise. Its ideal was Christian humanitarian service, not conversion.[43]

As a result, many conservatives withdrew from the denominations to form their own independent mission agencies. Unlike salaried missionaries appointed by denominational boards, a new model of "faith missions" led recruits to rely on God's provision for their financial support. Initially, faith missionaries understood themselves as complementing rather than replacing denominational personnel. They had long commissioned single women as well as those with insufficient education to be appointed by the denominational boards. With names such as China Inland Mission and Africa Inland Mission, faith missions left the cities and ports to established agencies and moved inland to "unreached" indigenous populations. They remained largely transdenominational and transnational, requiring only conservative doctrinal agreement. As Northern mainline denominations divided, however, faith mission came to serve less as a complement and more as an alternative to mainline missions.[44]

Despite a decline in finances and new candidates, the mainline boards still maintained ten times more missionaries than conservative independent agencies between 1920 and 1950. Asia dominated the missionary imagination. In 1919, Protestant mainline denominations made up more than 70 percent of the missionary force in the three largest "mission fields," China, India, and Japan.[45] In addition to missionary personnel, the movement invested millions of dollars—more than $2.5 million just in Japan and Korea in 1939 alone. Yet by the 1930s, new nationalisms, modernization, and maturing indigenous Christian communities began to question missionary motives. China fell into civil war beginning in 1927, Japan went to war with China in 1937, and India rebelled against British colonial rule in 1920. The loss of Asia devastated mainline missions.[46] Yet if closing countries and a loss of evangelistic zeal dampened mainline missions, these events allowed for a refocusing of institutional energies into the hope for a shared global Christianity. Ecumenical mission conferences debated indigenization principles, supported national Christian councils, and redefined social action as an essential part of the gospel.[47]

During the same period, faith missionaries expanded as fundamentalists continued to abandon denominational boards and form independent agencies. At the same time, they changed from a "generalized, self-sufficient missionary society model" into specialized agencies. While "evangelism" still dominated, new ministries included Wycliffe Bible Translators, which focused on linguistics, the Far East Gospel Broadcasting Company, which pursued radio evangelism, and the Mission Aviation Fellowship, which flew missionaries into remote locations. Often virtually invisible to mainstream culture, these organizations combined optimism, technology, and fundraising prowess to succeed at worldwide evangelization.[48]

The end of World War II brought both mainline and fundamentalist/evangelical missionaries into the mission field with ample finances and confidence in American exceptionalism. General Douglas MacArthur challenged American churches to send ten thousand missionaries to Asia, and the churches surpassed his goal.[49] Former U.S. soldiers returned to study in Bible colleges on the G.I. Bill, joined mission societies, and returned overseas. Dozens of religious entrepreneurs built specialized mission organizations. Young evangelists supported by new agencies such as Youth for Christ, the Navigators, the Billy Graham Evangelistic Association (BGEA), and World

Vision drew record crowds to month-long crusades in foreign cities. If the number of mainline missionaries once far outpaced evangelicals, by 1955 conservative missionaries constituted the majority as evangelicals moved from the margins to the mainstream of American culture.[50]

Cold War politics fanned the initial flames of the burgeoning international engagement of these post–World War II evangelicals. As they sought to reclaim their role in society, they also sought to win the world for Christ and America, spreading the gospel alongside democracy and capitalism. As William Imboden noted, "What they lack in institutional and intellectual credibility, they tried to compensate for with organization and energy."[51] Evangelicals, however, were not the only ones. By the early 1950s, all the large religious denominations had established anticommunist educational programs. Nationalism and anticommunism, couched in religious language, served as the glue binding a common Judeo-Christian tradition. Capitalism and communism were conflicting economic systems. American Christians also saw them as conflicting religious cultures to be engaged with missionary fervor. America's chief evangelist, Billy Graham, claimed, "Communism is not only an economic interpretation of life—Communism is a religion that is inspired, directed, and motivated by the Devil himself who has declared war against Almighty God."[52] As any politician would, President Harry Truman capitalized on such fervor to unite Americans behind a religious cause: faith and prosperity would overcome Soviet unbelief and communism.

Yet these two diametrically opposed ideological systems shared a common goal (global hegemony through modernization) as well the mechanisms to achieve it (technological advancement through the methods of production). These two global powers, the Western and Soviet blocs, fought over control of the nonaligned nations, the "third world," while economic development became a key tool of statecraft for both to garner support and gain the upper hand.

As Cold War politics led American Christians to a greater international focus, the place for social and economic issues on the missionary agenda again rekindled debate. Fundamentalists and modernists had already split over these issues decades earlier. Now new evangelicals and other mainliners sought to find a balance. Better technology and communication meant that periodicals with firsthand reports of global famines and photographs of malnourished children arrived in mailboxes while missionaries presented footage of shelled-out villages and leper colonies through films shown in local churches.[53] While theological debates continued, popular reports of American missions avoided the dichotomy between evangelism and social action that had ripped apart the Protestant missionary enterprise. Most evangelicals would claim that conversion was primary, but they also understood the need to meet physical needs first before addressing spiritual ones. In fact, many saw the two as linked, believing that conversion could even lead to material benefits, helping to alleviate poverty and warding off communism. Yet American Christians disagreed about the systemic character of poverty. Often Western missionaries illustrated global poverty one individual child at a time, juxtaposing a malnourished Korean orphan next to a well-fed, middle-class American child. The image of an innocent child helped bypass divisive theological debates and put a human face in the place of mind-numbing statistics. The result were new funding models such as child sponsorship programs. Rather than rely on government or denominational funds, new groups such as Christian Children's Fund, World Vision, and Compassion International appealed directly to the public for monthly support and offered an opportunity to correspond with a Christian child overseas. They met with overwhelming financial success and presented a new way for Americans to engage with one picture of a growing global Christianity[54]

By the mid-twentieth century, missions had evolved through various forms. Though missions had once been dominated by denominational boards, theological skirmishes and new funding models led to the rise of a number of new faith missions and independent agencies. As a prosperous America emerged from World War II to fight the Cold War, a new type of internationally focused parachurch agency emerged as well. The comingling and competition among these American mission institutions exposed American Christians to a world to which they might not have otherwise paid much attention. New funding models brought images of the developing world into their homes, offering them new opportunities to participate in a maturing global Christianity in ways that convinced many to open their pocketbooks.

The Rise of Faith-Based Humanitarianism and International Development

At the same time American mission agencies were expanding through renewed global interest and evolving through new forms and shifting constituencies, a new American style of global development was emerging as well. In many ways, Americans Christianity was also at the forefront of this movement. At the turn of the twentieth century, progressive reformers and Social Gospel proponents did not hide their belief in the superiority of Western civilization but rather channeled it into a responsibility to share modernity and social progress with the world. What some considered a decline in evangelism among mainline missions, others simply saw as an expansion of their Christian vision through development and progress. Often these same Protestant missionaries aligned themselves with governments, businesses, universities, and foundations to create what they deemed a better (and more modern) world. Philanthropist and liberal Protestant layman John D. Rockefeller Jr. again modeled such a turn. At the same time he was funding the Laymen's Study, which challenged traditional missionary methods, he was ardently supporting China's modernization through rural agriculture with missionaries deeply involved in the work.[55]

Through America's grand entry into international affairs and the West's slow transition away from colonialism, the history of international development has often focused on President Harry S. Truman's 1949 Inaugural Address as its beginning:

> More than half the people of the world are living in conditions approaching misery. . . . Their poverty is a handicap and a threat both to them and to more prosperous areas. For the first time in history humanity possesses the knowledge and the skill to relieve the suffering of these people.[56]

Establishing a new centerpiece of American foreign policy, Truman lent financial support, political power, and religious zeal to international development in order to contain communism and establish America's global hegemony. Yet what Truman proposed was nothing new. He was building upon a view of the world that Protestant missions had already established. Alongside traditional missions, however, a number of new religious humanitarian agencies emerged to assist in making Truman's vision a reality. Having enshrined "freedom from want" into his Four Freedoms, President Franklin D. Roosevelt had already helped to create new international institutions such as the United Nations (UN), International Monetary Fund (IMF), and World Bank. At home, Roosevelt established the American Council of Voluntary Agencies in Foreign Service (ACVAFS) to coordinate the relief work of American private voluntary organizations (PVOs). From the beginning, a "three-faiths consortium" of mainline Protestants, Catholics, and Jews maintained close ties with the U.S. government.

A host of religious philanthropies established under FDR's initiative honed their voluntary work during World War II and offered themselves in order to realize Truman's vision.[57] Catholic Relief Services (which began in 1943),

Church World Service (1946), Lutheran World Relief (1945), CARE (1945), and the American-Jewish Joint Distribution Committee (1914) captured the public imagination in the 1940s and attained wide recognition during the Cold War, especially through their work in Korea and Vietnam.[58] By 1947, 75 percent of private philanthropy overseas flowed through Protestant, Catholic, and Jewish agencies, and through the early 1950s, religious agencies received the majority of government support[59]

As a new stream of international religious humanitarian agencies emerged out of World War II, they offered a variety of approaches. Many of the largest religious humanitarian agencies served as arms of denominational or ecumenical bodies. Most of these worked in partnership with the U.S. government and received millions in grants, subsidies, and in-kind resources for the developing world. Others, largely new evangelistic and independent agencies, had little patience for government partnership. They worried that bureaucracy would quench the Spirit or require them to relinquish their evangelistic fervor. Officially registered religious agencies questioned their experience, evangelistic proclivities, and willingness to partner and often left them on the periphery of humanitarianism's inner circle.[60] Yet a set of shared religious motivations still led to a sense of responsibility for the world that united these disparate movements around a spirit of development.

With modernization and economic growth the unquestioned goal of development in the 1950s and 1960s, the United States alongside the UN, IMF, and World Bank poured money into large-scale development projects. They brought in Western technical and scientific knowledge to build highways, promote industry, and establish universities. Tackling macro-issues, they theorized that a growing gross national product (GNP) would trickle down to benefit everyone.[61] While all denominations, mission agencies, and faith-based relief and development organizations would not have used the same language, and some missionary voices worried that development was covertly spreading a secular social gospel, most left the Western approach of modernization unquestioned.

There were unique exceptions. Dan West, founder of Heifer International, got the initial vision to send livestock overseas instead of short-term aid or trickle-down development in order to help people move from dependence to self-sufficiency. With its original motto "A cow, not a cup," Heifer became one of the most well-known and respected faith-based development-oriented nonprofits. West's idea was to provide livestock so that those in need would have milk and food, and so that through animal husbandry they could create a continual, self-sufficient source of income and support. In the midst of World

War II, he proposed the plan at his Church of the Brethren congregation in northern Indiana. Soon three calves named Hope, Faith, and Charity were donated and shipped overseas. The project soon spread across the American heartland. By the end of 1942, the Heifers for Relief Committee brought together Mennonites, Presbyterians, Methodists, Lutherans, and Amish for the work. Farmers raised heifers at home specifically to ship overseas and do their part to alleviate global hunger.[62]

Occasionally Americans' international engagement forced them to step back and reflect on their unregulated optimism. In 1958, William J. Lederer and Eugene Burdick published *The Ugly American*. Serialized in the *Saturday Evening Post*, the novel topped the best-seller list for seventy-eight weeks and sold four million copies.[63] The book excoriated the incompetence and laziness of State Department officials, ambassadors, and aid workers who lived comfortably while refusing to learn local languages and customs. American Christians took the opportunity to hold up religious workers in clear contrast to ugly Americans. They were red-blooded Americans who built modern economies and democracies, but, having learned the language and local customs, they built local trust alongside their schools, orphanages, clinics, and churches.[64]

This expanding global outlook often led American Christians to compare themselves unfavorably with their global Christian brothers and sisters. Where was Christianity most alive? In the small and often persecuted churches of Asia. On a 1960 international crusade, Billy Graham reported, "My travels in Asia and Africa have enabled me to meet so many Christians whose spiritual commitment, sensitiveness, and discipline are greater than anything I find at home [and] I shall not be surprised if more and more of them come to Europe and North America as 'missionaries.'"[65] Americans' self-critique was often linked to prosperity and a lack of sacrifice. Global Christians suffered under persecution and poverty, while Americans sought wealth and comfort. Western modernization had strong advocates, but occasionally American Christians delimited its excesses as a stumbling block and held up global Christians as the ideal.

As religious and secular development models continued to gain steam, however, modernization was acquiring its share of global critics. Latin American dependency theorists claimed that development perpetuated Western domination and reinforced the same systems that had helped create poverty. Other Third World leaders did not refuse Western aid but advocated "self-reliance" that allowed them to make their own choices about how development should proceed in their countries.[66] When the United Nations declared the 1970s the Second Development Decade, it began to heed calls for change. Development policy moved from investments in governments and an obsession with GNP to the redistribution of wealth and consultation with local communities about what they saw as their needs.[67]

In 1973, the U.S. Foreign Assistance Act aligned the United States Agency for International Development (USAID) with this new agenda. Instead of awarding contracts for the distribution of relief goods or the building of infrastructure to a handful of established agencies, it asked all NGOs to propose grants for individual projects. The number of NGOs receiving grants skyrocketed. The United States valued their expertise and capacity to mobilize local resources. NGOs appreciated the ability to shape their own projects.[68] Most religious NGOs supported these new directions. The dependency theorists' critiques of Western development paralleled the rise of liberation theology among both Catholic and ecumenical Protestants, who called for solidarity with the poor in ways that facilitated participatory development. And at the same time that some theologians were praising community development because it represented solidarity with the poor, organizational networks in the NGOs nurtured their long standing relationships with local communities. The smaller NGOs lacked the resources for large-scale relief, but most religious agencies had decades of experience working with religious leaders in global towns and villages.[69]

Although evangelicals had once considered development as a form of "secularized missions" and often felt squeezed out of large-scale government funding, they now began to see how missions and development could work together. The overlaps allowed some to revisit their approach by adopting more holistic language, a focus on indigenous leadership, and an embrace of structural injustice.[70] Missionaries now talked of development projects in local communities, while evangelicals founded new development agencies that had no missionary past. These new evangelical agencies grew in number and began to overtake the long-established mainline agencies in size and scope. The organizational and funding models of the older ecumenical organizations struggled, as they had become too dependent on government funding or denominational offerings. The mainline, Catholic, and Jewish religious agencies that had partnered with America's global vision at the outset of the Cold War begin to take a backseat in size and prestige as postcolonial critiques led some to distance themselves from the U.S. government and reimagine the role of the United States abroad. Upstart American evangelical agencies were now more willing to partner, and they found themselves a major player in international development. At the same time, as these agencies began to professionalize, the broader field of global development came to appreciate their size, experience, and expertise. Forty-five percent of all religious INGOs are now evangelical, which is by far the largest percentage of any religious tradition.[71]

The numbers of secular and religious INGOs and their budgets continued to expand dramatically. From 1970 to 1990, government aid to NGOs increased from under $200 million to $2.2 billion. In the 1980s alone, the combined budgets of INGOs almost tripled from $2.3 billion to $6 billion.[72] Yet this was in larger part due to another change in the models of development. What was a focus on local communities and basic needs in the 1970s now demanded that developing nations make structural adjustments in order to receive foreign aid. With agencies such as the World Bank and the International Monetary Fund (IMF) now embracing neoliberal economics, they required the reduction of government spending, deregulation of public institutions, and free trade with international corporations. Linking underdevelopment with corruption and inefficiency, neoliberals believed if they could privatize the public sector, free markets would benefit everyone. In reality, however, the demands led governments to cut social services. Western aid once funneled directly to foreign governments now went to the INGOs.[73]

Amid the continued drastic growth in size and number of INGOs over the past few decades, religious agencies have grown increasingly important. More than a third of all international nongovernmental organizations (INGOs) are now religious organizations, making up almost half of all NGOs' annual revenue. Religiously affiliated agencies make up a growing percentage of the recent rise of small grassroots agencies. They also number among the largest in the industry. Over the past decade, six of the ten largest American international nongovernmental organizations (INGOs) were Christian organizations.[74]

Yet even as the growth and professionalization of faith-based organizations (FBOs) have drawn the attention of elites within the development sector, they have often overlooked the particularities of organizations' distinct religious identities in favor of broad categorizations. Some have continued to segregate FBOs from the field of more "secular" professional development. Most often, however, the development literature has simply added faith on to a largely Westernized elite development discourse that unwittingly perpetuates and privileges development as a secular and neutral enterprise that religion must engage on foreign ground. In contrast, religious studies scholars demonstrate that development frameworks themselves can be viewed as their own secular religious ideologies as they embrace modernization, neoliberal economics, or particular forms of globalization.[75]

The fluid religious identities of development institutions are vital to understanding the interactions and imaginations of American and global Christians. Through this broader lens, FBOs may professionalize by transitioning from missions to development, hire specialized staff, or take government funding, but this does not necessitate a universal secularization. The diversity of religious agencies likewise defies any attempt to universalize a single secular or religious approach to development. Finally, questions of religious identity affect more than an organization's mission statement, hiring practices, and reliance on government support. It cannot be separated from how an organization shapes its institutional structure, manages its staff, appeals to potential donors, and translates the need for global development in the public sphere.

In some cases, global Christianity led faith-based INGOs to confront the overtly Western forms of development practice and institutional governance before secular organizations. By the 1980s, the global fault lines were less East versus West and now more North versus South. As the global South critiqued Western development, some within religious agencies articulated the need for change through a theological lens. World Vision International serves as one example. While the organization had offices in Canada, Australia, and New Zealand by the late 1960s, it largely remained an American agency funding programs run by local missionaries and churches overseas. By the 1970s, these new offices wanted greater representation and participation. They also knew true internationalization would necessitate abandoning a provincial Americanism for a more global geopolitics. Yet, they argued that internationalization was more than a question of organization; it was a matter of theology. Evangelical missiology now viewed Western missionaries as partners or servants of indigenous churches. Attempts to "express spiritual internationalism in organizational terms" led to real structural change. By 1978, the United States office handed over control to create World Vision International. The U.S. office remained the most influential, but now sat at the table as one among several voices making decisions about strategic planning, field operations, and budget.[76]

Alongside shared control, internal diversity also challenged World Vision's traditional evangelical ethos. In adopting development practice and the critiques of fellow global Christians, World Vision began to rely less on American expatriates and more on an indigenous workforce. As a result, its in-country staff began to resemble the Christian communities in the countries where it worked. In expanding to Eastern Europe after the Soviet Union's collapse, it hired a number of Orthodox staff people. In Latin America, it hired Catholics. The percentage of Pentecostal staff grew alongside the movement's growth throughout sub-Saharan Africa. The majority of staff members still identified as evangelical, yet diverse donor and staff constituencies made room for a broader Christian language that no longer reflected only the dialect of an American evangelicalism. At times, in some predominantly Muslim countries, a commitment to indigenous employees has led World Vision to hire a majority Muslim workforce even while retaining its Christian identity.[77] The mixing of faith and economics sometimes led American agencies to export Western models and lag behind development trends. At other times, however, faith-based INGOs were out front as their intimate engagement with global Christian voices led them to embrace change in governance and leadership long before others. The question is how religion and the religious practices of those with whom these agencies interact, at home and abroad, shape the organization's development techniques, management strategies, and corporate branding, as well as the everyday lives of employees, donors, and aid recipients.

New Forms of American Christian Engagement Within a Global Economy

Trends in both markets and missions have led to continued international interest from American Christians, but the institutional forms have continued to evolve. As denominations and centralized agencies have declined, new specialized agencies emerged and crossed over traditional boundaries. Mission and humanitarian agencies now overlap with local churches, social enterprises, and short-term missions. Like the global economy, the global religious marketplace may still be dominated by the West, but the influences and fluidity of forms have become incredibly diffuse.

If Washington Consensus economic institutions like the World Bank and IMF came to adopt neoliberal economic outlooks by the 1980s, a number of American Christians explicitly turned to these economic principles as central to their global mission as well. Through increased productivity and profit, these proponents argue with a missionary zeal that beneficent markets enable everyone to rise out of poverty.[78] From this perspective, training global entrepreneurs and marketplace leaders in the keys of private enterprise may serve as a better investment than funding religious humanitarianism. Private enterprise became a virtue, and many Christian colleges, think tanks, and nonprofits sought to train the next generation of leaders in the United States and in developing nations to protect these virtues at home and promote them abroad. The School of Business at Pat Robertson's Regent University framed its mission as training business leaders "to revolutionize nations economically and provide platforms for spiritual revival."[79] Prominent private Christian philanthropy such as the DeVos and Kern family foundations have funded the American Enterprise Institute or the Heritage Foundation to cement neoliberal economic and neoconservative political policies while also creating programs such as the Acton Institute to train students, entrepreneurs, nonprofit leaders, and international leaders in the intersections of "liberty, faith, virtue and free-market economics."[80] For these prominent platforms, a particular global vision of faith and economics is clear.

More often, however, the connections are subtler. In recent years, the same Western management systems or leadership principles applied to churches at home have found a welcome reception overseas. John Maxwell, an evangelical pastor best-known as a motivational speaker and leadership expert, has traveled to conferences of pastors and business leaders from around the world in recent years. Leaders within the global South are perfectly capable of leading their own seminars, but sometimes the presumption that the West knows best still exist.[81] For example, with Saddleback Church pastor Rick Warren's *The Purpose-Driven Life* having sold more than 30 million copies and reportedly translated into more languages than any book other than the Bible, Warren was courted by global leaders throughout the world. His global recognition came at the same time he first visited Africa and felt God calling him to "the cause of ending global poverty." He soon confessed: "I have been so busy building my church that I have not cared about the poor." Rwandan president Paul Kagame invited Warren to make Rwanda the first "purpose-driven nation, and Warren accepted the challenge.[82] By 2005, Warren had established his PEACE plan, which aimed to "plant churches, equip servant leaders, assist the poor, care for the sick, and educate the next generation." Most development experts questioned Warren's methods if not his motives. Boston College political scientist Alan Wolfe criticized Warren's "considerable naïveté," but he also said that historians were "likely to pinpoint Mr. Warren's trip to Rwanda as the moment when conservative evangelical Protestantism made questions of social justice central to its concerns."[83] Over the past decade, a new generation of Western pastors discovered global outlets for their work and invitations to apply them abroad. The discoveries came well after many American Christian international agencies had spent decades engaged overseas, and they often rehashed old debates, but they led a new pockets of American Christians to turn their attention abroad.

Another subtler overlap of faith and markets is the growing "business as mission" movement. Often referring to themselves as "tentmakers" in reference to the Apostle Paul, who financially supported his own missionary work by making tents (Acts 18:3), these Christian workers support themselves through their skills in the marketplace. While tentmakers have existed throughout Christian history, they have expanded rapidly in recent years. First, with neoliberal economic principles in place, there is a predilection for the positive impact of free markets. Second, however, as the budgets and personnel support by traditional missionary societies have declined, the ability for Christian workers to support themselves is becoming a greater necessity. Third, starting businesses has often served as the entrée for Christians into countries closed to traditional missionaries, such as many in the Middle East. These businesses often serve as the legitimate cover for their otherwise outlawed evangelism. Finally, business as mission has allowed for a new type of missionary. If the mission enterprise was traditionally dominated by preachers, teachers, or doctors, now it is just as accessible to engineers, business executives, and entrepreneurs. Of course, business as mission is not simply an American export. It may be a South Korean tech entrepreneur just as much as a Houston petroleum engineer with a passion for engaging in Christian mission as their reason for working in places such as Saudi Arabia.[84]

While some of these businesses measure success by profit maximization as much as by evangelistic or humanitarian outreach, an increasing number also measure impact by an additional bottom line of social impact. In the United States, thirty states have now passed provisions explicitly allowing for this new type of for-profit entity, the benefit corporation. The trend is spreading to multiple countries, and while such corporations are not necessarily faith-based, many are tied to founders with faith at the core of their mission or have been frequented by Christians because of their shared values of the common good.[85]

Whether benefit corporations or not, some businesses specifically capitalize on international consciousness in order to build their brand as both stylish and philanthropic. In 2006, Blake Mycoskie founded TOMS Shoes with the pledge to give away one pair of shoes to a child in need for every pair purchased, and while not tied to a religious mission, the company has grown wildly popular with American Christian youth and often partnered with faith-based INGOs in order to deliver shoes in the developing world. As multiple companies like TOMS have emerged, they not only share a portion of their profits with those in need but also are selling the opportunity for American consumers to purchase an identity, namely, as someone who cares.

Many have critiqued these buy-one-give-one (BOGO) models, partly because they often naively flooded the developing world with shoes or eyeglasses that undermined local indigenous economies. Companies such as TOMS Shoes and Warby Parker eyewear have listened to such criticism and are now more aware of the value of helping local artisans create products instead of simply shipping their own products overseas.[86] As these companies make clear, it is not only direct global interaction of American Christians abroad, but it also the way in which business shapes the global imaginaries and types of engagement with the world in which they exist.

American Christians have often adopted the latest trends from popular culture. If true in the case of contemporary music or youth culture, it is also true in business. Christian bookstores and music labels are one thing, but a penchant for fair-trade products and micro-enterprise is another. Sometimes this is as simple as faith communities acknowledging their role in the global economy by shifting to serve fair-trade coffee in their worship centers, but it is often much more involved, with major faith-based humanitarian agencies such as World Vision and Opportunity International promoting microfinance. Building on the principles of Nobel Prize winner Muhammad Yunus, who has promoted ways in which individual Western donors can make small loans to individuals in the developing world, American Christian organizations have either supported giving through a leading nonprofit intermediary such as Kiva or else built their own direct peer-to-project online platform. The funds are not charity. Instead, they are an investment that promotes a personal connection between a donor and a budding entrepreneur in the developing world.[87]

American Christians have never relinquished their initial missionary impulse, but the ways in which they can take part in a global Christianity have become incredibly diffuse, from donating to a multimillion-dollar INGO to starting their own grassroots agency or investing in peer-to-peer micro-finance. American congregations, however, still remain the lifeblood of global engagement. While multiple forms of global engagement operate outside the confines of church culture—some having made this choice quite intentionally—the majority still find that their resources, whether information, finances, or personnel, most often flow through local congregations. At the same time, with the ease of travel and communication made possible through globalization, local churches have begun to connect directly with global Christians overseas without the need to work through denominations or missionary societies.

In fact, since the 1970s, the phenomenon of short-term missions (STMs) has led local church members to see the world for themselves. Sociologist Robert Wuthnow estimates that 2.1 percent of active church members in the United States (1.6 million individuals) travel to another country on a religious mission trip each year.[88] The short-term mission trips of individual American Christians have not replaced mission efforts overseas but rather complement the efforts of missionaries, development workers, social entrepreneurs, and indigenous churches. Scholars debate whether STMs drain the resources of local staff, disrupt local economies, and create further dependency or rather bolster greater global investment and financial giving.[89] Often STMs come to provide funding, knowledge, or labor. Others come strictly to develop relationships. A growing movement among U.S. churches have established official long-term relationships with "sister churches" abroad that allows for mutual learning and exchange.[90] Almost all STM participants return to America claiming that they received far more than they gave, but the flows of finances and people through STMs have created a market in itself. Faith-based travel agencies specialize in coordinating trips for churches, while staff from religious agencies at home and abroad are employed to manage volunteers full-time. In fact, an evangelical professional class has emerged in countries such as Ghana, South Africa, or Guatemala of indigenous leadership equipped with college educations, ministry and business backgrounds, and cross-cultural skills to serve as go-betweens connecting Western STMs and funders with the work of the religious agencies on the ground.[91] A pervasive economic and cultural modernization has made these exchanges possible amid the flows of a global Christianity.

Conclusion

As a result of globalization, the dynamic flow of resources demonstrate how ever-evolving markets dictate the interactions of power, people, and profits in the development of a global Christianity. These market exchanges also affect American Christians' own global imaginaries. Sociologist Robert Priest has argued that the increased international exposure unsettled "a confident American exceptionalism" and troubled "simplistic patriotism."[92] But global awareness did not always bring worries. Many have welcomed global Christian growth and felt an affinity with born-again believers abroad. Sometimes they embraced an "enchanted internationalism" that bolstered global solidarity but reintroduced an "imperialist-style imaginary" that exoticized the other it claimed to embrace.[93] After brief international experiences, Western evangelicals often claimed to "really know" their fellow global Christians. Shared beliefs often trumped real differences.[94] Global awareness, in short, has been a source of both discouragement and enthusiasm.

In this vein, while much more could be said about the expansion of global prosperity, American Christians' internationalism has also led to greater understandings of the shortcomings of the global economy. In conjunction with the United Nations' Millennium Development Goals (MDGs), which originally pledged to halve global poverty by 2015 and have continued apace into the future, new religious agencies such as Micah Challenge emerged to enlist evangelical support.[95] A generation ago, most evangelicals saw the UN as a liberal or even atheistic enemy. Now a number of evangelical NGOs and denominations integrated the Millennium Development Goals into their aims for mission. In 2004, with the help of celebrities such as Bono, frontman for the rock band U2, and the funds of the Bill and Melinda Gates Foundation, the agencies reorganized to launch the ONE campaign to end extreme poverty and the global AIDS epidemic. While the campaign's goal was to persuade the U.S. government to allocate 1 percent of its budget to the world's poorest countries, its biggest success was making global poverty an issue for a new generation. Young evangelicals bought "Make Poverty History" wristbands and attended benefit concerts in droves. Few stopped to think about distinctions between structural injustice and individual salvation or whether poverty was a religious or secular issue. Global fiscal policy had become a religious issue.

For most Americans, discussions of religious NGOs have been dominated by coverage of the federal funding for domestic faith-based initiatives initiated under President Bill Clinton and expanded under Presidents George W. Bush and Barack Obama, yet the debates over faith-based initiatives have rarely applied to the funding for large-scale international development. The finances are significant. Indeed, most religious aid agencies that operate overseas have benefited from government funding for decades and are accountable to multiple professional and humanitarian standards as a part of a shared field of relief and development. But professionalized development is only one aspect of an extremely fluid market of missionaries, INGOs, and faith-based businesses that take part in defining a global Christianity. These interconnected markets cannot escape the complexities of globalization from either the perspective of U.S. Christians or the increasingly global Christian communities around the world.

Notes

1. Moses O. Biney, *From Africa to America: Religion and Adaptation Among Ghanaian Immigrants in New York* (New York: New York University Press, 2011).

2. Robert Wuthnow, *Boundless Faith: The Global Outreach of American Churches* (Berkeley: University of California Press, 2009), 1.

3. Scholars have debated the terms *global Christianity* versus *world Christianity*. Yale missiologist Lamin Sanneh may most clearly capture how scholars tend to distinguish the terms. I follow Stephen Offutt's adaptation of Sanneh's distinctions. *World Christianity* tends to focus on the indigenous, local-level diversity of Christian communities. *Global Christianity* often focuses more on the macro-elements that define the international community (whether shared, held in tension, or initiated out of the West). Because the focus of this volume is predominantly American religious history, I focus here most often on how American Christians encounter or imagine a global Christian community. See Lamin Sanneh, *Whose Religion Is Christianity? The Gospel Beyond the West* (Grand Rapids, MI: Eerdmans, 2003); Stephen Offutt, *New Centers of Global Evangelicalism in Latin America and Africa* (New York: Cambridge University Press, 2015), 25. For arguments on why world Christianity is a more appropriate stance for teaching the history of Christianity, see my "Taking World Christianity into the Classroom: A Review Essay," *Theology Today* 7, no. 2 (2014): 246–251.

4. Pew Forum on Religion and Public Life, *Spirit and Power: A 10-Country Survey of Pentecostals* (2006), and Pew Forum, *Global Christianity: A Report on the Size and Distribution of the World's Christian Population* (2011). Referenced in Offutt, *New Centers*, 18.

5. Philip Jenkins, *The Next Christendom: The Coming of Global Christianity* (New York: Oxford University Press, 2011), xi. While less dramatic than Jenkins's, the statistics articulated by other scholars are similar. See David B. Barrett, George Thomas Kurian, and Todd M. Johnson, *World Christian Encyclopedia: A Comparative Survey of Churches and Religions in the Modern World* (Oxford: Oxford University Press, 2001). Counting populations through different statistical methods, other scholars have found Barrett's work fairly accurate. See Becky Yang Hsu, Amy Reynolds, Conrad Hackett, and James Gibbon, "Estimating the Religious Composition of All Nations: An Empirical Assessment of the World Christian Database," *Journal for the Scientific Study of Religion* 47, no. 4 (December 2008): 678–693.

6. Jenkins looks first to growth through conversion but notes that continual growth occurs through population increase. While their arguments are more nuanced, other scholars such as Kwame Bediako, Lamin Sanneh, Dana Robert, Andrew Walls, and Joel Carpenter largely fall into this scholarly paradigm. Offutt, *New Centers*, 27.

7. Wuthnow, *Boundless Faith*, 34–36.

8. Jenkins, *The Next Christendom*, 18–19.

9. Ibid., 15–18.

10. The best example may be David Stoll, *Is Latin America Turning Protestant? The Politics of Evangelical Growth* (Berkeley: University of California Press, 1990).

11. Steve Brouwer, Paul Gifford, and Susan D. Rose, *Exporting the American Gospel: Global Christian Fundamentalism* (New York: Routledge, 1996), 3.

12. I am indebted to Offutt (*New Centers*, 28–29), who frames this third paradigm as "global connectedness."

13. Mark Noll, *The New Shape of Global Christianity: How American Experience Reflects Global Faith* (Downers Grove, IL: IVP Academic, 2009).

14. Wuthnow, *Boundless Faith*.

15. Robert Wuthnow and Stephen Offut, "Transnational Religious Connections," *Sociology of Religion* 69, no. 2 (Summer 2008): 209–232.

16. Jehu Hanciles, *Beyond Christendom: Globalization, African Migration, and the Transformation of the West* (New York: Orbis, 2008), 2.

17. Wuthnow, *Boundless Faith*, 2.

18. James H. Mittelman, *The Globalization Syndrome: Transformation and Resistance* (Princeton: Princeton University Press, 2000). Referenced in Hanciles, *Beyond Christendom*, 15.

19. In the 1970s, Immanuel Wallerstein proposed his "world-system" theory. With class as his foundational unit of analysis, he articulated the growth of the modern capitalist world-system that began in western Europe and has now taken over the globe. Immanuel Wallerstein, *The Capitalist World-Economy* (Cambridge: Cambridge University Press, 1979). See also Peter Beyer, *Religion and Globalization* (London: Sage Publications, 1994), 15–21.

20. Beyer, *Religion and Globalization*, 8.

21. Frank Lechner and John Boli, *World Culture: Origins and Consequences* (Malden, MA: Blackwell, 2005).

22. To some scholars, this is known as "institutional isomorphism." P. J. DiMaggio and W. W. Powell, "The Iron Cage Revisited: Institutional Isomorphism and Collective Rationality in Organizational Fields," in *The New Institutionalism in Organizational Analysis*, ed. Walter W. Powell and Paul J. DiMaggio (Chicago: University of Chicago Press, 1991).

23. John Boli and David V. Brewington, "Religious Organizations," in *Religion, Globalization, and Culture*, ed. Peter Beyer and Lori G. Beaman (Boston: Leiden, 2007), 203–231; John Boli and George M. Thomas, "World Culture in the World Polity: A Century of International Non-Governmental Organization," *American Sociological Review* 62, no. 2 (1997): 171–190; Joshua J. Yates, "To Save the World: Humanitarianism and World Culture," Ph.D. diss., University of Virginia, 2006, 7–9.

24. José Casanova, *Public Religions in the Modern World* (Chicago: University of Chicago Press, 1994), 19–38.

25. Max Weber, *Max Weber on Charisma and Institution Building: Selected Papers* (Chicago: University of Chicago Press, 1968). Also see Mark Chaves, "Secularization as Declining Religious Authority," *Social Forces* 72, no. 3 (March 1994): 749–774; Mark Chaves, "Intraorganizational Power and Internal Secularization in Protestant Denominations," *American Journal of Sociology* 99, no. 1 (July 1993): 1–48.

26. Peter Berger, "Reflections on the Sociology of Religion Today," *Sociology of Religion* 62, no. 4 (2001): 443–454; Peter Berger, ed., *The Desecularization of the World: Resurgent Religion and World Politics* (Washington, DC: Ethics and Public Policy Center, 1999).

27. David Martin, *Tongues of Fire: The Explosion of Protestantism in Latin America* (Oxford: Basil Blackwell, 1990); Martin, *Pentecostalism: The World Their Parish* (Oxford: Blackwell, 2002). Also see Offutt, *New Centers*, 29–30.

28. Paul Gifford, *Ghana's New Christianity: Pentecostalism in a Globalizing African Economy* (London: Hurst, 2004): ix. Also quoted in Offutt, *New Centers*, 31.

29. Offutt, *New Centers*, 32.

30. Peter L. Berger and Samuel P. Huntington, eds., *Many Globalizations: Cultural Diversity in the Contemporary World* (Oxford: Oxford University Press, 2002), 6–8.

31. Mark Hutchinson and Ogbu Kalu, eds., *A Global Faith: Essays on Evangelicalism and Globalization* (Macquarie Centre, NSW: Centre for the Study of Australian Christianity, Macquarie University, 1998); Mark Hutchinson and John Wolffe, A *Short History of Global Evangelicalism* (Cambridge: Cambridge University Press, 2012).

32. Laurence R. Iannaccone, "A Formal Model of Church and Sect," *American Journal of Sociology* 94 suppl. (1986): S241–S298; Laurence R. Iannaccone, "The Consequences of Religious Market Structure," *Rationality and Society* 3 (April 1991): 156–177.

33. Roger Finke and Rodney Stark, *The Churching of America, 1776–1990: Winners and Losers in Our Religious Economy* (New Brunswick, NJ: Rutgers University Press, 1992).

34. Jan Stievermann, Daniel Silliman, and Philip Goff, "General Introduction," 1–29, and E. Brooks Holifield, "Why Are Americans So Religious? The Limitations of Market Explanations," 33–62, both in *Religion and the Marketplace in the United States*, ed. Jan Stievermann, Philip Goff, and Detlef Junker (New York: Oxford University Press, 2015).

35. Noll, *The New Shape of Global Christianity*.

36. Harry S. Stout and D. Scott Cormode, "Institutions and the Story of American Religion: A Sketch of Synthesis," in *Sacred Companies: Organizational Aspects of Religion and Religious Aspects of Organizations,* ed. N. J. Demerath, Peter Dobkin Hall, Terry Schmitt, and Rhys H. Williams (New York: Oxford University Press, 1998), 64.

37. Amy Reynolds, *Free Trade and Faithful Globalization: Saving the Market* (Cambridge: Cambridge University Press, 2015); Rebecca Todd Peters, *In Search*

of the Good Life: The Ethics of Globalization (New York: Continuum, 2004); Rebekah P. Massengill and Amy Reynolds, "Moral Discourses in Economic Contexts," in *Handbook of the Sociology of Morality*, ed. Steven Hitlin and Stephen Vaisey (New York: Springer, 2010), 485–501.

38. For an overview of Venn's ideas, see Wilbert R. Shenk, "Rufus Anderson and Henry Venn: A Special Relationship?," *International Bulletin of Missionary Research* 5, no. 4 (1981): 168–172; Jehu Hanciles, *Euthanasia of a Mission: African Church Autonomy in a Colonial Context* (Westport, CT: Praeger, 2002), 23–41.

39. Brian Stanley, *The World Missionary Conference, Edinburgh 1910* (Grand Rapids, MI: Eerdmans, 2009).

40. In 1900, former president Benjamin Harrison, New York governor Theodore Roosevelt, and President William McKinley all gave speeches at the Ecumenical Missionary Conference in New York City. Soon after, missionary leader John R. Mott participated in diplomatic negotiations under President Woodrow Wilson. Gerald H. Anderson, "American Protestants in Pursuit of Mission: 1886–1986," *International Bulletin of Missionary Research* 12, no. 3 (July 1988): 102; Sarah Ruble, *The Gospel of Freedom and Power: Protestant Missionaries in American Culture After World War II* (Chapel Hill: University of North Carolina Press, 2014).

41. Dana L. Robert, "The First Globalization? The Internationalization of the Protestant Missionary Movement Between the Wars," in *Interpreting Contemporary Christianity: Global Processes and Local Identities*, ed. Ogbu U. Kalu (Grand Rapids, MI: Eerdmans, 2008), 93–130.

42. William Hutchison, *Errand to the World: American Protestant Thought and Foreign Missions* (Chicago: University of Chicago Press, 1987), 146–175; Grant Wacker, "The Waning of the Missionary Impulse: The Case of Pearl S. Buck," in *The Foreign Missionary Enterprise at Home*, ed. Daniel H. Bays and Grant Wacker (Tuscaloosa: University of Alabama Press, 2003), 191–205; James A. Patterson, "The Loss of a Protestant Missionary Consensus: Foreign Missions and the Fundamentalist-Modernist Conflict," in *Earthen Vessels: American Evangelicals and Foreign Missions, 1880–1980*, ed. Joel Carpenter and Wilbert R. Shenk (Grand Rapids, MI: Eerdmans, 1990), 73–91.

43. The Laymen's Report itself was published as *Rethinking Missions: A Laymen's Inquiry After One Hundred Years*, ed. William Ernest Hocking (New York: Harper, 1932). Hutchison, *Errand to the World*, describes the impact of the Laymen's Report in detail, 159–175. In addition to religious periodicals, the popular press also covered the response to the Laymen's Report on the mood of missions at home. See "Re-thinking Missions," *Time*, November 28, 1932.

44. Dana L. Robert, "'The Crisis of Missions': Premillennial Mission Theory and the Origins of Independent Evangelical Missions," in *Earthen Vessels: American Evangelicals and Foreign Missions, 1880–1980*, ed. Joel Carpenter and Wilbert R. Shenk (Grand Rapids, MI: Eerdmans, 1990), 29–46; Klaus Fiedler, *The*

Story of Faith Missions (Oxford: Regnum Books International, 1994), 125, 172; Michael S. Hamilton, "More Money, More Ministry: The Financing of American Evangelicalism Since 1945," in *More Money, More Ministry: Money and Evangelicals in Recent North American History*, ed. Larry Eskridge and Mark A. Noll (Grand Rapids, MI: Eerdmans, 2000), 104–138.

45. "God and the Emperor," *Time*, September 9, 1940.

46. Kenneth Scott Latourette, "The Real Issue in Foreign Missions," *Christian Century* 48 (April 15, 1931): 506; "Nationalism Is Throttling Missions," *Christian Century* 50 (September 13, 1933): 1140; Robert E. Speer, "True and Abiding Basis of Foreign Missions," *Missionary Review of the World*, October 1929, 757.

47. Hutchison, *Errand to the World*, 175; Rodger C. Baasham, *Mission Theology, 1948–1975: Years of Worldwide Creative Tension—Ecumenical, Evangelical, and Roman Catholic* (Pasadena, CA: William Carey Library, 1979), 21–50.

48. Joel A. Carpenter, "Propagating the Faith Once Delivered: The Fundamentalist Missionary Enterprise, 1920–1945," in *Earthen Vessels: American Evangelicals and Foreign Missions, 1880–1980*, ed. Joel Carpenter and Wilbert R. Shenk (Grand Rapids, MI: Eerdmans, 1990), 128–130; Harold Lindsell, "Faith Missions Since 1938," in *Frontiers of the Christian World Mission Since 1938: Essays in Honor of Kenneth Scott Latourette* (New York: Harper & Brothers, 1962), 211–214.

49. Roy Robertson, *Developing a Heart for Mission: Five Missionary Heroes* (Singapore: NavMedia, 2002), foreword.

50. Robert T. Coote, "The Uneven Growth of Conservative Evangelical Missions," *International Bulletin of Missionary Research* 6 (1982): 118–123; Ralph W. Winter, *The 25 Unbelievable Years: 1945–1969* (Pasadena, CA: William Carey Library, 1970), 51–57; Joel Carpenter, "Appendix: The Evangelical Missionary Force in the 1930s," in *Earthen Vessels*, edited by Joel Carpenter and Wilbert R. Shenk (Grand Rapids, MI: Eerdmans, 1990), 335–342.

51. William Inboden, *Religion and American Foreign Policy, 1945–1960: The Soul of Containment* (Cambridge: Cambridge University Press, 2008), 73.

52. William Martin, *A Prophet with Honor: The Billy Graham Story* (New York: William Morrow, 1991), 115.

53. Heather Curtis, "Depicting Distant Suffering: Evangelicals and the Politics of Pictorial Humanitarianism in the Age of American Empire," *Material Religion: The Journal of Objects, Art and Belief* 8, no. 2 (June 2012): 154–183; John Robert Hamilton, "An Historical Study of Bob Pierce and World Vision's Development of the Evangelical Social Action Film," Ph.D. diss., University of Southern California, 1980.

54. David King, "World Vision, Religious Identity, and the Evolution of Child Sponsorship," in *Child Sponsorship: A Critical Discussion*, eds. Matthew Clarke and Brad Watson (New York: Palgrave Macmillan, 2014), 260–279.

55. David Ekbladh, *The Great American Mission: Modernization and the Construction of an American World Order* (Princeton: Princeton University Press, 2010), 31–37.

56. Harry S. Truman, Inaugural Address, January 20, 1949, https://www.trumanli-brary.org/whistlestop/50yr_archive/inagural20jan1949.htm.

57. Several significant relief agencies were founded earlier in response to conditions after World War I. They included the American Friends Service Committee (1917) and the Mennonite Central Committee (1920)

58. Nichols, *Uneasy Alliance*, 63. CARE was the only secular international PVO among the eight largest between 1950 and 1960. While CARE is now a secular agency, it was originally a coalition of religious and secular organizations such as Church World Service, American Friends Service Committee, American-Jewish Joint Distribution Committee, and International Rescue and Relief Committee. The religious agencies pulled out in the 1950s because they felt CARE's objectives both became too closely aligned with U.S. politics and infringed on their own individual agencies' work. Rachel M. McCleary, *Global Compassion: Private Voluntary Organizations and U.S. Foreign Policy Since 1939* (New York: Oxford University Press, 2009), 25–28; Rachel M. McCleary, "Private Voluntary Organizations Engaged in International Assistance, 1939–2004," *Nonprofit and Voluntary Sector Quarterly* 37, no. 3 (September 2008), 521; Wallace J. Campbell, *The History of CARE: A Personal Account* (New York: Praeger, 1990), 55–56.

59. The 1954 Food for Peace legislation (PL 480) allowed registered organizations to apply for U.S. surplus goods and remittance for shipping and transportation costs of goods. Only registered organizations could participate. The International Cooperation Administration succeeded the ACVAFS in 1953 to coordinate distribution efforts and became the forerunner to the establishment of USAID in 1961. McCleary, *Global Compassion*, 64, 77; Nichols, *Uneasy Alliance*, 84.

60. One early exception was World Relief. In 1944, the National Association of Evangelicals established the War Relief Commission to transport food and clothing to displaced Europeans; they renamed it World Relief in 1950 and officially registered to receive government aid in 1956.

61. Walt Rostow, *The Stages of Economic Growth, a Non-Communist Manifesto* (Cambridge: Cambridge University Press, 1960). Rostow proposed development as a tool to help counter the rise of communism. He hypothesized that traditional societies would reach a point of economic growth that would allow them to "take off" and modernize, and it was up to the West to bring Third World societies to this point. Gilbert Rist, *The History of Development: From Western Origins to Global Faith* (New York: Zed Books, 2008), 80–85.

62. Jan West Schrock and John Haman, "Dan West Monologue," www.brethren.org/resources/dan-west-monologue.pdf (accessed January 15, 2015).

63. Clive Christie, *The Quiet American and The Ugly American: Western Literary Perspectives on Indo-China in a Decade of Transition, 1950–1960*, Occasional Paper no. 10 (Canterbury, Kent: University of Kent at Canterbury, Centre of East Asian Studies, 1989).

64. Bob Pierce, "We Need More 'Ugly' Americans," *Washington Post and Times Herald*, April 12, 1959.

65. Billy Graham quoted in Paul Rees, "The Remaining Life or the Removed Candlestick," *World Vision*, April 1960, 4.

66. Tanzanian president Julius Nyerere became best known for popularizing "self-reliance" into development parlance. In the Arusha Declaration in 1967, he used the term and also called for autonomy and auto-centered development. Rist, *History of Development*, 123.

67. Ibid., 123–168; Hefferan, *Twinning Faith and Development, Catholic Parish Partnering in the Haiti*. Bloomfield, CT: Kumarian Press, 2007, 46.

68. McCleary, *Global Compassion*, 103–105.

69. The 1968 Medellín Conference affirmed the preferential treatment of the poor and liberation. Theologians Gustavo Gutiérrez and Leonardo Boff popularized such claims. Both noted that the poor were dignified when they participate in their own liberation—hence the importance of the formation of base ecclesial communities. Kevin Norman York-Simmons, "A Critique of Christian Development as Resolution to the Crisis in U.S. Protestant Foreign Missions," Ph.D. diss., Vanderbilt University, 2009, 75.

70. Ronald J. Sider, ed., *Evangelicals and Development: Toward a Theology of Social Change* (Philadelphia: Westminster Press, 1982), 99.

71. McCleary, "Private Voluntary Organizations Engaged in International Assistance, 1939–2004," 518–519.

72. Tara Hefferan, Julie Adkins, and Laurie A. Occhipinti, *Bridging the Gaps: Faith-Based Organizations, Neoliberalism, and Development in Latin America and the Caribbean* (Lanham, MD: Lexington Books, 2009), 4; Roger Riddell, *Does Foreign Aid Really Work?* (New York: Oxford University Press, 2007), 48.

73. Sharon Harper, ed., *The Lab, the Temple, and the Market: Reflections at the Ection of Science, Religion, and Development* (Ottawa: IDRC, 2000), 71–72; Colin Leys, "Rise and Fall of Development Theory," in *The Anthropology of Development and Globalization: From Classical Political Economy to Contemporary Neoliberalism*, ed. Angelique Haugerud and Marc Edelman (Malden, MA: Blackwell, 2005), 113.

74. In 1940, the composition of faith-based relief and development INGOs was 38 percent Catholic, 25 percent Jewish, 15 percent mainline Protestant, 7 percent evangelical, and 6 percent faith-founded. In 2004, the percentages demonstrated large-scale evangelical growth: the breakdown was 45 percent evangelical, 13 percent faith-founded, 11 percent mainline Protestant, 9 percent Catholic, 7 percent ecumenical, 5 percent Jewish, 2 percent Muslim, and 1 percent Orthodox. In addition, while secular organizations made up the vast majority of development aid in the 1960s–1970s, now Christian NGOs account for more than 50 percent of real revenue. See McCleary, *Global Compassion*, 25.

75. Gerard Clarke, "Faith Matters: Faith-Based Organisations, Civil Society and International Development," *Journal of International Development* 18, no. 6 (2006): 835–848; Wendy Tyndale, *Visions of Development: Faith-Based Initiatives* (Aldershot, England: Ashgate, 2006); Jill deTemple, "Imagining Development: Religious

Studies in the Context of International Economic Development," *Journal of the American Academy of Religion* 81, no. 1 (March 2013): 107–129.

76. McCleary, *Global Compassion*, 117.

77. In a survey of staff in 1999, WVI found that 57 percent identified as evangelical, 19 percent as mainline, 16 percent as Catholic, 1 percent as Orthodox, and 7 percent as other. WVI, "The Commission of the Church Report," 2002. Presently, WVUS uses the five divisions employed by the ecumenical organization Christian Churches Together (Protestant, Roman Catholic, evangelical, Orthodox, and Pentecostal). The 2002 WVI "Commission of the Church Report" does not clarify if Pentecostals are included in the evangelical category or who is included within the "other."

78. Wuthnow, *Boundless Faith*, 79–81.

79. Regent University, *Graduate Catalog, 1994–1996* (Virginia Beach, VA: Regent University, 1994), 61, quoted in Linda Kintz, *Between Jesus and the Market: The Emotions That Matter in Right-Wing America* (Durham, NC: Duke University Press, 1997), 232; Bethany Moreton, *To Serve God and Wal-Mart: The Making of Christian Free Enterprise* (Cambridge, MA: Harvard University Press, 2009), 250.

80. Acton Institute, "Acton University" webpage, http://university.acton.org/about-au (accessed March 20, 2016).

81. Offutt, *New Centers*, 104–105.

82. Holly Lebowitz Rossi, "Rick Warren Publicly Pursuing Programs Against World Poverty," *Christian Century* 122, no. 14 (July 12, 2005): 15–16; Timothy C. Morgan and Tony Carnes, "Purpose Driven in Rwanda: Rick Warren's Sweeping Plan to Defeat Poverty," *Christianity Today* 49, no. 10 (October 2005): 32–36; Marc Gunther, "Will Success Spoil Rick Warren?," *Fortune*, October 31, 2005; David Van Biema, "Warren of Rwanda," *Time*, August 15, 2005; Cynthia McFadden and Ted Gerstein, "Rick Warren's 'Long-Term Relationship' with Rwanda," *Nightline*, ABC News, July 31, 2008.

83. Alan Wolfe, "A Purpose-Driven Nation?," *Wall Street Journal*, August 26, 2005. Warren has also faced criticism from fellow evangelicals for his naïveté and "amateur" approach to humanitarian work. For example, see Andrew Paquin, "Politically Driven Injustice: Fixing Global Poverty Requires More than Rick Warren's Peace Plan," *Christianity Today*, February 2006, 22. Warren's PEACE Plan has gone through several changes as he has responded to a number of these criticisms. The biggest change has been in the first initiative, "planting churches." After much criticism, Warren changed it to "promote reconciliation." Today it is "planting churches that promote reconciliation."

84. David Bronkema and Christopher M. Brown, "Business as Mission Through the Lens of Development," *Transformation* 26, no. 2 (April 2009): 82–88.

85. B Lab, "B Corporation," https://www.bcorporation.net (accessed March 12, 2016).

86. Amy Costello, "TOMS Shoes: A Closer Look," *Tiny Spark*, March 15, 2012, http://www.tinyspark.org/podcasts/toms-shoes.

87. Ken Walker, "The Kiva Effect," *Christianity Today*, December 10, 2009.

88. Wuthnow, *Boundless Faith*, 170–171.

89. Robert J. Priest, Terry Dischinger, Steve Rasmussen, and C. M. Brown, "Researching the Short-term Mission Movement," *Missiology* 34, no. 4: 431–450.

90. Janel Kragt Bakker, *Sister Churches: American Congregations and Their Partners Abroad* (New York: Oxford University Press), 2013.

91. Offutt, *New Centers*, 70–71.

92. Priest quoted in Brian Howell, "The Global Evangelical," *Immanent Frame*, July 28, 2008, http://blogs.ssrc.org/tif/2008/07/28/the-global-evangelical.

93. Melani McAlister, "What Is Your Heart For? Affect and Internationalism in the Evangelical Public Sphere," *American Literary History* 20, no. 4 (2008): 870–895.

94. Brian M. Howell, "Mission to Nowhere: Putting Short-Term Missions into Context," *International Bulletin of Missionary Research* 33, no. 4 (October 2009): 206–211; Wuthnow, *Boundless Faith*, 181–182; Wuthnow and Offutt, "Transnational Religious Connections."

95. Micah Challenge takes its name from the biblical passage Micah 6:8, "He has shown you O man what is good. And what does the Lord require of you? To act justly, and to love mercy, and to walk humbly with your God." See http://www.micahchallenge.org (accessed April 23, 2012).

4

Liberty and Order

THE MORMON STRUGGLE
WITH AMERICAN CAPITALISM

Matthew Bowman

IN MAY 2009 a federal grand jury indicted the Mormon Rick Koerber for mail fraud, wire fraud, and tax evasion in Salt Lake City. Over the previous five years, Koerber had attracted more than $200 million in investments into his FranklinSquires real estate firm, mostly from small contributors. He promised each investor a 5 percent return, and all seemed well until late 2007, when the housing bubble burst, investment dried up, and Koerber's backers stopped receiving checks.

Koerber's indictment made the front page of local papers. He was well known in Utah for billboards and advertising announcing him as the "Latter-day capitalist" and declaring that his investments were guided by a metaphysical system. "Principles Govern!" announced the billboards, even in the rough-and-tumble marketplace. He hosted a local radio show on which he devoted time to explaining his theory that, based on his reading of scripture, "God himself is clearly a capitalist." According to prosecutors, Koerber routinely invoked his membership in the Church of Jesus Christ of Latter-day Saints as a means to build trust with his investors, a ploy called "affinity fraud." He took money from Hartman Rector, a former high-ranking member of the Mormon leadership, and later had cameramen project Rector's image on-screen during FranklinSquires real estate seminars. He claimed he had learned the "principles" governing the marketplace during his time in Mormon youth programs. The day before he was arraigned on these charges,

Koerber changed the heading on his website from "Capitalist. Mormon. Dad." to simply "Capitalist."[1]

Though Koerber's scam was unusually successful, it is hardly the only such scheme to flourish in Utah. A number of journalists and commentators have noted that the Mormon state seems particularly susceptible to Amway-style multilevel marketing businesses, get-rich-quick strategies, and other such monetary schemes.[2] In 2008 two Mormon bishops, Val Southwick and William Hammons, were sent to prison for bilking investors of more than $100 million—including many members of the congregations they supervised—over more than twenty years, promising them shares in Southwick's never-quite-materializing real estate development firm.[3] Utah County, where Brigham Young University is located, is a hotbed of multilevel marketing firms: it is the home of Xango vitamin juice, NuSkin Enterprises, and DoTerra essential oils.[4] As far back as 1884, the Mormon John Koyle sold 114,000 shares of stock to raise money to open up the "Relief Mine," a repository of treasure near Provo, Utah, that he said was used by the ancient American civilizations the Book of Mormon describes. Koyle claimed angels had shown him the location in a vision and he needed only enough money to purchase equipment and labor. No such wealth was ever found.[5]

All these episodes evince a peculiar relationship between Mormonism and money, at least in the United States. Mormonism seems to have made Koerber a more rapacious and talented fund-raiser and turned his focus to a particular type of free market American capitalism. In 2014 his website still quoted the mid-twentieth-century Mormon leader Stephen Richards's defense of the free market system, and claimed "the very truths enshrined in the man-labeled philosophy 'capitalism' are in fact the same universal truths proclaimed in scripture as the Gospel."[6] But at the same time, their faith in Mormonism rendered his victims less capable capitalists, less inclined to exercise skepticism in the marketplace, and more inclined to trust Koerber (and Southwick, and many others) because he draped his scheme in Mormonism's language and sold it in Mormonism's communities. This curious double-mindedness exists because Mormon theology and philosophy lend themselves quite well to the individualistic, classically liberal rhetoric of someone like Koerber, but in practice, Mormon lifeways bend in a quite different direction: toward a communitarian, mutually supportive community in which the sort of trust Koerber abused is taken for granted. Mormonism's relationship with money has reflected both impulses: there is a philosophic basis for a strong, atomistic individualism in Mormon theology, but there is also powerful historical precedent for less market-oriented economic organization. And, as legions of witnesses against Koerber, Southwick, and others testified in the trials of these men, their abuse of the trust of a religious community in the name of principles they believe that community testifies of has created conflict within the faith. When exposed, scam artists revealed to the scammed that there were in fact multiple forms of Mormonism, and multiple forms of capitalism. Koerber and his victims seemed hardly to be practicing the same faith at all.

During Mitt Romney's 2012 campaign for the presidency, several media outlets published essays declaring Romney's conservative politics to be somehow un-Mormon, because they were unlike the economic communalism appearing in the Mormon past. For instance, David Mason, a professor of theater at Rhodes College, wrote in the *Washington Post* that Romney's opposition to the Affordable Care Act was a sign that "Romney's not that Mormon," because in the nineteenth century "Joseph Smith himself developed a collectivist system in which all were to have everything in common so that no one would be poor."[7]

It is an oversimplified argument, but in one sense Mason's point is apt. In 1832, two years after he organized his new faith, Joseph Smith established what he called the United Order, an economic system centered on an institution called the United Firm. Run by nine Mormon leaders, the United Firm supervised what one of Smith's revelations called "the common property of the whole church." It oversaw various church endeavors: a publishing house, a sawmill, and various mercantile enterprises. It also managed residential real estate for church members and an institution called the "bishop's storehouse," which took in excess property for redistribution to the poor. Mormons were asked to deed their property to the United Firm but would continue living in the houses and working the land they deeded as "stewards" on behalf of the entire community.[8]

Later, in 1860s Utah, Brigham Young found himself trying to hold together a Mormon community that economic forces seemed determined to pull apart. The gold rush in California was tempting hundreds of Mormons to leave Utah; the transcontinental railroad brought non-Mormon merchants to Salt Lake City. In response Young tried to revive the United Order. He declared, "They say they are going to California; and I thank the Lord they are. Why? Because I would rather be in this community with one hundred families of poor honest hearted saints than one hundred million who mix up with devils and go to California. . . . The doctrine of Brother Joseph is that not one dollar you possess is your own, and if the Lord wants us to use it let it go and it is none of your business what he does with it."[9] In the early 1870s a host of Utah towns established a range of cooperative ventures, from a revived version of the United Firm in the town of Brigham City to purer form of utopian socialism in the aptly named Orderville, where there was no private property and the citizens lived in dormitories.[10] Like many other nineteenth-century economic radicals, particularly those in the West, Brigham Young was a determined producerist and localist, suspicious of entanglement with large financial institutions and government alike and instead in favor of self-sufficiency and a people capable of producing all they needed themselves rather than depending on imports. He sent Mormons all over the Great Basin to establish "iron missions" and "cotton missions" to ensure that the Saints would need to buy those raw materials from no other community, and he designed the city blocks of Salt Lake wide enough to ensure that every house lot would have room for an orchard in the back. There was to be no economic inequality in Utah.[11]

None of these utopian communities survived very long; if they did not fall to the unwillingness of individual Latter-day Saints to turn over their property to their church, they fell to the pressure of the burgeoning American capitalism that surrounded them. Nonetheless, they reflected Brigham Young and Joseph Smith's impulse that the health of the Mormon community as a whole should trump the financial success of the individual. Indeed, in the efforts of the United Order explicit commitment to that principle was required of each Mormon convert. As Joseph Smith's revelations commanded, "Thou wilt remember the poor, and consecrate of thy properties for their support." Another explained why: "For according to the law every man that cometh up to Zion must lay all things before the bishop in Zion."[12] The Mormons' commitment to Zion often collided with the law and mores of American society surrounding them. Two examples of nineteenth-century Mormon dissent illustrate the origins of the tensions that Koerber and other twentieth-century con artists exploited; in each, a Mormon attempt to build Zion crashed up against a very American desire for independent wealth and economic development, and in each, the weight of the collision tore Mormonism apart.

The first example is the failure of the Kirtland Safety Society, in Kirtland, Ohio, headquarters of the church for much of the 1830s. Joseph Smith was notoriously careless about finances. He was in debt through much of his life, often living on the charity of his followers, and sometimes his personal financial habits affected his community. In January 1837, having been denied a bank charter by the Ohio legislature, Smith founded the Kirtland Safety Society Anti-Banking Company, a joint-stock company designed to function as a bank despite not being legally chartered as one. The Ohio legislature that refused Smith a charter was dominated by followers of Andrew Jackson, hostile to the sort of speculation and counterfeiting they associated with banks, and only a few months later the Panic of 1837 seemed to justify their suspicions. Smith, on the other hand, stood at the head of a church that was possessed of little capital and was struggling for currency to pay debts from the construction of a large temple in Kirtland.[13] He issued an open letter in the church's periodical, *The Messenger and Advocate*, inviting Mormons to "call at Kirtland, and receive counsel and instruction upon those principles that are necessary to further the great work of the Lord, and . . . we invite the brethren from abroad, to call on us, and take stock in our 'Safety Society.'"[14] For Joseph Smith, gathering his community together and furthering its progress justified the staggering economic risk of the Safety Society.

But to others, the risk teemed too great. In November 1837, the Kirtland Safety Society—perhaps inevitably—crumbled, victim of a bank rush that erupted when word spread throughout Kirtland that it was unable to redeem the notes it issued. Over the course of that year and the next, the Mormon community splintered. Smith and some close associates fled to Missouri, where another group of Mormons was attempting to implement the United Order. Left behind in Kirtland, a company of Mormon dissidents established what they called the Church of Christ, the original name of the church Joseph Smith had since renamed the Church of Jesus Christ of Latter-day Saints. Its leader, Warren Parrish, had once served as Smith's clerk, and expressed indignation that Joseph Smith and his associates had such "influence over this Church in this place, that they have filched the monies from their pockets." He declared that Smith believed "man has no more agency than a wheelbarrow," and professed disbelief that "men of common sense and common abilities, should be so completely blinded as to dispense entirely with the evidence of their senses, and tamely submit to be led by such men."[15] More than the failure of the Safety Society itself, what incensed Parrish was that the Mormon leader presumed that his religious leadership gave him authority over his followers' financial choices.

But Parrish did not renounce Mormonism when he renounced Joseph Smith. Rather, the Church of Christ declared Joseph Smith to be a fallen prophet, and offered instead a purer form of his religion that renounced Smith's communalism in favor of a more individualistic form of Christianity. According to a Mormon elder who encountered them later, "They thought there was enough of them to establish a pure religion that would become universal," and hoped to "unite all the Christian churches" through propagating a form of Christianity that appealed to human reason rather than resting its claims on authority. The elder heaped scorn upon Parrish for taking a job as a clergyman and portrayed him as hypocritically denying his past allegiance to Joseph Smith in order to maintain his salary.[16] Whether or not the story is true, the distinction drawn is telling. Parrish and his followers could not tolerate a religion that presumed to supplant the individualistic thrust of American capitalism, and as a consequence, they drew back from the Mormonism of the late 1830s, a Mormonism increasingly devoted to Joseph Smith's prophetic authority. And yet the fact that Parrish maintained some sense of Joseph Smith's restorationism and claimed to be embracing a purer form of Mormonism in rejecting the Kirtland Safety Society shows that David Mason's argument that pure Mormonism is economically communal is overly simplistic, because it presumes the existence of a Platonic form of Mormonism that never truly existed.

Another episode of Mormon dissent occurred in the late 1860s, as Brigham Young was reviving the United Order. Even more explicitly than does the Safety Society affair, it illustrates how Mormon theology could justify more than one sort of financial system. In 1869 Brigham Young ordered William Godbe excommunicated. Godbe was one of Salt Lake City's richest merchants, and leader of a circle of businessmen and intellectuals increasingly dissatisfied with Young's leadership. As Young began instituting policies readying the Mormons for a revived United Order—advising against trade with non-Mormons, protecting home industries, discouraging large-scale mining—Godbe and his friends grew increasingly dismayed. In 1868 they founded the *Utah Magazine* and challenged what an early issue called "a great encroachment of power" on the part of the "ruling priesthood of our Church." The magazine worried that "a steady and constant decline was taking place . . . in the spirituality of our system as a whole."[17] Echoing Parrish, the Godbeites claimed that Brigham Young's rule was choking off both individual spiritual lives and the financial health of the Utah Territory. The Godbeites ardently supported the industrialization of Utah and the integration of Utah into the national marketplace. Godbe published an article in *Utah Magazine* in October 1869 suggesting that if the equipment and training to run mines could not be found in Utah, "it will pay to buy it of Jew or Gentile." The article urged the mineral development of Utah's mines and mountains as a way to gain financial strength in the face of encroaching American capitalism, but at the same time encouraged them to use that strength to become players in the national marketplace rather than to stand aloof from it. "Without something of this kind to bring us money, we must always be a bartering community," Godbe warned.[18] Of course, that may well have been what Brigham Young had in mind all along.

The Godbeite argument for capitalism as a religious principle differed from those of Parrish and his fellows; they were grounded in the concepts about human nature that Joseph enunciated. Toward the end of his life Smith published new works of scripture, the Books of Abraham and Moses, which presented themselves as the memoirs and visions of those figures. These books explained that the souls of human beings existed in God's presence before the creation of the world, and that in order to preserve human freedom God had expelled Satan from his premortal court in a conflict Mormons call "the war in heaven." Satan fell to earth, but his goal remained to "destroy the agency of men."[19] In the last year of his life Smith taught that the human soul was uncreated, was as eternal as God himself, and indeed was of the same type of being that God is, merely eons behind in progression. The moral trial of life on earth, then, was designed to refine humanity toward a state of divinity. The preservation of human agency was thus critical for reasons divine as well as mundane. Collectively, these ideas are sometimes called Joseph Smith's Nauvoo theology, for they were publicized and taught while the Mormons were headquartered at that Illinois city.[20]

The Nauvoo theology overturned traditional Christian notions of original sin in favor of a radically optimistic vision of human potential and destiny. But it also gave the Godbeites and other Mormons (like Rick Koerber) the foundation on which to build a version of Mormonism that downplayed Brigham Young's commitment to communalism and Zion in favor of an emphasis on individual potential, accomplishment, and effort. By the 1870s, for instance, some of the Godbeites, particularly William Godbe himself, had drifted into sympathy with spiritualism, arguing that the spiritualist movement more fully expressed the intentions of Joseph Smith than did the church that Brigham Young presently led. An editorial in the *Utah Magazine* argued as early as 1868 that Joseph Smith was essentially a spiritualist. "He admitted in the main the truth of spirit manifestations, but pointed to the fact of the untellable millions of spirit intelligences appertaining to the earth," the editorial argued, and revealed that such manifestations could provide "correct transmission of truth."[21] During a trip to New York in the winter of that year, Godbe and his friend E. L. Harrison visited a medium, who spoke to them in the voice of Heber C. Kimball, a Mormon leader who had died only months before.

After this astounding experience, Godbe and Harrison returned to the medium several times, encountering Joseph Smith, Jesus Christ, the apostle Paul, and dozens of other spiritual leaders who counseled them how best to deal with Brigham Young.[22] They emerged with a revitalized vision of

Mormonism that discarded Young's clannishness and theocracy, his emphasis on priestly authority, and his economic communalism, and emphasized instead Joseph Smith's vision of progress and human potential. This form of Mormonism elevated rationality, freedom, and spiritual growth. It was fiercely individualistic. It could also be adduced to support the industrial forms of capitalism Godbe had fought for.

By December 1868, Godbe and Harrison were claiming that Joseph Smith's real mission was to create "an inspirational people," a "church like unto Joseph"—that is, a group of believers who were open to communication with the spiritual realm and ready to act upon its advice to build a more perfect society. Mormonism had emerged, they claimed, because "there were no tens of millions of spiritualists in Christendom." If not for Brigham Young ruling the church with an iron fist rather than promoting individual progress and spirituality, Harrison claimed, Mormonism would be well on its way toward "a new spiritual dispensation to this inspirational people . . . [which would] surprise most of our friends abroad who have believed nothing in the Divinity of Mormonism."[23] Such a thing had become possible now that Brigham Young's tyranny stood exposed. W. H. Sherman, a Godbeite journalist, connected the Godbeites' spiritual agenda with their preferred economic system, declaring that "the evils of this policy [the United Order] were not, until recently, so apparent"—until, that is, Godbe and Harrison received their revelations. "We have always claimed ours to be the most democratic church on earth," wrote Sherman, but the United Order revealed "exercises of despotic power the crowned heads of Europe would not venture upon today."[24]

The Godbeites ended up excommunicated from the church and their version of the faith withered, as had Warren Parrish's Mormonism. But the impulses that had driven all of these actors—Smith, Young, Parrish, Godbe—remained alive in Mormonism and ensured that its seemingly contradictory relationship with capitalism endured into the twentieth and twenty-first centuries. In the remainder of this chapter, I will outline three examples: the sacralized libertarianism embraced by some Mormon leaders and activists in the mid-twentieth century, the prophetic jeremiads against capitalism of Hugh Nibley, Mormon's foremost apologist, and, finally, the establishment of the Church Welfare System, another uneasy attempt to balance these competing impulses.

The most powerful advocate for the individualistic approach of Parrish and Godbe was, ironically enough, a president of the church, Ezra Taft Benson. Before his presidency (from 1985 to 1994), he was a successful Idaho farmer who eventually served several decades as a member of the Quorum of the

Twelve Apostles, the second-highest council of his church, and eight years as secretary of agriculture in Dwight Eisenhower's cabinet. Of similar mind and similar popularity as a writer and speaker was Cleon Skousen, who worked variously as an FBI agent, professor at Brigham Young University, popular speaker against communism, and police chief in Salt Lake City during the 1950s and 1960s. Between the two of them, they synthesized a libertarian form of Mormonism that might be called a political theology.

Both Skousen and Benson read Mormon theology, particularly the Nauvoo synthesis of Joseph Smith, through the lens of the Cold War. They became prominent national figures in the cultural struggle against communism—a fight they interpreted broadly as the struggle against large government more generally. Two of Skousen's books, 1958's *The Naked Communist* and 1981's *The 5000 Year Leap*, garnered wide readership, particularly on the right wing of American politics; *The Naked Communist* was particularly popular within the far-right John Birch Society, whose founder had accused Dwight Eisenhower of communist sympathies, and Skousen frequently spoke at Birch Society events. He founded several anticommunist organizations, including one called the All-American Society and one called the Freeman Institute, both of which widely distributed his pamphlets warning of communist infiltration into American culture and agitated for shrinking the size of government.[25]

Through the 1930s and 1940s, Benson climbed the ranks of Idaho's agricultural world, serving as a county agricultural agent, working for the University of Idaho, and eventually becoming national secretary of the National Council of Farmer Cooperatives. In 1943 he joined the Quorum of the Twelve Apostles, and ten years later Eisenhower's cabinet. After he left government he became a vocal advocate for many of the same principles and organizations Skousen endorsed. Like Skousen, he spoke frequently in public venues about the threat of communism and lambasted John F. Kennedy's administration for its socialist tendencies. He endorsed the John Birch Society, though his church position restricted him from taking up actual membership, and in 1966 sought permission from the president of the church to run for president of the United States in 1968 on a third-party anticommunist ticket with Strom Thurmond, the ultraconservative senator from South Carolina.[26]

Given their involvement in the broader American anticommunist movement, both of these men might seem to be fairly typical agitators for their era—not so different from Robert Welch, the founder of the Birch Society, or the evangelical Fred Schwarz.[27] Like many other anticommunists in the period, they accused communists of crimes far in excess of the political threat communism posed—they understood communism to be an existential challenge to a divinely ordained way of life. Both would have thoroughly endorsed, for instance, Whittaker Chambers's declaration that communism "is the vision of materialism . . . Communism restores man to his sovereignty by the simple method of denying God."[28]

The difference between someone such as Chambers and other anticommunists in the era is the extent to which Skousen and Benson's rhetoric about freedom and bondage derives from their reading of Mormon theology. While Chambers accused communism of enabling human pride, rejecting human limitation, and denying the fall of Adam and Eve, Mormons instead condemned it for its totalitarianism, for exerting too much control—the same accusations that Godbe and Parrish had leveled at the church they were expelled from. When they spoke to Mormon audiences, Benson and Skousen invoked Mormon doctrine explicitly; when they spoke to non-Mormon audiences, the ideas were still present, but muted and translated. These two men gave Mormon theology a particular cast, emphasizing certain aspects, framing the sacred narratives of Mormon scripture, premortal life and the conflict with Satan in heaven, in the light of current geopolitics. They invoked traditional Mormon teachings that the Constitution was inspired by God, emphasizing particularly that the founders intended to defend freedom of religion, speech, and democracy. They reiterated the Book of Mormon's promises that this "promised land" of the Americas would be preserved in liberty as long as its people were righteous.[29] And they invoked the Mormon theology of agency.

For instance, in *The Naked Communist*, Skousen approaches communism as essentially a theology, calling it "a framework of ideas designed to explain everything in existence." The theory of dialectical materialism, Skousen said, could be reduced to a philosophy of matter that governed human action. According to Skousen, communism taught that "after the brain receives impressions from the outside world, it automatically moves the individual to take action." Thus, "man could not arbitrarily choose any one of several forms of society but only that one which promotes the prevailing mode of production." Communism, it turned out, not only created dictatorships but was actually premised upon a philosophy that rejected the notion of agency fundamental to Mormon theology. As Skousen said, "Communist leaders have suppressed the natural desires of their people and have tried to motivate them to action through fear." Capitalism, on the other hand, promoted freedom. Skousen said, "This is one of the greatest blessings of free enterprise capitalism. To a remarkable extent it allows a man to do just about whatever he wants to do." Because Skousen associated religious belief with the preservation of freedom, he believed the "dynamic power of religious convictions is precisely what prevents a soundly religious person from accepting Communist oppression and Communist mandates."[30] Religion and capitalism both promoted freedom, while communism and atheism taught enslavement.

In works and speeches designed for Mormon readers, Skousen much more explicitly linked these ideas to Mormon theology and scripture: he was particularly fond of the first two books of Nephi in the Book of Mormon, which contain apocalyptic visions of the future of the Americas. One passage was particularly important to Skousen, in which a prophet named Lehi declared that "men are free according to the flesh . . . they are free to choose liberty and eternal life, through the great Mediator of all men, or to choose captivity and death."[31] Skousen linked this declaration to Nephi's vision of the future of the American continent, declaring that America had a divine mandate to oppose communism because of the teachings of the Book of Mormon, which promised that nobody "would have a permanent inheritance in America unless they obeyed God's commandments and accepted the gospel which would be restored to America."[32]

Cleon Skousen read contemporary global geopolitics into the Book of Mormon's teachings and the struggle with communism into scriptural endorsements of free agency. Ezra Taft Benson, on the other hand, read the Cold War into the "war in heaven." As an apostle, Benson traditionally addressed the entire church with his fellow apostles twice a year at the church's General Conference. Tens of thousands were listening to him in person, over radio, and in print when in 1961 he delivered one of his most famous addresses: "The American Heritage of Freedom—A Plan of God." Here he stated quite frankly that "communism is turning out to be the earthly image of the plan which Satan presented in the pre-existence. The whole program of socialistic-communism is essentially a war against God and the plan of salvation—the very plan which we fought to uphold during 'the war in heaven.'" Benson understood communism to be a war on "the plan of salvation," by which he meant the process of choice, refinement of souls, and repentance that would lead human beings back to the presence of God. Communism was a spiritual threat as well as a political threat. Benson then declared that "the devil . . . is enticing some men, both in and out of the Church, to parrot his line by advocating planned government guaranteed security programs at the expense of our liberties." His solutions were, accordingly, both political and spiritual. He called for regular family prayer, church attendance, and scripture study—but also that each Mormon "should use his influence in the community to resist the erosion process which is taking place in our political and economic life."[33]

Mormons should vote, run for office, and participate in politics in other ways, and they should use their religion to understand what they should do while in office.

Skousen and Benson were loud voices, but their political theology did not enlist all Mormons. In the middle 1960s, David O. McKay, the president of the church, dispatched Benson to Europe to supervise mission work there—but also, it was widely speculated, to get him out of the country at a politically turbulent time. Similarly, in 1979 the church leadership sent a circular to the congregations of the church warning that the reams of material Skousen produced should not be considered representative of Mormon doctrine, and that church membership rosters and facilities should not be used to further the work of Skousen's Freeman Institute.[34] After the Cold War Skousen sank into obscurity—until the popular television personality Glenn Beck revived him posthumously by endorsing his writings on the air early in Barack Obama's presidential administration.[35] Benson became president of the church in 1985, but despite the fears of some politically liberal Mormons that he would turn the church into a force for conservative politics, he served a largely quiet term of office, emphasizing humility and scripture study rather than politics until his death in 1994.

Nonetheless, their theories have provided much grist for Mormons such as Koerber, convinced that Mormonism endorses unfettered capitalism at a metaphysical level. While Benson and Skousen confronted communism, since the end of the Cold War many of their arguments have been employed to endorse capitalism rather than assail communism. The Mormon libertarian Connor Boyack, chairman of the Libertas Institute, a libertarian think tank in Utah, has relied heavily on their work. In his two volumes *Latter-day Liberty* and *Latter-day Responsibility* (both of which were blurbed by former Libertarian Party presidential candidate Ron Paul) Boyack constructed a political theology quite similar to that of Skousen and Benson; indeed, the forward to *Latter-day Liberty* was by Cleon Skousen's son Mark, who writes that it is "sure to become an important guidebook to those seeking to better understand just how to 'abide . . . in the liberty wherewith [we] are made free' (D&C 88:86)." Benson appears twenty-one times in the bibliography, and in the opening chapter Boyack declared that "Latter-day Saints are blessed with an increased understanding of who were are, why we're here on earth, and what consequences our mortal actions have. . . . A gospel-based understanding of liberty is unique in many ways from the world's definition of the term, primarily due to the revelations we have been given regarding God's plan of salvation and the War in Heaven."[36] Boyack argued that capitalism is deeply linked to the sacred notion of agency: he made the case that "we cannot simultaneously be independent while also being dependent upon others," and endorsed entrepreneurialism as a moral good, arguing that "a necessary characteristic of one's God-given agency is the ability and opportunity to act independent of external coercion ... Entrepreneurialism is not so much a destination as it is a process and a mindset."[37] Rick Koerber agreed, writing on his website that capitalism is a "moral revolution" that aided "individuals in their own personal efforts to live a principle-centered life, established upon a sound economic foundation, as a necessary prerequisite to meaningful citizenship." He quoted David O. McKay, longtime president of the LDS Church in the mid-twentieth century: "The fostering of full economic freedom lies at the base of our liberties."[38] And "liberty" to Mormons, as Boyack indicated, is a theologically loaded term.

But even in the mid-twentieth century, at the height of the Cold War, this thoroughly articulated form of libertarian theology was not Mormonism's only option. Several prominent Mormons of the period, most visibly the Canadian Hugh B. Brown, of the church's governing First Presidency, and Stewart Udall of the Democratic Arizona political dynasty, leaned to the political left. But the most vehement and the most intellectually interesting Mormon to articulate an economic philosophy closer to that of Brigham Young than of Parrish or the Godbeites was Hugh Nibley, a Berkeley PhD in ancient languages and a polymath professor of religion at Brigham Young University. He was best known as the founder of Mormon apologetics, devoting much of his time and scholarly energy to demonstrating through archaeology, linguistics, and historical parallels the historical veracity of the Book of Mormon, but it is quite possible that his theological writings on the notion of Zion will outlive his apologetics.[39]

Nibley's views were not so much those of a midcentury American liberal as they were those of a nineteenth-century utopian. As was Brigham Young, he was a determined producerist, disdainful of wage labor and particularly scathing about consumerism. For a university professor in Cold War America, supported by tuition money and hardly an independent farmer himself, this may seem a strange position to take, but Nibley took as his model both Brigham Young and the Hebrew prophets; his role was to enunciate ideals, not to propose practical economic reform. As he wrote, "In its present state, the world is far from qualified to receive a celestial society into its midst. But if we today cannot achieve Zion, we can conceive of it." The concepts central to Boyack and Benson and Skousen remained important to Nibley: agency, freedom of choice, and the moral weight of those things. However, he interpreted the role agency should play in economics differently than did these other Mormons. For Boyack or Benson, free agency was a theological imperative toward free markets; for Nibley, it was an imperative to opt out of the American marketplace entirely. He blasted what he called the "rhetorical sleight of hand" of the "work ethic," and "the corollaries that anyone who has wealth must have earned it by hard work and is, therefore, beyond criticism; that anyone who doesn't have it deserves to suffer," he declared in a speech at Brigham Young University. "The activities of the modern world that go by the name of work may not have been as spectacularly destructive as those of the barons of the middle ages, yet we are beginning to find out now that they *are* destructive." Thus for Nibley, a devoted acolyte of Brigham Young who mourned the loss of nineteenth-century communalism, the temptations of modern American consumerism were precisely as destructive, as grim a temptation, as Soviet totalitarianism might be. He said that he despaired to walk down the streets of Salt Lake City and see the names of the stores: "Zion's Loans, Zion's Real Estate, Zion's Used Cars, Zion's Jewelry, Zion's Supermart, Zion's Auto Wrecking, Zion's Outdoor Advertising, Zion's Gunshop, Zion's Land and Mining, Zion's Development, Zion's Securities—all that is quintessentially Babylon now masquerades as Zion."[40]

For Nibley, the association of the marketplace with free agency was a myth that actually destroyed the purpose of true agency. Again he invoked the Hebrew Bible: "Though generosity cannot be legislated, no one in Israel could get out of taking the proper test, to show how far he was willing to go, granted complete free agency, in carrying out God's express wishes regarding the distribution of his bounties." Unlike Boyack, for whom economic independence was necessary to properly exercise agency, and who thus ascribed a moral imperative to success in the free market, Nibley believed that even the pursuit of wealth was sinful, and that human agency could not be rightly exercised in any economy other than that of a perfected Zion society, where work was performed not for personal gain but for the good of the community. "God has placed whatever we have in our hands only to see what we will do with it—whether we will waste, hoard, or bestow it freely," he said, and he believed the correct answer was the last. The title of Nibley's most famous speech was "Work We Must, but the Lunch Is Free." Zion, he declared, indeed required everybody to work—but not for their lunch. Rather, he said, "In Zion you labor, to be sure, but not for money, and not for yourself, which is the exact opposite of our present version of the work ethic."[41]

His prominence as president of the church made Benson's political views somewhat more known among Mormons than those of Nibley, whose books are famous among but not often read by American Mormons. Both men attracted some disciples; Boyack is not the only Mormon who advocated a Bensonian form of libertarianism, and Nibley remains a favorite of many Mormon academics and intellectuals. However, neither can be said to represent the mainstream of Mormon attitudes about money. Rather, they present two polarities, and the vast majority of Mormons lie somewhere in the middle, far more comfortable in the managed capitalism of the United States than either man was.

For instance, the 1970s and 1980s saw a spate of publications by and for Mormons that closely modeled such popular how-to guides for business success as those produced by Zig Ziglar, Napoleon Hill, and other mainstream American gurus of wealth.[42] The most famous of these was Stephen R. Covey, whose *The 7 Habits of Highly Effective People* exemplified the form of Mormon success writing that even more aggressive capitalists such as Koerber borrow from. *The 7 Habits* insists that true success comes through grasping what Covey calls "correct principles," or "natural laws," promising that "to the degree that we align ourselves with correct principles, divine endowments will be released within our nature in enabling us to fulfill the measure of our creation."[43] This language—"the measure of our creation," "divine endowments," "correct principles"—is all Mormon jargon, phrases coined for the most part by Joseph Smith. Covey's first book, *The Spiritual Roots of Human Relations* (1970), is explicitly a work of Mormon theology and was published by the LDS Church–owned Deseret Book. *7 Habits* borrows extensively from it, lifting, at points, entire anecdotes and complete passages.

The foundation of Covey's theology is Joseph Smith's Nauvoo theology. *7 Habits* maintains that God achieved divinity through mastery of the moral laws governing the universe, and that God has taken the responsibility to guide human beings, also morally independent agents, along the same path. As one of Joseph Smith's revelations declares, "Whatever principle of education we attain unto in this life, it will rise with us in the resurrection"; further, "There is a law irrevocably decreed in heaven before the foundations of this world upon which all blessings are predicated—and when we obtain any blessing from God, it is by obedience to that law upon which it is predicated." The conception of success in *7 Habits* closely follows Joseph Smith. "They represent the internalization of correct principles upon which enduring happiness and success are based," Covey writes of these habits. That internalization "produces happiness, 'the object and design of our existence.'"[44] This notion of moral law is central in the ways Mormons such as Covey talk about money; for instance, the Mormon author Doug Christensen's *The Right to*

Riches declared, "Three of the laws for obtaining financial wealth are the law of the Sabbath, the law of the fast and the law of tithing. . . . Each blessing is dependent on the recipient's first observing the law that governs it. That law is foreordained, irrevocable, and invariable. When the law is complied with God cannot and will not withhold the appropriate blessing."[45]

Covey and Christensen's association between right conduct and consequent success reflects Mormonism's strong commitment to the cultivation of self-discipline and ethical behavior, traits ultimately rooted in Joseph Smith's Nauvoo theology. It is also reflected in the Church Welfare System, which is perhaps the greatest institutional expression of mainstream Mormon attitudes toward money.

The Welfare System was instituted under the direction of Heber Grant, president of the church from 1918 to 1945. Grant was a self-made millionaire who founded an insurance agency in his twenties and was wealthy enough to take a large hit in the Panic of 1893 and remain capable of aiding the church through financial turmoil in the same decade.[46] He was a staunch advocate of the gospel of wealth as preached by many late nineteenth-century religious leaders, from Russell Conwell to Dwight Moody: if an American desired success in business, that person must first embrace moral rectitude. He became a great advocate for the temperance movement, and as he said when he endorsed abstinence from alcohol to the young men and women of the church, "We, the youth of Israel, if we shall accomplish anything for the reformation of the world, must accomplish a reformation first in ourselves."[47]

And yet Grant also bore sympathy for Brigham Young's old dream of an independent, self-sustaining Mormon Zion. He spent much of his presidency struggling to save various floundering companies founded in the nineteenth century and either in full or in part supported by the church: a sugar company, the Salt Lake Theatre, newspapers, a life insurance company, various other agricultural investments. In 1923, Grant organized the Corporation of the President of the Church to better manage the various properties and interests of the church. His efforts reflected his personal confidence in capitalism but also his awareness of and sense of responsibility for the economic health of Utah.

The Church Welfare System sought to reconcile these two impulses. Though he grew up a Democrat, Grant was deeply suspicious of the New Deal. In 1941, in his role as president of the church, he and his two official counselors sent a letter to the Roosevelt administration declaring, "The Church has not found it possible to follow along the lines of the present general tendency in the matter of property rights, taxes, the curtailment of rights and liberties of the people, nor in general the economic policies of what is termed 'the New Deal.'" Grant's main complaint against the New Deal was that its programs were overweening and too powerful, and threatened to choke off the sense of self-reliance and free agency that had sustained the Mormon settlements. In this way Grant understood himself to be the heir of Brigham Young; though he combined Young's devotion to communalism with a stern Victorian morality, he saw no competition between the two. As the letter declared, explaining the values he feared the New Deal was destroying, "The hardship of pioneer life thus built into the warp and woof of the grandparents and parents of the present generation the sterling qualities of thrift, industry, honesty, integrity, sobriety, independence, love of liberty, and all the sterling virtues that go to make up a great people. The support of 'home industry' was one of the cardinal principles of the great commonwealth they were founding."[48] In 1936, Grant seized upon a program some local leaders of the church had begun in Salt Lake City, expanded it churchwide, and dubbed it the Church Security System, a name soon changed to the Church Welfare System.

The Welfare System was designed to do three things. First and second, it sought to preserve some semblance of Brigham Young's Zion. The Welfare System revived some of the church-owned industries Grant had struggled to maintain, but rather than profit, these new institutions sought simply to provide work and necessities for the poor. Additionally, bishops' storehouses, where material aid for the poor had been held since the time of the United Order, were revitalized. While in the nineteenth century they had been filled with the surplus donated by church members, now Mormon leaders began stocking them with the product of church-owned farms, church-owned canneries, and eventually a pasta factory, a soap factory, and a thrift store. Lastly, those who received welfare were asked to contribute labor to these establishments. When Grant announced the program to the church he declared that "our primary purpose was to set up, in so far as it might be possible, a system under which the curse of idleness would be done away with, the evils of a dole abolished, and independence, industry, thrift and self-respect be once more established amongst our people. The aim of the Church is to help the people to help themselves. Work is to be re-enthroned as the ruling principle of the lives of our Church membership."[49]

Grant's rhetoric invoked the welfare system primarily as a defense against idleness, and as a way to revive a long list of virtues strikingly similar to those he feared the New Deal was exhausting. This was to be accomplished through labor; for Grant, moral development dependent upon the exertion of effort. Here was an early articulation of the economics of Mormons such as Benson or Koerber: an emphasis upon self-reliance as a moral good. It remains a common language among Mormon leaders today. On the seventy-fifth anniversary of the Welfare System, in 2011, the First Presidency of the church issued an open letter declaring, "To provide in the Lord's way, we must develop our own self-reliance and then seek to help others become self-reliant. . . . When we live these principles, we are better able to alleviate suffering, build character, and foster unity."[50]

But seen through a slightly different prism, the ways in which Mormons now talk of the Welfare System could hark back to a brand of Mormonism reminiscent more of Hugh Nibley than of Rick Koerber, a brand evident in the phrase "foster unity." Mormons such as Grant were as hostile to consumerism as they were laudatory of individualism, and believed the Welfare System was as much a guard against the corruption of capitalism as it was against the degradations of idleness. The Welfare System provided plain supplies, encouraged mutual aid, and was premised on the notion that consumer debt was a great evil. By the mid-twentieth century, Mormon leaders were distancing themselves from consumer capitalism and endorsing instead Grant's middle way: an individualism that was virtue-based rather than consumption-based, sympathetic to Nibley's hostility to American culture but also committed to an economic ethic of self-reliance. The apostle Dallin Oaks warned, "We are told to be self-reliant, to provide for ourselves and those dependent upon us. But success at that effort can easily escalate into materialism . . . I believe this relationship identifies materialism as a peculiar Mormon weakness."[51] But while Nibley assailed consumer capitalism for encouraging individualism, these middle-way Mormon leaders assailed it for harming the same. The apostle Marvin Ashton warned, "We live in a self-indulgent, me orientated, materialistic society. Advertisements entice young buyers by demonstrating how easy it is to get credit and buy on time." Rather, Ashton declared, "God will open in the windows of heaven to us in these matters if we will but live close to him and keep his commandments."[52] True prosperity was to be achieved through personal rectitude, not the reckless pursuit of financial gain.

In the early twenty-first century, it was the Grant synthesis that best represented the mainstream Mormon approach to money. It was neither so easy in the boom-and-bust world of twenty-first-century American capitalism as Rick Koerber's approach was, nor was it as prophetic and skeptical of the modern economy as Hugh Nibley's. In fact, it resembled nothing so much as Max Weber's classic Protestant work ethic, emphasizing frugality, diligence, and commitment—those nineteenth-century virtues Brigham Young endorsed, but stripped away from his resolute communalism and wedded instead to a salvation theology of individual virtue. The Grant synthesis was awkwardly born, and bears within it a number of potential Mormon approaches to wealth, so much so that both Rick Koerber and Keith Woodwell, a Mormon and Utah's chief investigator of investment fraud who testified against Koerber, could claim the mandate of the faith when they faced each other in court. Woodwell denounced Koerber for skewing the notion that "if you pay your tithing and do what you're supposed to do, the windows of heaven will be open to you and God will pour you out a blessing." According to Woodwell, in fact, Mormonism teaches that "there are no shortcuts to wealth. You work hard, make good decisions, and inch forward."[53]

At sentiments like this Koerber only sniffed. The "individualistic, capitalistic, free enterprise system has been the God inspired means of enabling men to raise to a level of prosperity unprecedented in all historic time," he would write later. "No one," he said, "can prosper without being mindful of these truths, and the degree to which we are mindful determines the degree to which we prosper."[54]

Notes

1. Eric Peterson, "Free Capitalist Rick Koerber," *Salt Lake City Paper*, September 30, 2009; Tom Harvey, "Latter-day Capitalist Rick Koerber: Rags to Riches and Back Again," *Salt Lake Tribune*, October 17, 2009.

2. Anson Shupe, *The Darker Side of Virtue* (New York: Prometheus Books, 1986), 16–17; Matthew Heller, "Healthy, Wealthy, but Wise? How the Dietary-Supplement Trade Became Utah's Third-Largest Industry," *Los Angeles Times Magazine*, February 1, 2004, 1–10.

3. Ben Winslow, "Val Southwick's Victims Tell Stories of Shattered Lives," *Deseret News*, December 17, 2008.

4. Jon Taylor, "Multilevel Marketing Is Top Scam," *Deseret News*, March 19, 2008.

5. Kevin Cantera, "A Currency of Faith: Taking Stock in Utah's Dream Mine," MA thesis, University of Utah, 2008.

6. Rick Koerber, "Isn't 'Capitalism' Inconsistent with the Basic Doctrines of Christianity?," The Free Capitalist Project, January 13, 2009, http://www.freecapitalist.com/2009/01/13/isnt-capitalism-inconsistent-with-the-basic-doctrines-of-christianity/.

7. David Mason, "Romney, Obamacare, and Mormonism," *Washington Post*, July 17, 2012.

8. Doctrine and Covenants 82:3. Along with the Book of Mormon and the Pearl of Great Price, the Doctrine and Covenants are Mormon scripture, available in a variety of formats including those published by the LDS Church in 2013.

9. Brigham Young, "Extracts from a Discourse Given December 5, 1853," Church History Library and Archives, Salt Lake City, Utah.

10. The best exploration of these experiments is Dean L. May, Leonard Arrington, and Fermorz W. Fox, *Building the City of God: Community and Cooperation among the Mormons* (Urbana: University of Illinois Press, 1992).

11. On producerism generally see Michael Kazin, *The Populist Persuasion* (New York: Basic Books, 1995), 27–49; Lawrence Goodwyn, *The Populist Moment* (New York: Oxford University Press, 1978), 55–95. On Brigham Young's economics, see Leonard Arrington, *Great Basin Kingdom: An Economic History of the Latter-day Saints, 1830–1900* (1958; Urbana: University of Illinois, 2005), 96–131.

12. Doctrine and Covenants 46:30, 72:15.

13. On banking and fear of counterfeiters in Jacksonian America, see Steven Mihm, *A Nation of Counterfeiters: Capitalists, Con Men, and the Making of the United States* (Cambridge, MA: Harvard University Press, 2007). Mihm discusses the Kirtland Safety Society struggle with the Ohio legislature on 181–182.

14. Reprinted in "Autobiographical Remarks of Ebenezer Robinson," Church History Library, Salt Lake City, Utah. The Kirtland Safety Society is discussed in Mark L. Staker, *Hearken, O Ye People: The Historical Setting of Joseph Smith's Ohio Revelations* (Salt Lake City: Kofford Books, 2009), 463–543. Its utopian aspects receive treatment in Marvin S. Hill, Keith C. Rooker, and Larry T. Wimmer, "The Kirtland Economy Revisited: A Market Critique of Sectarian Economics," *Brigham Young University Studies* 17, no. 4 (Summer 1977), 389–471, and its failure in D. A. Dudley, "Bank Born of Revelation: The Kirtland Safety Society Anti-Banking Company," *Journal of Economic History* 30 (1970): 848–853.

15. Warren Parrish, "To the Editor of the *Painesville Republican*," *Painesville Republican*, February 15, 1838.

16. George A. Smith, "Divine Origins of Mormonism," in *Journal of Discourses* (London: George D. Watt, 1854–1886), 7:111.

17. "Manifesto," *Utah Magazine*, November 27, 1869, 470. Young's revival of the United Order is discussed in May, Arrington, and Fox, *Building the City of God*; in Leonard Arrington, *Brigham Young: American Moses* (Urbana: University of Illinois Press, 1986), 377–392; and in John G. Turner, *Brigham Young: Pioneer Prophet* (Cambridge, MA: Harvard University Press, 2012), 397–405. His confrontation with the Godbeites receives book-length treatment in Ronald W. Walker, *Wayward Saints: The Godbeites and Brigham Young* (Urbana: University of Illinois, 1998).

18. "The True Development of the Territory," *Utah Magazine*, October 16, 1869, 377.

19. The Pearl of Great Price, Moses 4:1–3.

20. On Joseph Smith's Nauvoo theology, see Richard Bushman, *Joseph Smith: Rough Stone Rolling* (New York: Knopf, 2005), 333–337; Terryl Givens, *Wrestling the Angel*, vol. 1 of *The Foundations of Mormon Thought: Cosmos, God, Humanity* (New York: Oxford University Press, 2014), 19–20, 157–160; Van Hale, "The

Doctrinal Impact of the King Follett Discourse," *BYU Studies* 18, no. 2 (Winter 1978): 209–225; and Donald Q. Cannon and Larry Dahl, *The Prophet Joseph Smith's King Follett Discourse: A Six Column Comparison of Original Notes and Amalgamations* (Provo, UT: Brigham Young University Printing, 1983). On the concept of "agency" in Mormon theology, see David Paulsen and Donald Musser, eds., *Mormonism in Dialogue with Contemporary Christian Theology* (Macon, GA: Mercer University Press, 2007), 44–46, 190–198.

21. "Spiritualism and Priesthood," *Utah Magazine*, November 20, 1868, 453.

22. Walker reviews these visits in *Wayward Saints*, 118–123.

23. "Joseph Smith and His Work," *Utah Magazine*, December 18, 1868, 520.

24. W. H. Sherman, "Tendencies of Our System to Despotism," *Utah Magazine*, December 18, 1868, 524–525.

25. Skousen's career is discussed in "Roundtable Review: The Naked Capitalist," *Dialogue: A Journal of Mormon Thought* 6, no. 3 (Autumn/Winter 1971): 99–116, and O. Kendell White, "A Review and Commentary on the Prospects of a New Mormon Christian Right Coalition," *Review of Religious Research* 28, no. 2 (December 1986): 182–185. His involvement with the John Birch Society is discussed in D. Michael Quinn, *The Mormon Hierarchy: Extensions of Power* (Salt Lake City: Signature Books, 1994), 82–87, 103–104.

26. Benson's early career is reviewed in the hagiography by Sheri Dew, *Ezra Taft Benson: A Biography* (Salt Lake City: Deseret Book, 1987), and in D. Michael Quinn, "Ezra Taft Benson and Mormon Political Conflicts," *Dialogue: A Journal of Mormon Thought* 26 (Summer 1993): 1–87, and Gary James Bergera, "'This Great Thing Which Has Come to Me a Humble, Weak Farmer Boy': Ezra Taft Benson's 1943 Call to the Apostleship," *Mormon Historical Studies* 9, no. 2 (Fall 2008): 155–164.

27. On anticommunism in the 1950s and 1960s, helpful are Seymour Martin Lipset and Earl Raab, *The Politics of Unreason* (New York: Harper and Row, 1970), and more recently Lisa McGirr, *Suburban Warriors: The Origins of the New American Right* (Princeton: Princeton University Press, 2001), 147–187.

28. Whittaker Chambers, *Witness* (1952; New York: Regnery, 2002), 10. See also Sam Tanenhaus, *Whittaker Chambers: A Biography* (New York: Random House, 1997), 117–119.

29. Doctrine and Covenants 101:76–80; Book of Mormon, 2 Nephi 1:5.

30. Skousen, *The Naked Communist*, 31, 32, 36, 51, 327. This reading of communism was shared by other American Christians; see for instance Patrick Allitt, *Catholic Intellectuals and Conservative Politics in America, 1950–1985* (Ithaca: Cornell University Press, 1993), 60–70; Jonathan P. Herzog, *The Spiritual Industrial Complex: America's Religious Battle Against Communism in the Early Cold War* (New York: Oxford University Press, 2011), 39–75.

31. Book of Mormon, 2 Nephi 2:27.

32. Skousen, *The Cleansing of America* (Salt Lake City: C&J Investments, 1981), 15.

33. Ezra Taft Benson, "The American Heritage of Freedom—A Plan of God," *Conference Report*, October 1961, 73.

34. Gregory A. Prince and William Robert Wright, *David O. McKay and the Rise of Modern Mormonism* (Salt Lake City: University of Utah Press, 2005), 228.

35. See, for instance, Sean Wilentz, "Confounding Fathers," *New Yorker*, October 10, 2010, 32–37.

36. Connor Boyack, *Latter-day Liberty* (Orem, UT: Cedar Fort, 2011), 2, 17.

37. Connor Boyack, *Latter-day Responsibility* (Orem, UT: Cedar Fort, 2012), 67, 71.

38. Rick Koerber, "What Is the Free Capitalist Project?," The Free Capitalist Project, May 20, 2008, http://www.freecapitalist.com/2008/05/20/freecapitalist-project. The McKay quotation is one often cited but never published in the original; it was first referenced in Benson, "The American Heritage of Freedom—God's Plan," 75.

39. Nibley's apologetic works were eventually collected and published by his associates at Brigham Young University as *The Collected Works of Hugh Nibley*, 19 vols. (Salt Lake City, UT: Deseret Book, 1984–2010). Volume 9, *Approaching Zion* (Salt Lake City: Deseret Book, 1998) contains his writings on economics. His authorized biographer Boyd Peterson explores his political views in *Hugh Nibley: A Consecrated Life* (Salt Lake City: Kofford Books, 2002).

40. Nibley, *Approaching Zion*, 25, 13, 27, 49.

41. Ibid., 335, 37.

42. Zig Ziglar, *See You at the Top* (Gretna, LA: Pelican Publishing, 1975); Napoleon Hill, *Think and Grow Rich* (Cleveland, OH: Ralston, 1937). Both are rooted in a Christian form of New Thought that was later incorporated into the prosperity gospel; see Donald B. Mayer, *The Positive Thinkers: Religion as Pop Psychology from Mary Baker Eddy to Oral Roberts* (1965; New York: Knopf, 2013) and Kate Bowler, *Blessed: A History of the American Prosperity Gospel* (New York: Oxford University Press, 2013), 55–60.

43. Stephen R. Covey, *The 7 Habits of Highly Effective People* (New York: Free Press, 1989), 314.

44. Doctrine and Covenants 130:18–21; Covey, *7 Habits,* 23, 48.

45. Doug Christensen, *The Right to Riches* (Salt Lake City: Doug Christensen, 1986), 24.

46. The best biography of Grant is Ronald Walker, *Qualities That Count: Heber J. Grant as Businessman, Missionary, and Apostle* (Provo, UT: Brigham Young University, 2004).

47. Heber J. Grant, "Temperance—Inspirations to Progress," *Young Women's Journal* 20, no. 9 (September 1908): 506.

48. Heber J. Grant, J. Reuben Clark, and David O. McKay to William Fitzgibbon, Chief of Staff to the U.S. Treasury, October 11, 1941, Marriner Eccles Papers, Special Collections, Marriott Library, University of Utah. The letter was likely written by Clark.

49. Heber J. Grant, "The Welfare System." *Conference Report*, October 1936, 3. The development of the Welfare System is discussed in Garth L. Mangum and Bruce D. Blumell, *The Mormons' War on Poverty: A History of LDS Welfare, 1830–1990* (Salt Lake City: University of Utah Press, 1993).

50. *Providing in the Lord's Way* (Salt Lake City: Church of Jesus Christ of Latter-day Saints, 2011), n.p.

51. Dallin H. Oaks, "Our Strengths Can Become Our Downfall," *Ensign*, May 1995.

52. Marvin J. Ashton, *One for the Money* (Salt Lake City: Deseret Book, 1975), 6, 11.

53. Tom Harvey, "Preying on the Faithful," *Salt Lake Tribune,* May 1, 2010; James Sterngold, "When Exotic Investments Are Too Good to Be True," *Fortune*, December 10, 2012.

54. Rick Koerber, "God Is a Capitalist: Answering Ruble Fisher," The Free Capitalist Project, October 27, 2008, http://www.freecapitalist.com/2008/10/27/god-is-a-capitalist-answering-ruble-fisher.

5

A Business Turn in American Jewish Religious History

WOMEN AND THE EMERGENCE
OF POPULAR PHILANTHROPY

Deborah Skolnick Einhorn

IN 1654, the first community of Jews landed in New Amsterdam with the intent to settle, having dodged the Inquisition, privateers, and rough seas. Their arrival set off a volley of heated letters between New Amsterdam's director general, Peter Stuyvesant, and his sponsors at the Dutch West India Company in Amsterdam. Stuyvesant appealed to the directors' religious sensibilities, asking permission that "the deceitful race—such hateful enemies and blasphemers of Christ" be required "in a friendly way to depart." But he also appealed on financial grounds: "Owing to their present indigence they might become a charge in the coming winter." New Amsterdam's leader expressed a profound concern about the potential economic burden the poor, new immigrants, "with their customary usury and deceitful trading with the Christians," could pose to his burgeoning outpost.

The company directors were sympathetic to Stuyvesant's appeal but had their own pocketbooks to consider. Jewish investors in the West India Company had interceded on behalf of their coreligionists, citing their own investments and the company's potential profits from the expansion of new world populations. Ultimately, the Jewish investors' petition was granted, but with one caveat: "Granted that [the Jews] may reside and traffic, provided they will not become a charge upon the Deaconry or the Company." On this condition of self-reliance, the first twenty-three Jews permanently settled in New Amsterdam.

The realistic but reluctant directors broke the news to Stuyvesant gently, stressing the business considerations and the fiscal conditions of the agreement:

> We would have liked to effectuate and fulfill your wishes and request that the new territories should no more be allowed to be infected by people of the Jewish nation, for we foresee therefrom the same difficulties which your fear. But after having further weighed and considered the matter, we observe that this would be somewhat unreasonable and unfair, especially because of the considerable loss sustained by this nation and also because of the large amount of capital which they still have invested in the shares of this company. Therefore after many deliberations we have finally decided and resolved to apostille upon a certain petition presented by said Portuguese Jews that these people may travel and trade to and in New Netherland and live and remain there, provided the poor among them shall not become a burden to the company or to the community, but be supported by their own nation. You will now govern yourself accordingly.[1]

The directors thus mandated Stuyvesant's governance vis-à-vis the Jews, while insisting on Jewish communal self-care and self-reliance.

As the early part of this chapter will explore, the business of taking care of their own—first through mutual aid and eventually through a sophisticated system of charitable organizations—has been at the core of American Jewish life and history. This was foreshadowed by the original entrance agreement, but it is also a reflection of a strong tendency toward peoplehood and civil religion.[2] The Jewish polity has an "auxiliary" Jewish life that supplements, and oftentimes supplants, Jewish religious practice.[3] American Jews' modes of affiliation, organization, and connection have been, and continue to be, diverse and not necessarily "religious" in nature. Synagogues are but one type in a constellation of Jewish institutions:

> Through their ostensibly "secular" organizations, American Jews have undertaken to govern themselves as a component of k'lal Yisrael, the peoplehood of Israel. In so doing, they have achieved unity, purpose and identity as a moral community which transcends (without excluding) the overtly religious ideology and practice of the denominational movements of American Judaism.[4]

Jewish law and texts reflect this blending of sacred and profane. Financial transactions infamously took place in the Temple in Jerusalem. The Talmud, compilations of rabbinic commentary on the Hebrew Bible that are ultimately codified into rabbinic law, spends countless pages legislating loans, debt, and payment of workers, as well as contributions to community institutions and funds. I would argue that this cultural and religious tradition, thousands of years old, impacts historians' approach as well.

These structures and cultural idiosyncrasies help explain why American Jewish history has not experienced the same dramatic "business turn" as the historical study of other religious groups. American Jewish history has addressed religion, lived religion, and Jewish life beyond religion from its early days because these were foundational ways of being Jewish. Whereas other faith traditions' histories may have been more focused on theological evolutions, changes in rites, and religious adaptations in the New World, Jewish "religious" history has been a record of Jewish religion and Jewish community organizations, and the resources necessary to run them.[5]

This is not to say, however, that the historiography of American Jews has always been inclusive of all lived religion, or of all the business of Jewish life. Widening the business lens exposes large areas of neglect, particularly when it comes to gender. Despite women's great contributions to Jewish life, and particularly to fund-raising and institution building, almost all of American Jewish history marginalized their contributions: "Women form a critical part of [American Jewish] history, a part that has, for far too long, been obscured."[6] In this way, an essential piece of the Jewish organizational economy was excluded from the American Jewish narrative. Of course, this was typical in the American milieu until the 1970s, when social history made its mark and women's numbers in graduate history programs grew. Yet, like much of feminism's impact on Jewish life and Judaism, a broader view of women's role in the business of Jewish life did not take shape until later.

Despite this lag, by the 1980s prominent scholars of American Jewish history began to tell women's stories and acknowledge their place in the Jewish polity. By integrating more social and feminist history, scholars of American Jewish life began to draw a more complete picture of lived Judaism in the United States. American Jewish women's early philanthropy and organizations— formalized as early as 1819—laid the groundwork for Jewish educational, social service, and health organizations today. This more inclusive view of American Jewish history broadens and deepens the business lens, yielding a richer understanding of several centuries of American Judaism and American Jewish life.

Jewish Women's History: Widening the Lens

Women have always been an equal part of the past. They just
haven't been part of history.

GLORIA STEINEM

In 1981, "pressured into it by colleagues and associates," Jacob Rader Marcus published *The American Jewish Woman, 1654–1980.* Afterward, he was "grateful to them."[7] His generation's foremost scholar on American Jewish history, Marcus articulated the need for this type of inquiry:

> The Jewish woman has been ignored in the standard chronicles of this country's Jewry. There are exceptions, of course, but the few women included can be counted on the fingers of one hand. There can be no questions: there is an American Jewish woman's history that goes back to September 1654. All American Jewish annalistic works deal with men, a numerical minority among the Jews; there has been no full-length, scientifically conceived, source-based book retailing the lives and adventures of American Jewesses. They were, they still are, a majority of all Jews in this land.[8]

Ultimately, he deemed it "a privilege, with the resources at hand, to present a history that will serve—if for nothing else—as a point of departure." Marcus predicted that "ten years from today, another history of the American Jewish woman will have to be written . . . I hope. A new school of Jewish historians is now rising; many of them are women; they will do justice to their sex. Books on the Jewish woman will appear; they must be written."[9] Indeed, the field has taken off over the last twenty-five years, with scholars, book series, and organizations dedicated to bringing women's contributions to light.

Nonetheless, fifteen years later, feminist scholars were still raising questions about the depth of the impact, and the particular lag for Jewish history: "Feminist historical scholarship is almost twenty years old, yet its impact on the writing of modern Jewish history has been remarkably limited. This is not so because of male malevolence, but because of the very conceptualization of the field of Jewish history. History is a conservative discipline, and Jewish history especially so."[10] Though historian Paula Hyman thus critiques the progress, she and her colleagues have made significant contributions to uncovering women's contributions, both inside and outside the home.

Earlier generations of Jewish historians failed to capture women's contributions of time and money to Jewish causes for these academic and cultural reasons, but also because of historical class norms. In addition to the conservative nature of history as a discipline, and the patriarchal religious context of Jewish history, twentieth-century women did their part to camouflage their work so that they could be seen to adhere to class norms. Privileged women used domestic rhetoric to "spin" their volunteer work (including fund-raising, social work, event planning, and settlement of immigrants), thereby protecting it; this complicates somewhat the task of uncovering that work. In a landmark article, Beth Wenger argues that women used class-appropriate rhetoric to describe what were actually gender norm challenges. Women legitimated their "public participation by defining the world as home-enlarged":[11]

> While Jewish women had long been expected to act as benevolent nurturers, female benevolence in the United States evolved into a sophisticated volunteer movement. Beginning in the nineteenth century, German Jewish women, whose middle-class status afforded them the necessary leisure time for volunteer work, founded the first female Jewish benevolent societies and women's clubs. As volunteers and clubwomen, women fulfilled the traditional duties of "women of valor"[12] by dedicating themselves to the betterment of families and communities. At the same time, Jewish women's clubs often belied the norms of traditional female behavior which had inspired the founding of their organization. Volunteer work, initially designed for women's selfless activities, allowed women to acquire a sense of selfhood and gender consciousness while sharpening leadership and organizational skills. Jewish women who began as behind-the-scenes workers gradually emerged as public agents. Behind the myth of self-sacrificing female benevolence existed a quietly radical redefinition of behavioral norms for Jewish women. Without overtly challenging inveterate notions of Jewish womanhood, Jewish clubwomen assumed new roles and responsibilities within the Jewish community.[13]

Jewish women thus expanded "hearth and home" to encompass all those in need, while also expanding their sphere, responsibilities, and talents. This creative subversion has in some cases complicated discovery of women's full role in the business of Jewish life in America.

The Business of Jewish Women's
Philanthropy: A Historical Case Study of the Turn

Having thus opened the door to women's history, feminist scholars immediately looked to their impact on the organizational and fiscal landscape of
American Jewish life. This chapter presents one case study of how broadening
the business lens of American Jewish history to include women's contributions also changes our understanding of Jewish philanthropy and religious
history overall. By understanding women's role in universalizing charitable
giving in the World War I and postwar periods, historians can better understand the landscape of Jewish philanthropy as a whole, how Jewish community chest organizations became a dominant mode of giving in the American
Jewish world, and the impact of war and suffrage on women's volunteer work.

When immigrants from Eastern Europe began flooding American shores
in the 1880s, fleeing pogroms and rampant discrimination, their more settled
coreligionists worked tirelessly to help them settle into their new country.
Help came from landsmen, people originating from the same area of Eastern
Europe, as well as "uptown" German Jews. These more established Americans
created countless micro-organizations to serve every need. Sewing societies
provided clothing and linens, settlement homes housed and trained young
workers, loan societies made interest-free loans to business that were just
starting out, and small schools called *heders* educated young boys.

At the same time as domestic needs grew dramatically, the needs of families still living in Eastern Europe ballooned. Americans expanded their
support for those relatives as well, often going door-to-door, collection box
in hand. Ultimately, the demands on those donating for Jews at home and
abroad became too frequent, too disruptive, and too overwhelming. In hopes
of avoiding what we now label "compassion fatigue," the Boston Jewish
community brought many small groups under one umbrella in 1895. Using
community-chest-style fund-raising and allocations, the Federation of Jewish
Charities of Boston sought to expedite philanthropy for donors, organizations, and recipients. As social work and charity became professionalized
during this time,[14] the federation model spread to other Jewish communities.
Each sought to communicate a sense of collaboration and unity, choosing
names beginning with adjectives such as *federated*, *united*, or *associated*.

Despite these descriptors, in the early years the campaigns attracted only
a small percentage of each city's Jews. Boston's first drive raised $11,909 from
489 donors. At the time, the city had an estimated 20,000 Jewish residents,
14,000 of whom were new immigrants.[15] In the early years, Jewish federated

philanthropy remained an elite enterprise. But during the World War I era, American propaganda and rhetoric around the war effort encouraged universal participation, and the Federations followed suit.

To win the war, the government preached, everyone on the home front had to pitch in. Propaganda posters encouraged women in particular to buy war bonds, plant gardens, knit socks, and try their hand at a variety of vacant jobs on the home front and on the war front. Many featured women with a shovel in hand or greeting Uncle Sam with a willingness to pitch in. The YWCA proclaimed, "For every fighter, a woman worker." Another, from the National League of Women's Service, features a woman saluting Uncle Sam with the tag line "Miss American reports for service, sir." "Our boys need sox, knit your bit," proclaimed the Red Cross. The National War Garden Commission and the Woman's Land Army promoted victory gardens, charging women to "Sow the Seeds of Victory, Plant and Raise your own Vegetables." President Wilson's prediction that "food will win the war," in particular, weighed heavily on women's shoulders. The country could not do it without them.

The Federation's Women's Division and the Emergence of Popular Philanthropy

Jewish organizations faced a spike in needs at home and overseas and sought to bring this wartime ethos to bear on Jewish charitable work. As tensions escalated abroad and the United States joined the Allies in World War I, Jewish women heeded the universal call to action. As men and women were recruited to their respective roles in the war effort, Jewish women mirrored these calls in their new fund-raising efforts. The Federation's Women's Division of Boston, and counterparts in Philadelphia, New York, and Chicago, initiated their first-ever campaigns during this period. Their groundbreaking work was both a response to unprecedented wartime and postwar needs and a reflection of the sudden shift in gender expectations. A sharpened historiographic gender lens helps us to see the full picture of the evolution of American Jewish philanthropy more clearly within the context of these shifting norms. During World War I, federations turned to popular philanthropy—striving for universal giving—as a means of creating communal solidarity and serving dramatically increased needs. Through their federation divisions, women were essential to a strategic and timely shift in the business of American Jewish philanthropy, from an elite to a mass movement. Women were thus at the forefront of the emerging, modern era of popular Jewish philanthropy.

Despite their early existence and impact during World War I, most scholars either completely neglect or misdate the founding of local women's divisions.[16] Those sources that do address their establishment, typically in just one sentence or paragraph, often mistakenly attribute the founding to the World War II era.[17] This misinformation has long been perpetuated in scholarly articles as well as in the popular press, thus erasing women's early federation fund-raising work from collective memory.[18] With the help of local Jewish newspapers and organizational records, this chapter traces the development of the earliest Federation women's divisions and their participation in World War I–era, postwar, and Depression-era campaigns. Thus equipped, we will explore women's early participation in the dramatically shifting landscape of Jewish giving.

As we have begun to see, the World War I and immediate postwar era witnessed a massive sea change in Jewish communal philanthropy. Internally, Jewish needs, growing both at home and abroad, stimulated an explosion of mass giving in the Jewish community. Externally, the mass movements for war relief seem to have inspired a more inclusive Jewish communal fund-raising structure.[19] Combined, such internal and external factors catalyzed a shift from elite philanthropy to mass giving in the Jewish community. In contemporary terms, the "major gifts" philosophy, focused on established Jewish families and their large donations, gave way to pushes for universal participation. Considering the size of the ever-growing American Jewish population—by 1918 the number of Jews in the United States had swelled to almost 3.8 million[20]—the potential collective impact of small gifts was indeed significant. Federations took note of this potential and embarked on new strategies for soliciting and collecting gifts from all segments of the Jewish community. This move away from elite, patrician philanthropy and toward mass giving remains one of the most critical turning points in Jewish organizational history.

Not only were Jewish women part of the federation structure at this historic moment, but their presence was one key to a successful transition. Women's formal, mass entry into the federation system during the World War I era, through women's divisions, helped change the direction of Jewish philanthropy. Just as federations sought mass participation in the campaign, women volunteered by the hundreds and thousands. Since organizational and community historians have virtually ignored the existence of women's divisions during this period, they have also missed the impact of those new organizations on the changing philanthropic landscape. But in at least three major American cities, women's divisions and their hundreds of volunteers were introducing the giving potential of half the Jewish community to the new approach of federations.

The Jewish community followed the lead of other American organizations of the period both in its shift to broad-based campaigns and in the inclusion of women therein. Catalyzed by wartime needs, both new and existing philanthropies moved to more efficient, mass-based efforts. These efforts broke social and financial barriers by reaching untapped communities and raising unprecedented sums. Wartime needs prescribed the shift to "a short, intensive campaign with a definite end goal, under the leadership of well-known financiers, industrialists, and merchants—appeals on behalf of War services were made to the whole community, treating it as if it were a constituency."[21] Such community building through fund-raising inspired Jewish leadership to consider this strategy to promote Jewish unity: "The possibility that a sense of solidarity might grow from the routine of fund raising dawned upon [New York's] wealthy philanthropists as they watched all Americans, Jewish and Gentile, respond to the mass appeals for wartime relief. They realized that philanthropy and the machinery of fund raising could express American Jews' sense of community and not merely their religious responsibilities."[22]

Both these general and Jewish efforts capitalized on women's community mobilization power, albeit seemingly somewhat later in the Jewish community. "[In] those days, when the whole philanthropic system was undergoing a thorough shake-up, new fields of women's usefulness were discovered."[23] The impact of innovative, inclusive, community-building campaigns, both general and Jewish, reached far beyond the conflict's end. The goal of universal giving during wartime helped change the country's philanthropic culture from elite to mass giving: "Tax returns for the period show that the American public had been trained to give 'something' almost irrespective of income, during the war, and that now the habit had been established."[24] Federation and other mass Jewish relief campaigns likewise inculcated this habit in all segments of their community, including the women's. This era of groundbreaking philanthropy would set the stage for future iterations of American Jewish philanthropy, characterized by its inclusive, community-building philosophy.

Women's Division of Philadelphia's Federation of Jewish Charities, 1918

Immediately after the close of World War I, Philadelphia's Federation of Jewish Charities ushered in this new philanthropic era. A December 1918

Jewish Exponent article heralded the shift from representing "only a part of the community" to representing "all of the community."

> The drive for the support of the Jewish Charities of Philadelphia, which will take place in January, 1919 . . . represents a new era in Jewish communal institutions. The Great War has awakened our community to its duties and to its possibilities. The Philadelphia Federation, up to this point, has represented only a part of the community. It is now proposed that it shall represent all of the community. We have learned through War Chest, through the United War Work drive, through the Liberty Loan campaigns, through the American Red Cross, to work with all our fellow citizens of every origin and creed in doing war work. This seems to have taught the Jews of Philadelphia the lesson that they must work together. . . . There can be no two opinions as to the usefulness of this cause. No valid reason can be alleged against all the Jewish people working together and hundreds of reasons can be advanced in favor of it.[25]

Inspired by heightened needs and the impressive cooperation of wartime campaigns, the city's federation sought to create Jewish unity through philanthropy. Americans working across religious and racial boundaries thus set an example for Jews working across denominational and cultural lines as a unified Jewish community.

The shift from communal exclusiveness to inclusion, with the Great War as catalyst, included the launch of Philadelphia's Women's Division. In fact, the final paragraph of the same *Exponent* article announced the creation of the new division. This single article connects the beginning of a "new era" with the introduction of the Women's Division. The connection attests both to women's presence and to their role in helping to usher in the federation's new strategy. The new division took their charge seriously, planning a house-to-house canvass "to get subscriptions from women and children."[26] One thousand women, divided into seven districts, canvassed Philadelphia for the ten days of the campaign. They undertook to help their federation make its move toward inclusiveness: "It is the duty of all Jewish women to assist this great project by their contributions. Everyone in the household should become a member of the Federation."[27] This call for universal participation, although perhaps an unattainable goal, nonetheless communicated the federation's new, postwar message of unity, inclusion, and philanthropy by *all*.

In the immediate postwar period, Philadelphia thus followed the lead of other anchor Jewish communities' new mass-giving business model. Almost as a postscript, the final paragraph of an article titled "The $750,000 Federation Campaign" announced, "Women to Aid in Drive: A women's division has been formed to aid the campaign, beginning January 5. The division, which will be composed of 500 Philadelphia women, will be headed by Mrs. Arthur Loeb, chairman, and Mrs. Cyrus Adler, vice chairman."[28] The third and final sentence of the historic announcement goes on to list the division's six "district chairmen" and their constituent neighborhoods. Though no known histories of Philadelphia acknowledge Jewish women's formalized role in fund-raising, *The Jewish Exponent* reported consistently about the Women's Division launch.

The *Exponent's* weekly "Womankind" column, always located on page 5, both praised and preached about women's campaign participation. In a January 3, 1919, column, editor Emma Brylawski boldly asserted the drive's dependence on its female fund-raisers:

> It has become generally recognized that no work of whatever nature can be successfully carried out unless it is participated in by the women. . . . The women of the community are now asked to take part in the Federation of Jewish Charities drive for $750,000. . . . The women [solicitors] are most enthusiastic and are anticipating wonderful results.[29]

Solicitors planned to canvass their districts, making "house-to-house visits," a seeming signature of the early Women's Division campaigns.[30] Prescriptions for universal participation soon followed in the *Exponent*. Five days into the campaign, the first in Philadelphia to include systematic solicitations by women, the *Exponent* printed a heavy-handed recommendation: "It is the duty of all Jewish women to assist this great project by their contributions. Everyone in the household should become a member of the Federation."[31] Campaign leaders had charged the new division with gaining "subscriptions" not only from their female peers but also from neighborhood children.

The *Exponent's* coverage, always touting the women's enthusiasm in glowing terms, succeeded in generating even more excitement. Within one week of their first report, the number of Women's Division volunteers doubled from five hundred to one thousand.[32] To inspire and instruct this new army of federation solicitors on the eve of the campaign, the Women's Division invited a New York emissary to speak. "The principal speaker was Mrs. Alexander

Kohut, of New York city, who stirred the large audience with graphic accounts of how the recent campaign was conducted in New York."[33] The Philadelphia women thus called upon a New York (lay) expert for guidance in their first Women's Division campaign.

After its inception in 1918 and first campaign in 1919, the Philadelphia's Women's Division of the Federation of Jewish Charities continued to be a force in that city's fund-raising. The division made headlines throughout the 1920s. Leading up to the January 1925 campaign, the *Jewish Exponent* proclaimed competitively: "The Jewish women of our city will not permit the men to outclass them in the campaign, which is about to be launched with a view to raising one million, five hundred thousand dollars."[34] Unlike their early *Jewish Exponent* appearances, the women were no longer confined to the "Womankind" column or to the final paragraph of an article about the Federation. The women's campaign had gained popular recognition, an appreciation seemingly matched within the federation structure. In 1925, Mrs. Arthur A. Loeb, chairman of the Women's Division, was also named the associate chairman of the overall campaign.[35] In 1926, the new Women's Division chairman delivered an "eloquent address at Federation's opening dinner," making the *Jewish Exponent*'s front page.[36] Thus, for more than a decade before their earliest acknowledgment in federation and more general histories, the Women's Division in Philadelphia thrived, made headlines, and helped their local Federation reach its ever-growing fund-raising goals.

Women's Division of New York's Federation for the Support of Philanthropic Societies, 1920

The 1917 New York Emergency Relief Campaign seemingly set the pace for federation's philosophy shift and for the creation of a permanent Women's Division. According to Rebekah Kohut, campaign leaders prided themselves on the "'pull together' spirit of the different classes of Jews."[37] This unified wartime giving foreshadowed the federation's near future of mass philanthropy. Women's active campaign participation likewise set a precedent for the genders "pulling together." Women's "small, individual contributions," even in their first mass drive, accounted for 5 percent of campaign totals.[38] Despite their relatively small contributions, women delivered mass participation and likely also played a part in encouraging donations from spouses and family members. These two factors were undoubtedly keys in the quest for universal Jewish giving, both during World War I and in the immediate postwar era.

Although New York's federation was only born in 1917, the postwar era catalyzed a rebirth in 1920.[39] In that year, the creation of a Business Men's Council signified a shift in federation philosophy: "To substitute all-year-around propaganda for the sporadic efforts of drives is the plan of the Business Men's Council."[40] This move away from brief, intensive campaigns reveals a desire to draw subscriptions from an even larger segment of the Jewish community. "Their plan is to reach every member of every industry at some time during the year to interest him in the work that is being done by the institutions affiliated with Federation."[41] The new group assured the community that federation's universally felt work made universal participation possible: "The work is so varied and so all inclusive that no Jew can say that he is not interested or that he does not care to help. Federation has a place for everyone and a part for everyone to play."[42]

Rebekah Kohut, whose visit kicked off these early Philadelphia successes, did not yet belong to a women's division of her own. In fact, New York's Federation for Support of Jewish Philanthropic Societies would not form its own women's division for another year and a half.[43] The *Jewish Exponent*'s vague description of Kohut's work aiding "in directing the recent Jewish charity drive"[44] actually referred to her tenure as head of the Women's Division for the New York Emergency Relief Campaign,[45] not in the as-yet-uncreated Women's Division of Federation.[46] Nonetheless, that relief campaign helped to prove New York women's fund-raising aptitudes, likely setting the stage for the forthcoming federation division.

As the *American Hebrew* reported in December 1917, "women's teams" raised 5 percent of New York's $5 million relief goal. Acknowledging the "splendid work of women's teams," the weekly Jewish periodical noted: "The women, fourteen teams of them, did wonderful work, raising over $250,000, largely in small, individual contributions."[47] Such small but independent donations would characterize women's division campaigns for years to come, moving the campaigns closer to the goal of universal participation. In 1916, even before the relief campaign, before the official launch of New York's federation, Kohut and other well-known New York women gathered to discuss their future role: "A meeting of prominent women to discuss plans of the projected Federation for the Support of Philanthropic Societies in New York City was held at the home of Mrs. Felix Warburg."[48]

Despite this early groundwork, New York's women remained within the general campaign structure for its first two years, 1918 and 1919.[49] Women volunteers constituted half of the team-leading "colonels" for the 1918 subscription drive,[50] and were charged with spreading "the gospel of Federation throughout the city."[51] Although men and women's campaigns were not yet formally divided, neither were they completely integrated. As in the precedent-setting Emergency Relief Campaign, women likely subscribed only other women.

The 1920 Business Men's Council launch indicated a major shift in the new federation's structure. "Persistent continuous work" and "all-year-around propaganda" displaced the "sporadic efforts" of aggressive two-week campaigns.[52] *The American Hebrew* heralded and praised this tactical shift on its front cover in May of 1920.[53] Still, the ensuing consequences for fund-raising by women, who were obviously excluded from the men's council, remained to be seen.

During the summer months, though, "around festive tea tables" and on the "summer hotel porch rocker," a parallel Women's Division swung into action. Praising this shift away from "fancy work"[54] in fund-raising, *American Hebrew* author Zelda Popkin mocked traditional campaign gender roles: "And the *ladies*—God bless 'em—they will make fancy work and hold a bazaar or bake cakes for a Kaffee Klatch or card party. That will be enough for them to do." Having chided the federation for formerly depriving women of opportunities "to stand shoulder to shoulder with the men,"[55] she praised the recent development of a formal Women's Division:

> The program of the Women's Division is supplementary to that undertaken by the men through their Business Men's Council, and its significance is that an exact division of the burden of raising Federation's annual four million dollar budget has been made and women are recognized as the equals of men, in Federation as at the polls.[56]

The author jumps between praise of equality and perhaps unconscious admission of its limitations. She cites women's "supplementary" role in raising an "exact," but not equal, portion of the budget: "The Women's task is to bring Federation into the homes of New York Jewry, as the men bring it to factory and office."[57] The article thus reflects a timely, triumphant feeling of having achieved "equality," however separate or conditional.

New York women thus took their place in the reimagined federation structure. The Women's Division held the key to half the Jewish population. In its first year, New York's Women's Division undertook a census of Jewish New York toward the creation of a master solicitation list. Volunteers committed to canvassing their assigned district, "listing the name of every Jewish resident and shopkeeper," and then to soliciting all prospective donors in that area.[58] "One hundred per cent is the goal of the women workers. They have pledged themselves not to cease their efforts until New York Jewry supports a Federation with the full contributing strength of every man, woman and child."[59] In the case of New York, then, the women strived to engage even more than "their half" of the population. Like their male counterparts, the Women's Division embraced the move toward mass giving, striving for efficiency, thoroughness, and the ideal of universal participation.

The Jewish women of New York took their new charge seriously and approached their task scientifically. "The city is divided into 65 districts, each in [the] charge of a chairman and her committee of ten or more workers. The plan of work has the marks of thorough organization and is so 'business-like' that milady before the war would have shrunk from it in fright and given up the task before it was begun."[60] Efficiency and professionalism, seemingly universal sources of Women's Division pride, marked this first independent women's campaign in New York. The author considered the Women's Division to be "more than time and dollars. It will be a proof of women's ability in hitherto untried fields with new working methods."[61] Fund-raising would thus become the battlefield on which postwar Jewish women would prove their mettle.

In the decade that followed its founding, still invisible to history, the New York Women's Division continued to mechanize and motivate. In 1922, one volunteer collected $10,000 in pledges within days of the campaign's launch.[62] The Women's Division "Heart Club" entitled her to proudly wear 400 hearts, one for every $25 in pledges.[63] By 1928, the New York campaign drew just short of 10 percent of its funds from the Women's Division. The federation's drive that year, which raised $5.3 million, broke records for women's involvement: "The largest sum ever raised by women's teams for annual maintenance work of philanthropies was secured by the Women's Division of the New York Federation for the Support of Jewish Philanthropic Societies, which, according to a summary of 1928 work by Mrs. Sidney C. Borg, chairman of the Women's Division, secured $510,586."[64] Reaching the half-million-dollar mark, New York's Women's Division truly became a model to emulate. And Boston women took advantage of this New York prototype as they prepared to relaunch their Women's Division in 1930, thirteen years after its first brief foray.

Boston: Women's Division of Boston's Federated Jewish Charities, 1917, and Women's Division of Boston's Associated Jewish Philanthropies, 1930

After more than two decades of fund-raising in Boston, the Federated Jewish Charities shifted gears during World War I. In 1917, the leadership undertook to widen its small fund-raising base of just twelve hundred donors. As in Philadelphia and New York, the local press heralded this move away from elite philanthropy and toward mass giving and communal solidarity. On April 12, 1917, the *Jewish Advocate's* banner headline proclaimed: "The Slogan: 'A United Israel for Charity.' We want first to unite all the Jewish of Boston. Irrespective of what their religious, social or economic views are, the vehicle in which they can all ride is charity."[65] One editorial urged the "rank and file of our people" to respond to the federation's appeal: "Our charities must not depend for support on the generosity of a few benevolent and well disposed persons."[66] This shift, from the federation's historical dependence on the few to solicitation of the rank and file, perfectly encapsulates the wartime changes in Jewish giving. Jews of all social and economic classes, these journalists insist, should shoulder their portion of the communal burden, no matter how small. A second column therefore called upon *every* member of the community, men and women alike: "For this purpose, it will be necessary that every Jew in Boston tax himself or herself . . . so that all Boston Jewry may be united in one mighty effort."[67]

A midcentury history of Boston's federation considered 1917's new, broad-based constituency the audience for the city's "first modern fund-raising campaign."[68] The 1916 Report of the Welfare Committee recommended changes "that shaped that modern Federation."[69] Characterized by efficient systems, new committee structures, and districting of the city, the "first popular fund-raising campaign" began "to make good the claim of being the community's representative Jewish charitable organizations."[70] During the brief campaign, federation subscriptions skyrocketed from twelve hundred to eight thousand, quadrupling the dollars typically collected.[71]

Boston women helped to usher in this philanthropic "modernity" and the first popular federation campaign in their city. The federation created its Women's Division, or Ladies' Teams Committee, specifically to aid in this ambitious new work. Newly efficient systems and committees thus integrated community women, albeit in a separate leadership structure. Granting access to half the city's Jewish population and their pocketbooks, the Women's Division was essential in the federation's striving toward the ideal of universal participation. Their contributions, although likely small for the most part, undoubtedly helped to raise the federation's financial and membership bottom lines.[72]

No matter the size of their gifts, women's participation helped to create "A United Israel for Charity" across traditional class and gender boundaries. "Men and women, old and young, who had not known each other, worked together and celebrated at a triumphant dinner the new solidarity among Boston's Jews."[73] Such communal unity through philanthropy, a goal of the Boston, Philadelphia, and New York campaigns, helped both to fulfill wartime needs and to empower new federation donors. The impact of this new age of Jewish philanthropy, however, would last far beyond the World War I era.

The 1917 women's campaign in Boston significantly predates that city's 1930 inauguration of a permanent Women's Division.[74] The division's own records and annual reports document the early wartime campaign. A 1946 overview of the Boston Women's Division work pays homage to its World War I–era roots:

> The Boston Women's Division had its inception in 1917 when the first effort was made to conduct an educational program for the agencies of the Associated Jewish Philanthropies. In addition, a fund-raising campaign among the women of the city was conducted. From this nucleus has grown the present Women's Division ... which has created an ever-growing awareness among women of their own responsibility in giving out of their own incomes or household allowance.[75]

A somewhat obscure 1956 history of the Associated Jewish Philanthropies confirms this institutional memory. In 1917, for "the first time, wives and daughters of Federated leaders organized a separate women's division under the chairmanship of Mrs. Harry Liebman. No resources were left untapped."[76] In fact, the *Jewish Advocate* lists Mrs. Liebman as the "ladies' teams committee" chairman for the 1917 $200,000 drive.[77] Later newspaper articles likewise confirm the existence of an early women's drive in Boston. [78] When Boston women reinitiated their federation fund-raising in 1930, the *Jewish Advocate* reported: "More than doubling the amount ever turned in by their group before, the Women's Division has contributed nearly $50,000 to the campaign total."[79] Thus, the group's record-setting work in 1930 confirms the existence of an earlier Women's Division record to be broken.

After a seeming period of hibernation during the 1920s boom, the Boston Women's Division reemerged in 1930 as part of the renamed Associated Jewish Philanthropies (AJP). With the Depression looming and drastically increased demand for services, the AJP commissioned another "long-range planning study."[80] In the meantime, the community's women initiated their own strategy. The *Jewish Advocate* announced the "birth" of its city's Women's Division, albeit in the final paragraphs of an extensive campaign article: "The

Women's Division was formed at a tea given recently by Mrs. Louis E. Kirstein at her summer home in Devereaux. The suggestion for such a division came from Lina Frankenstein and Mrs. Henry Ehrlich and was heartily seconded by almost 100 women who were present."[81] Just as in New York, the summer months had proved fertile ground for the regrowth of the women's division concept in Boston. Within a few months the women had officially created a permanent division: "A meeting of the temporary organization of the Women's Division of the Associated Jewish Philanthropies for the purpose of forming a permanent Women's Division was called to order by the Chairman, Mrs. Hyman Freiman, at 2.15 o'clock on Wednesday, January 14 in the Community Center of Temple Ohabei Shalom, Marshall and Beacon Streets, Brookline."[82] Notably, neither the *Advocate* nor the early minutes of the organization acknowledge the group's 1917 roots.

During this period of increased needs, the Federation called upon the reinvented Women's Division to help alleviate the Depression deficit. Executive Committee minutes from February 1931 report: "Dr. Selekman told of the great need for temporary relief and of the necessity of double expenditures in this field. Because of this added expense there will be a deficit of about $110,000. To meet this deficit he told of the projected special campaign. . . . The co-operation of the Women's Division was requested."[83] The women agreed to participate and raised $38,425 that year, more than one-third of the projected shortfall.[84] Like their predecessors who initiated a women's campaign during the First World War, Boston women reincarnated Women's Division during the national crisis that followed.[85]

Conclusions

In at least three major northeastern cities, Federation Women's Divisions emerged simultaneously with popular Jewish philanthropy. Their thousands of volunteers helped to launch mass Jewish giving and to encourage women's own independent giving. The two were inextricably linked. The Federation's "modern" philanthropic strategies answered the calls for communal solidarity, for increased funding to meet beneficiaries' wartime and postwar needs, and for gender "equality" in "Federation as at the polls." Critical moments in American history also marked crucial turning points for Jewish communal structures and for women's status therein.[86] The most recent business turn in Jewish historical scholarship has thus widened the lens to include women's impact, illuminating their contributions of time, money, and the potential of universal giving. Without that broader view, the shift from elite (male) philanthropy toward universal Jewish communal giving would remain unclear. Though much of the impact of women's mass entry into the workforce was reversed "when the boys got back," in Jewish communities the Women's Divisions continued to raise a growing percentage of community funds, and the trend became universal by the end of the Second World War.

Today, as Jewish demographers chart lower rates of affiliation and giving to Jewish causes, the elite model of Jewish federation philanthropy has been making a comeback, reliant on family foundations and mega-donors—an efficient necessity. The sense of a Jewish communal tax, paid in the form of donations to the local federation, has waned. Donors seek meaning, connection, and community through their giving, making them less likely to feel outright obligation or even latent social pressure.

Historiographically, the feminist lens has begun to encourage scholars to examine other marginalized groups and movements as well.[87] Rather than simply observing or forecasting declining connection to the religious and business sides of Jewish life today, contemporary scholars seek alternative explanations. By looking at grassroots movements, communities with new ways of connecting Jewishly, and Jewish minority populations, scholars will begin to understand contemporary ways that Jews are finding and creating Judaism for themselves, including through new organizations[88] and giving to non-Jewish causes.

Heeding that original condition of entry into America, Jews have indeed succeeded in caring for their own, per Stuyvesant and his sponsors' request. As Jews reinvent the giving and fund-raising wheel yet again, historians will need to shift the categories to include a more diverse group of Jews raising and channeling funds into new and renewed organizations. Only with that broader view can scholars expect to amplify the "margins," understanding the religious, communal, and philanthropic connections of a new generation of American Jews.

Notes

1. Jacob Rader Marcus, *The American Jewish Woman, 1654–1980* (New York: KTAV, 1981), 32–33.
2. Robert Bellah, "Civil Religion in America," *Daedalus: Journal of the American Academy of Arts and Sciences* 96, no. 1 (Winter 1967): 1–21.
3. Daniel Elazar, *Community and Polity* (Philadelphia: Jewish Publication Society, 1976).
4. Jonathan Woocher, *Sacred Survival: The Civil Religion of American Jews* (Indianapolis: Indiana University Press, 1986), vii.

5. For example, Salo Baron, *A Social and Religious History of the Jews* (New York: Columbia University Press, 1969); Ismar Elbogen, *A Century of Jewish Life* (Philadelphia: The Jewish Publication Society, 1944); Paul Mendes-Flohr and Jehuda Reinharz, *The Jew in the Modern World* (New York: Oxford University Press, 1995); Jacob Rader Marcus, *The Jew in the American World* (Detroit: Wayne State University Press, 1996).

6. Pamela Nadell and Jonathan Sarna, *Women and American Judaism: Historical Perspectives* (Hanover, NH: Brandeis University Press, 2001), 12.

7. Marcus, *The American Jewish Woman*, xi.

8. Ibid.

9. Ibid., xii.

10. Paula E. Hyman, "Feminist Studies and Modern Jewish History," in *Feminist Perspectives on Jewish Studies*, ed. Lynn Davidman and Shelly Tenenbaum (New Haven: Yale University Press, 1994), 120.

11. Beth Wenger, "Jewish Women and Voluntarism: Beyond the Myth of Enablers," *American Jewish History* 79, no. 1 (Autumn 1989): 17.

12. The concept of 'woman of valor' derives from Chapter 31 of Proverbs in the Hebrew Bible, which includes a description of the ideal wife. This praise is traditionally offered by chanting part of the chapter (*Eishet Hayil*) on Friday nights before Sabbath dinner.

13. Wenger, "Jewish Women and Voluntarism," 16–17.

14. Notably, the professionalization of aid work and social work hampered some women's participation in work they had been doing as volunteers for decades, as they were deemed underqualified for this more "scientific" brand of outreach. A review of Regina Kunzel's work on this issue summarizes a parallel process: "Kunzel analyzes how evangelical women drew on a long tradition of female benevolence to create maternity homes that would redeem and reclaim unmarried mothers. She shows how, by the 1910s, social workers struggling to achieve professional legitimacy tried to dissociate their own work from that earlier tradition, replacing the reform rhetoric of sisterhood with the scientific language of professionalism."

15. "Our History," Combined Jewish Philanthropies of Greater Boston, www.cjp.org/about-us/our-history, accessed July 28, 2015.

16. For examples of omission, see Harry L. Lurie, *A Heritage Affirmed* (Philadelphia: Jewish Publication Society, 1965); Jewish Social Service Association, *Fifty Years of Social Service* (New York: Clarence S. Nathan, 1926); Rhoda Rosen, ed., *The Shaping of a Community: The Jewish Federation of Metropolitan Chicago* (Chicago: Spertus Press, 1999). Also Daniel Elazar, "The Federations Step Forward," *Jewish Political Studies Review* 7, nos. 3–4 (1995): 13–31. In omitting or setting back the development of Federation Women's Divisions, both institutions and scholars have virtually erased up to thirty years of women's involvement in community fund-raising, education, and leadership. Before most histories even acknowledge they exist, local women's divisions were collectively raising millions of dollars. Perhaps more

important, this erasure camouflages women's collective impact on major shifts in the business of Jewish fund-raising.

17. Likely because of a confusion or confluence with the founding of United Jewish Appeal's National Women's Division in 1946. Examples of misdating to World War II include Federation Steven J. Gold, "Women's Changing Place in Jewish Philanthropy," *Contemporary Jewry* 18 (1997): 61, and Barry A. Kosmin, "The Political Economy of Gender in Jewish Federations," *Contemporary Jewry* 10, no. 1 (1989): 18 ("Women's Divisions of Jewish Federations came into existence following World War II"). Philip Bernstein's Federation history comes closer in its dating of the Women's Division to the 1930s, labeling New York as an early trendsetter. Philip Bernstein, *To Dwell in Unity* (Philadelphia: Jewish Publication Society of America, 1983), 262.

18. For one example of perpetuation in the popular press, see Amy Stone, "The Locked Cabinet," *Lilith*, Winter 1976, 17–21.

19. For example, see "The $750,000 Federation Campaign," *Jewish Exponent*, December 27, 1918, 10.

20. *American Jewish Yearbook*, 1920–1921.

21. John R. Seeley, *Community Chest: A Case Study in Philanthropy* (Toronto: University of Toronto Press, 1957), 19–20.

22. Deborah Dash Moore, "From Kehillah to Federation: The Communal Functions of Federated Philanthropy in New York City, 1917–1933," *American Jewish History* 68, no. 2 (1978): 131.

23. Zelda F. Popkin, "Women to 'Sell' Philanthropy: The Ladies, God Bless 'Em, Used to Hold Bazaars, but Not Now," *American Hebrew*, September 10, 1920, 440.

24. Seeley, *Community Chest*, 21.

25. "The $750,000 Federation Campaign."

26. "Womankind," *Jewish Exponent*, January 3, 1919, 5.

27. Ibid.

28. "The $750,000 Federation Campaign."

29. "Womankind."

30. Ibid.

31. Ibid.

32. "Federation's Great Drive a Big Success," *Jewish Exponent*, January 10, 1919, 10.

33. Ibid.

34. "Jewish Women in Federation Drive," *Jewish Exponent*, January 2, 1925, 13.

35. Ibid.

36. "Whirlwind Campaign Sweeps to $4,000,000," *Jewish Exponent*, January 22, 1926, 1.

37. "Federation's Great Drive a Big Success."

38. "$5,000,000 and Over the Top," *American Hebrew*, December 21, 1917, 206.

39. Notably, since New York's Federation was only founded in 1917—when other Federations were making the change to popular philanthropy—some of the

principles of mass giving were integrated in its original structure. The 1920 shift looked to widen the constituency further. Lurie, *A Heritage Affirmed*, 79.

40. "Federation to Eliminate Campaigns," *American Hebrew*, May 21, 1920, 3.

41. Ibid.

42. Ibid.

43. Popkin, "Women to 'Sell' Philanthropy," 440.

44. "Federation's Great Drive a Big Success."

45. Henry H. Rosenfelt, *This Thing of Giving* (New York: Plymouth Press, 1924), 217.

46. "New York Relief Campaign," *American Hebrew*, November 16, 1917, 1.

47. "$5,000,000 and Over the Top."

48. "Women Discuss Federation Plans," *American Hebrew*, November 10, 1916, 12.

49. Although New York's Federation was founded in 1917, it conducted its first annual campaign in 1918.

50. "50,000 Members for Federation," *American Hebrew*, January 11, 1918, 286.

51. "Federation Campaign a Success," *American Hebrew*, January 25, 1918, 351.

52. "Federation to Eliminate Campaigns."

53. Ibid.

54. The author described "fancy work" as "[holding] a bazaar or bak[ing] cakes for a Kaffee Klatch or card party." Popkin, "Women to 'Sell' Philanthropy," 440.

55. Ibid.

56. Ibid.

57. Ibid.

58. Ibid.

59. Ibid., 482.

60. Ibid.

61. Ibid.

62. "No Let-Up in Federation Round-up," *American Hebrew*, October 27, 1922, 630.

63. This phenomenon of wearing one's pledge continues as a highly successful (and critiqued) tactic of fFederation women's philanthropy in the form of the Lion of Judah pin, which recognizes annual gifts of $5,000 or more.

64. "Women's Division of Federation Raised Record Sum During 1928," *Jewish Tribune*, January 25, 1929, 13.

65. "The Slogan: 'A United Israel for Charity,'" *Jewish Advocate*, April 12, 1917, 1.

66. H. H. Rubenovitz, "Solidarity and $200,000," *Jewish Advocate*, April 12, 1917, 8.

67. P. Israeli, "Thoroughness and Philanthropy," *Jewish Advocate*, April 12, 1917, 8.

68. Barbara Miller Solomon, *Pioneers in Service* (Boston: Court Square Press, 1956), 95.

69. Susan Ebert, "Community and Philanthropy," in *The Jews of Boston*, ed. Jonathan Sarna (Boston: Combined Jewish Philanthropies, 1995), 226.

70. Solomon, *Pioneers in Service*, 96.

71. Ibid., 95; Ebert, "Community and Philanthropy," 226.

72. Like other new contributors, though, they also helped bring down the average donation from approximately $58 to $31. In 1916, twelve hundred donors contributed $70,000. In 1917, eight thousand donors contributed $250,000.

73. Solomon, *Pioneers in Service*, 96.

74. Ebert, "Community and Philanthropy," 226.

75. "Boston Women's Division," report, July 9, 1946, Collection of the American Jewish Historical Society (New England Branch), I-220, IX/2-18.

76. Solomon, *Pioneers in Service*, 96. In this research, Solomon's history of the Associated Jewish Philanthropies of Boston was the only text to correctly date a local Federation Women's Division chapter/campaign.

77. "The Slogan: 'A United Israel for Charity,'" *Jewish Advocate*, April 12, 1917, 4.

78. A scan of Boston's *Jewish Advocate* from that year yielded no direct references about women's collective role in that year's annual campaign, held in April. In 1917, the *Advocate* logically overflowed with information about happenings abroad, a possible reason for the failure to include mention of the newly created Women's Division. In her autobiography, Rebekah Kohut lamented this same phenomenon during the Second World War: "No, my name isn't in the papers, but it would be a pleasant surprise if I could at least run across the names of friends and neighbors in the papers occasionally (in something besides the obituary columns) . . . this is a lost pleasure in New York, where the papers . . . seem to be published mainly as a record of the World Crisis rather than for the day-to-day pleasure of people living in New York." Rebekah Kohut, *More Yesterdays* (New York: Bloch, 1950), 6.

79. "$536,950 Total Raised to Date for Charities," *Jewish Advocate*, November 4, 1930, 4. Also, "Jews of Boston Responding Generously to Charities Drive, Now Past Half Million Mark," *Jewish Advocate*, October 31, 1930, 1.

80. Ebert, "Community and Philanthropy," 228.

81. "Philanthropies to Open Drive for $750,000," *Jewish Advocate*, September 19, 1930, 2. Eerily, despite more than a decade passing in between, both local newspapers report the creation of their Women's Divisions in the final paragraph of an article announcing their drive for $750,000.

82. Women's Division Minutes from January 14, 1931, Collection of the American Jewish Historical Society (New England Branch), I-220, IX/2-18.

83. Executive Committee Meeting Minutes from February 18, 1931, Collection of the American Jewish Historical Society (New England Branch), I-220, IX/2-18.

84. "Women's Division Team Figures 1930–1944," Collection of the American Jewish Historical Society (New England Branch), I-220, IX/2-18.

85. Federations were not alone in calling upon community women during this period of increased need. "As the Depression deepened, synagogue sisterhoods shouldered an increasing financial load and a greater responsibility for maintaining synagogue activities." Beth Wenger, *New York Jews and the Great Depression* (New Haven: Yale University Press, 1996), 176.

86. This connection has been explored vis-à-vis American women, although in the opposite direction: "When women finally got the vote in 1920, they did so more as a measure of gratitude for their participation in the war effort than as a matter of social justice." S. J. Kleinberg, *Women in the United States, 1830–1945* (New Brunswick, NJ: Rutgers University Press, 1999), 202.

87. Nadell and Sarna, *Women in American Judaism*; Beryl Lieff Benderly and Hasia Diner, *Her Works Praise Her: A History of Jewish Women in America from Colonial Times to the Present* (New York: Basic Books, 2002); Melissa Klapper, *Ballots, Babies and Banners of Peace* (New York: NYU Press, 2013); Deborah Skolnick Einhorn, "Power of the Purse: Social Change in Jewish Women's Philanthropy," Dissertation, Brandeis University, 2012.

88. *The Slingshot Guide,* which is produced annually by the Slingshot Fund, tracks this growing field and helps potential donors and volunteers find cutting edge Jewish organizations.

6

The Business of Asian Religions

GURU ENTREPRENEURS AND GODMEN CEOS

Michael J. Altman

IN HIS 1941 autobiographical account of his time in America, Gujarati writer Krishnalal Shridharani described his "brief career as a yogi." While visiting a high-society woman in Rhode Island, Shridharani offhandedly remarked that meditation came more naturally outdoors in the early morning. "Every time I visited her sea-side sanctuary after that unfortunate remark," he wrote, "I was expected to get up at five in the morning, parade across the lawn in her company to the water front, and sit on the pebbles for half an hour meditating." Later, the woman gathered some friends together and asked Shridharani to give a lecture on meditation, proper breathing, and "Yoga in general." Americans expected that every Indian they encountered knew something about yoga and something about meditation, and was a guru in the making.[1]

For his part, Shridharani hoped to dispel these myths about Indians. "Not all Indians enjoy a religious station. They are not all Swamis, or Yogis, or Sadhus, or Rishis," he wrote. Shridharani blamed the stereotype of Indian religiosity on the American marketplace, which allowed some Indians to profit from American expectations of Hindu spirituality. He described how Americans "may hear about one Yogi Tincanwalla, advertising himself as 'The Einstein of Spiritual Relativity,'" or be "invited to attend classes ('$2.00 for each attendance; $35.00 for the series of fifteen') in 'Yogic breathing.'" Shridharani expresses a tongue-in-cheek ridicule of these gurus whom he found "dragging spiritual qualities down to the market place." Yet, despite their place in the marketplace, many Indian swamis answered a "dire American need." They provided a "serenity of mind" to Americans caught up in the "uncertainties of an industrial economy, the speed and noise of the modern city, the dreadful stresses and strains of modern times."[2] The swami sold his lectures, yoga poses, and meditation in the marketplace as a solution to the stress of the market economy.

As historians of religion in America have turned their attention to the role of markets and money in religious history, their focus has rarely moved beyond American Christianity. Much of this work has been dominated by a Weberian approach that sees the roots of capitalism in Protestant religion and the destruction of religion in a tide of secularism brought on by modernity. In his study of India, Weber described how the country's caste system limited its capacity to produce a rational capitalist marketplace. There was "no indication that by themselves they could have created the rational enterprise of modern capitalism."[3] India needed British colonial power to establish capitalism. Weber blamed this lack of rational capitalism on India's mystical religion. Mystical religion led to "world indifference," which then assumed "the form of a flight from the world, or, indeed, in an inner-worldly manner."[4] Mystical Asians, according to Weber, did not see the need to work in the world through their actions and so they never achieved the rational this-worldly asceticism of the Protestant work ethic and capitalism.

The Weberian link between Protestantism and capitalism has kept American historians from paying sustained attention to the role of money, markets, and business in Asian religions in America. The industrious this-worldly Protestants of American history have been given attention, while Asian religions have been left unexplored. Yet the American marketplace is chock full of Asia and Asian religions. Americans buy yoga in its infinite forms, merchandise branded with the image of gods and goddesses, and books on subjects ranging from Zen to Tibetan Buddhism. What Thomas Tweed has described as the "Buddhification of America" could be expanded to the "Asianization of America."[5]

Yet it is important to resist any explanation of this Asianization that sees it as a one-way or even back-and-forth movement of culture and capital between America and Asia. Taking the business turn in the study of Asian religions in America means taking a global view of networks and circulation. As Andrea Jain has argued regarding yoga, it was not a matter of transplanting yoga from a static East to a static West, but "a movement that developed in response to transnational cultural developments, namely developments in consumer culture."[6] When it comes to Asian religions in America, following the money means taking a global view of interconnected marketplaces. Asian religions in the United States continue to be part of larger global movements that connect social, economic, and cultural developments in Asia with those in North America. As Arjun Appadurai argued, "The new global cultural economy has to be seen as a complex, overlapping, disjunctive order that cannot any longer be understood in terms of existing center-periphery models (even those that might account for multiple centers and peripheries)."[7] Thus, taking the business turn means shifting from the study of Asian religions *in* America to the study of Asian religions *and* America. It means paying particular attention to the global flows moving through, within, and around both continents.[8]

Taking the Business Turn in the Study of Asian Religions in America

Most scholarship about Asian religions in America has used a travel or arrival metaphor in interpretations of the encounter between Asia and America. For example, in the introduction to *Asian Religions in America: A Documentary History*, Thomas Tweed organizes his introduction around the themes of mapping, meeting, and migration. These spatial themes reflect the "images connected with perceptions of place and movements though space" that Tweed and Stephen Prothero saw in their documentary sources.[9] Similarly, Prema Kurien's sociological study of Hinduism in America described how "Hinduism arrived in the United States long before Hindu immigrants did."[10] Kurien's use of "arrival," along with the title of the chapter, "Transplanting Hinduism in the United States," signals a model where a thing in the world called "Hinduism" somehow made its way to the geographical space we call the United States. Like Tweed, it is a from-here-to-there metaphor of Asian religions in America in which the story of "Hinduism" in America begins with its arrival.[11]

These arrival models for Asian religions in America do a good job capturing the history of how and when people, texts, and practices from Asia found their way to the United States. That is, there really was a from-here-to-there movement. But there are two problems with the arrival narratives of Asian religions in America. First, they do not account for the process of construction and representation that produced Asian religions in America. When Kurien describes the arrival of Hinduism she means that missionary reports, translations of Sanskrit texts, and descriptions of religion in India had traveled from India to the United States. Yet until the last decades of the nineteenth century Americans did not call these things "Hinduism." They called them "heathenism," "brahmanism," "the religion of the Hindoos," and "paganism" instead. As Richard King has argued, Hinduism as a "world religion," comparable to Christianity and other world religions, did not exist until the nineteenth century.[12] The same can be said for Buddhism, as Philip Almond argued in the aptly titled *The British Discovery of Buddhism*.[13] Asian religions—"Hinduism," "Buddhism," "Sikhism," et cetera—did not arrive in the United States. Rather, people and practices from the continent of Asia were represented and constructed in a variety of ways for a variety of ends in American culture. The model of essential and sui generis "Hinduism" or "Buddhism" or "Daoism" arriving in America misses this process of representation and construction.

Second, by focusing on the arrival and growth of Asian religions in America, scholars have emphasized themes of acculturation, assimilation, Americanization, and other processes of change and adaptation by Asian immigrants in America. Thus the questions have been things like: Is there an "American" Buddhism? How have Hindus adapted to American culture? How has Asian religion transformed American culture? These questions are all well and good, but they remain in the narrow register of travel, movement, immigration, and assimilation. Tweed has recently offered a path toward the next stage in the study of Asian religions in America, specifically Buddhism, in what he called a "translocative" approach. Such an approach focuses on how "religious rituals, stories, metaphors, institutions, and artifacts" are propelled "back and forth between the homeland and the new land."[14] But the translocative still privileges the homeland/America dyad. I argue that a better next step would be to pull the lens back to a wider angle and pay more attention to the global processes, systems, flows, and networks in which Asia and America are but nodes. The movement between the homeland and the United States may still play a central role in such a study, as it does in Tweed's translocative, but always within larger global systems. Taking the business turn in the study of Asian religions means following money, trade, and labor through global markets, between nation-states, and through multinational corporations. In what follows, I offer an example of how the business turn realigns the study of Asian religions in America through an analysis of two Indian entrepreneurs: Swami Vivekananda and Sathya Sai Baba.

Swami Vivekananda and "Guru" Entrepreneurs

"Learn business, my boy. We will do great things yet!" Swami Vivekananda wrote from Chicago to one of his supporters back home in India.[15] The young Hindu monk came to America in 1893 and represented "Hinduism" at the World's Parliament of Religions. As historian Carl Jackson described him: "Demonstrating a fluent command of English, impressive stage manner, and a gift for the memorable phrase, the Hindu spokesman was a sensation from his first address."[16] In his speeches at the Parliament and, later, in his lecture tour around the United States, Vivekananda presented a universal adaptation of Vedanta philosophy, a philosophy based in the Sanskrit texts of the Upanishads and Vedanta. His message appealed to his American audience by "emphasizing the more universal elements in the Hindu tradition . . . he spoke in favor of a Hinduism that was reasonable, philosophical, universal, and even scientific."[17] It was a Hinduism aimed at upper middle-class Americans looking beyond the usual forms of American religion.

Yet Vivekananda did not come to America as a missionary. He came as a fund-raiser. He explained the reasons for his trip in a letter to Ramakrishnanda, a fellow monk, in 1894:

> Suppose some disinterested Sannyasins, bent on doing good to others, go from village to village, disseminating education and seeking in various ways to better the condition of all down to the Chandâla, through oral teaching, and by means of maps, cameras, globes, and such other accessories—can't that bring forth good in time? . . . To effect this, the first thing we need is men, and the next is funds.[18]

Vivekananda described how he traveled around India in search of the funds to carry out this project but could not find anyone to support him. "Therefore I have come to America," he wrote, "to earn the money myself, and then return to my country and devote the rest of my days to the realization of this one aim of my life."[19] Vivekananda was more of a migrant worker than he was a missionary.

Fund-raising concerned Vivekananda for most of his time in America. His letters home to India from the United States stress his fiscal needs again and again. For example, even before the Parliament, he reported in an August 1893 letter to friends in Madras how he was living in Boston with a woman he had met on a train. Thus he was "saving for some time my expenditure of £1 per day, and she has the advantage of inviting her friends over here and showing them a curio from India!"[20] In the same letter he compared himself to Pandita Ramabai, an Indian convert to Christianity who had begun raising money among Protestant women's societies. However, Vivekananda quickly realized he could not rely on handouts but must work for his funding. "Mendicancy has no vogue here, and I have to labour," he wrote Ramakrishnanda. "A lecture fetches from two hundred up to three thousand rupees. I have got up to five hundred."[21] For Vivekananda, his work in the United States was part of a global exchange between American capital and Indian spirituality: "As our country is poor in social virtues, so this country is lacking in spirituality. I give them spirituality, and they give me money."[22] Vivekananda realized he could sell spirituality to Americans to save his people in India.

Vivekananda formed a small Vedanta Society in 1895 and began to surround himself with a circle of disciples. He found support among prominent men and women of the upper-middle and upper classes of American cities: George and Belle Hale in Chicago; Thomas Palmer, a wealthy Detroit businessman; Walter and Frances Goodyear, of the Goodyear Rubber Company; Sara Bull, the wife of Ole Bull, a famous Norwegian violinist; soprano Emma Thursby; and Francis Legget, a New York businessman.[23] At times the high-society status of his supporters caused Vivekananda problems, as they were concerned that his behaviors might embarrass them or himself. When Vivekananda returned to India in 1897, the affluent circle of followers became a source of funds for his work in India building a social reform movement that became the Ramakrishna Math and Mission.

His friends in America had been so helpful that when he returned to America and settled in Los Angeles in 1899 he came for two purposes: "the primary one was the hope that it would improve his exceedingly poor health; another was his never-ending need to raise money for his Indian work."[24] But Vivekananda's fund-raising proved fruitless. Francis Legget attempted to raise $100 annual subscriptions from Vivekananda's followers but found that they took offense at her interference between themselves and the swami. As Vivekananda told his English disciple Sister Nivedita, "A very polite but cold letter came to her [Legget] in reply from Mrs. Hale, written by Mary, expressing their inability and assuring her of their love for me."[25] Vivekananda's fund-raising in the West was a project of little success but great hope. He consistently believed funds would appear. "The moment we are fit," he told Nivedita, "money and men must flow to us. . . . This time good is coming in chunks, I am sure. We will make the foundations of the old world shake this time."[26] Vivekananda's work in the United States may have built a lasting institution in the Vedanta Society, but that was a side effect. The spiritual training of the Vedanta Society in America was meant to fund the social work of the Ramakrishna Mission in India.

The business of selling Indian spirituality to Americans was more than just an exchange of money. As Peter van der Veer has argued, Vivekananda's distinction between Western materialism and Indian spiritualism was central to a growing nationalist discourse in India that was itself a reaction to British colonial power:

> The typical strategy of Vivekananda was to systematize a disparate set of traditions, make it intellectually available for a Westernized audience and defensible against Western critique, and incorporate it in the notion of "Hindu spirituality," carried by the Hindu nation that was superior to "Western materialism" and brought to India by an aggressive and arrogant "British nation."[27]

Social reform brought together this "Hindu spirituality" with a call for revitalizing the Hindu nation. The Ramakrishna Mission created spiritual ascetics fit to the social reformist tasks of the nation. "National self-determination, social reform, and spiritual awakening were all linked" in Vivekananda's plans for India's future.[28] And he needed American dollars for all of it.

Vivekananda entered the United States as an entrepreneur in search of investors to help him fund his vision for a new India. By exchanging spirituality for money he was able to return to India and jump-start a nationalist movement that still shapes Indian politics. The swami is thus better understood as a businessman than as a guru. While railing against Western materialism and championing the superiority of Hindu spirituality, he used American dollars to build an anticolonial and nationalist movement. Through the frame of the business turn, his moment on stage at the World's Parliament of Religions becomes more than just the entrance of "Hinduism" into America. Rather, it becomes the beginning of a fund-raising tour, the first step in the business of exchanging spirituality for money, and an important moment in colonial Indian history and the rise of the Indian nation-state.

From Gurus to Godmen

Swami Vivekananda's fund-raising trips to the United States and his reform work at home in India mark him as the first in a line of global gurus who built networks between India and America. Like Vivekananda, the gurus who followed him functioned quite differently in the American and Indian contexts. As Joanne Waghorne has argued, these global gurus had two public faces: "their function as spokespersons, apologists, and unifiers of the Hindu religion for Hindus in India and heritage Hindus in the United States as well as the broad-minded international public (for which they are respected) and their role as synthesizers and creators of newer and more universalized religious forms that break the bounds of territory, race, and ethnicity (for which they and their followers are often treated with suspicion."[29] Vivekananda, and the gurus who followed him, balanced a universalist religion around the globe with a nationalist religion at home.

Along with this global expansion, Vivekananda was also part of a larger process of "sadhuization" that occurred in late nineteenth- and twentieth-century Indian culture, a period anthropologist Agehananda Bharati and others have called the Indian Renaissance. Through this process, "the sadhu [an ascetic Hindu holy man], as itinerant or *āśram*-bound full-time religious specialist, expert in salvation-giving mediation, as opposed to the ritualistic specialist, the hereditary brahman . . . is at the helm of things."[30] Religious authority began to shift during this period of colonial Indian history from the hereditary and orthodox brahman priests to monks and sadhus that proclaimed a modernist and nationalist Hinduism. This Hinduism claimed that "all religions are one, and the theological differences, the varying concepts of God are unimportant; yet, of all these concepts, the Indian concept is the noblest and the most profound; it is the most 'scientific,' it is universal."[31] But more important, sadhuization realigned Hindu religion by transplanting Western ideals of the value of the individual into Indian modernity and Indian religious philosophy (especially Vedanta). There was a "newly established dignity of an empirical, social, and autonomous individual."[32] Sadhuization produced a modern autonomous individual fit for nationalist politics, individual religion, and liberal economic markets.

Vivekananda's work in the United States should be seen, then, as a global overflow of this process of sadhuization. Luckily for him, his modern Hindu message in America flowed alongside a larger cultural trend that American religious historian William Hutchinson called the "modernist impulse" in American Protestantism.[33] This impulse among Protestant modernists shared Vivekananda's desire to adapt religious ideas to modern culture and his vision of progressive social reform. Vivekananda developed a modern Hinduism in the midst of the Indian Renaissance that translated well among urban religious liberals in America. In need of funds for the social reform agenda of his modernizing work, he parlayed that modern Hinduism into lecture tours and a group of wealthy liberal supporters in the United States.

Sadhuization in India that began in the nineteenth century led to new movements of so-called godmen by the middle of the twentieth. Unlike Swami Vivekananda, whose authority derived from his position as a disciple of the guru Ramakrishna and a monk within the Ramakrishna Order, the "first salient characteristic of godmen, whose prophetic charisma is completely individual, is that their divinity is virtually asserted de novo, without any systematic attempt to validate the clam by tracing spiritual descent from a predecessor."[34] The rise of these godmen coincided with larger economic and political changes in India. Godmen arose in Indian society as the Indian economy emerged as a liberal economy in global markets. Their authority as gurus formed "a nexus of knowledge, power, and wealth in Indian society," as Lise McKean argued.[35] That nexus expanded globally and included the United States.

Twentieth-century godmen were global entrepreneurs. They possessed what McKean described as "entrepreneurial flair for building networks of institutions and followers."[36] Indeed, McKean has argued that these godmen are economically rational business managers:

> Gurus share with managers and employers the desire to control subordinates. They all rely on the labor of others to secure their profits. Devotees donate money and labor to the guru in the hope of earning the guru's favor and grace. Through deferential behavior and conscientious work, employees hope to earn favors from bosses, favors that might supplement their often inadequate wages. The guru's teachings about disciplined and simple living complement the interests of employers. Managers and employers may or may not reinforce their authority by demonstrating these virtues in their own lives. However, they rely on references to the virtues of hard work and abstemious habits for moral legitimation of employee's low wages. Through deference and service to superiors, who belong to larger and more powerful social networks, subordinates hope to earn assistance in procuring desired goods and services that may be financially or socially beyond their personal means.

Taking McKean's point, the Indian godmen who have taken their networks global should be understood as CEOs of multinational corporations. These global guru organizations have extended from India and Asia to the United States.

Sai Baba, Global CEO and God Incarnate

Sathya Sai Baba was one of the most prominent of these global guru entrepreneurs at the turn of the twenty-first century. Clouds of mystery and hagiography swirl around and shroud Sai Baba's biography. As anthropologist

Lawrence Babb put it, "no supposedly 'real' Sathya Sai Baba can be any more real than an imagined character in fiction. All that is available are his public surfaces, his self as formally presented as an object for the devotion of his followers."[37] Nevertheless, a few facts are known about the man turned godman and guru. He was born Sathyanarayana Raju in 1926 in the small village of Puttaparthi to a pious but poor family in the southern part of Andhra Pradesh. But these facts "are but the framework; the real tale is told by the elaborations . . . Sathya Sai Baba's entire life has been one of signs and portents, uncanny occurrences," and miracles.

Three miraculous revelations mark the transition from Sathyanarayana Raju to Sathya Sai Baba. In 1940, at the age of thirteen, a scorpion sting rendered young Sathyanarayana unconscious for several days. When he awoke he had been transformed and went around singing in Sanskrit, reciting Vedanta philosophy, weeping, or falling into catatonic states. A couple of months later, after a series of exams and exorcisms by "village doctors," Sathyanarayana magically materialized some sugar candy and milk, considered luxuries during this time in India, and told his father, "I am Sai Baba." He demanded people call him Sathya Sai Baba, connecting him to a popular Muslim mystic saint named Shirdi Sai Baba who died in 1918. After these two initial revelations, Sai Baba demonstrated magical powers, such as manifesting sacred ash and healing people. Thus "the transformation of the rural peasant boy into the local guru was complete."[38] Sai Baba's network of devotees grew throughout India even as partition separated the subcontinent. He built a new ashram, or sacred residence, Prasanthi Nilayam, in 1950 on the outskirts of his home village that attracted devotees from throughout India. Then in July 1963, Sai Baba made his third important revelation: he was God. After a bout of disease that he claimed he took on himself to relieve a devotee, Sai Baba appeared to heal himself and then claimed that he was an avatar, a divine incarnation, of Shiva and Shakti—male and female divinity, respectively. He was not only a guru, he was not only divine, he was all of divinity—every aspect of it—in one body.

The claim to universal divinity launched Sai Baba from national guru to international godman. In the decades that followed, Sai Baba developed a specifically middle-class following around the world that was attracted to his miraculous ability to manifest objects ranging from sacred ash to trinkets, consumer goods, gold jewelry, and money. He was, as historian of religion Hugh Urban aptly termed him, "a kind of *One Man Cargo Cult*."[39] On one level, these miracles served to authorize Sai Baba's divinity, but as Urban pointed out, these miracles also affirmed the divinity of consumer goods and consumerism itself. These miracles helped "his large urban middle class, upwardly mobile and affluent followers *to trust modern capitalism and consumerism*, as well."[40] As India joined global economic markets in the latter half of the twentieth century, the growing Indian middle-class and global South Asian immigration fueled Sai Baba's transformation into a global godman with devotees around the world. When Sai Baba died in 2011 he left behind a global network of devotees and organizations.

In her study of Sai Baba's global movement, Tulasi Srinivas described it as "a global religious empire."[41] Rather than "empire," Baba's global organization is better understood as a multinational corporation. Sai Baba's organization began as small devotional groups called *samiti* in India and Sai Centers in the rest of the world. The organization was global from the start. The first samiti was registered in Bombay in 1965, the first Sai Center founded in Sri Lanka in 1967, and the first American Sai Center established in Tustin, California, in 1969.[42] From its early charter in 1965, Sai Baba's organization has grown into a multinational guru corporation.

The Sai Baba corporation is divided into three major branches with numerous regional subsidiaries and local organizations. At the top of the structure sit the Sri Sathya Sai Central Trust (SST), the Sri Sathya Sai Seva Organization (SSSO), the International Sathya Sai Organization (ISSO), and the Prasanthi Council. The SST controls the finances for the major institutions of Sai Baba's Indian social work. It finances the various schools, colleges, and hospitals run by the organization. The SSSO sits atop the network of regional state Seva organizations in India. Meanwhile the ISSO split off from the SSSO in the 1990s and now acts as an international wing that oversees the global network of Sai centers. Sai Baba established the SST and SSSO in the 1960s as the movement made its international leap, but the Prasanthi Council was not established until 2003, in the wake of a murder scandal at the organization's ashram.[43] The role of the Prasanthi Council seems unclear. In 2010, Tulasi Srinivas wrote that "while the Prasanthi Council was convened to prevent future problems, many devotees are still unclear about its function, as it adds to the list of overlapping Sai organizational bodies and charters."[44] The overlapping authority and ambiguous relationships between these branch organizations have left observers confused. As Srinivas commented, "I found it was difficult to understand how the organization is run given its confusing complexity—its many overlapping organizations, its myriad and interlocking lines of control, its lack of structural clarity, its muddied hierarchy, and its lack of articulated direction—but operationally it seems to function seamlessly."[45] Like many other multinationals, Sai Baba's corporation works inscrutably and powerfully.

Since Sai Baba's death in 2011, the organization has streamlined and the Prasanthi Council has taken on a central governing role. The global wing of the organization is now controlled by the Sri Sathya Sai World Foundation, which deals with the financial and legal matters of the ISSO. Just below this, the Prasanthi Council governs the rules and regulations of the ISSO. Below the Council, the ISSO is divided into geographical zones, regions, and countries. The American branch of Sai Baba's corporation is located in Zone 1, Region 11 of the global ISSO. Zone 1 consists of the United States, Israel, West Indies, and Canada. Within regions and countries, the Sai Centers are divided into smaller regions with a Central Council or Coordinating Committee overseeing these subregions and officers overseeing each center. The ISSO has built a tightly structured hierarchy from the individual center all the way to the organization's governing bodies in India.[46]

This massive global corporate structure has been built through the global movement and exchange of money, people, and commodities. To begin with, Sai Baba's middle-class Indian following has given generously to Baba's organizations. While Baba himself does not own property or accept donations, the SST has "streamlined the donation process to such a degree that donations can be immediately made at any branch of the Canara Bank and directly deposited into the Trust's account." Devotees may make such donations whenever they "feel the 'spiritual prompting' of Sai Baba's grace."[47]

In the United States, Sai Centers are prohibited from accepting donations or charging any fees for membership or services. Indeed, Baba himself said, "Fund collection is as much opposed to this movement as fire is to water."[48] Mirroring the Indian organization, American donations to Sai organizations are made to the Sathya Sai Society of America (SSSA), a non-profit 501(c)(3) charity based in California. According to filings with the Internal Revenue Service, the SSSA began in 1968, about the time when the first Sai Center was founded in California. As Table 6.1 shows, nearly all of the money donated to the SSSA by American devotees goes to various Sai organizations in India, mostly the SST. The list of contributors to the SSSA includes both Indian American and Euro-American surnames, reflecting the mix of Sai Baba devotees in the United States. Furthermore, SSSA Internal Revenue Service filings indicate that it accepted donations from Sai organizations in Trinidad, Guyana, and Canada. Thus, the SSSA serves as a branch of the Sai Baba corporation through which money flows across national boundaries back to the central SST in India, where it is used for various religious and social projects. It is the same model Vivekananda worked for at the turn of the twentieth century, Western money for Eastern spirituality, but on a global scale.

Table 6.1 Donations to and Disbursements
from SSSA, 2001–2014 in USD[67]

Year	Donations	Total Disbursements	Disbursements to India
2001	1,095,653	293,311	248,311
2002	1,272,738	3,832,367	3,812,362
2003	1,746,996	1,500,951	1,500,951
2004	4,033,019	3,831,729	3,831,729
2005	6,697,172	6,780,565	6,735,565
2006	4,167,417	4,457,763	4,457,763
2007	1,343,811	1,428,553	1,428,553
2008	1,089,490	1,287,164	1,277,164
2009	825,089	773,012	773,012
2010	3,759,767	3,954,112	3,951,612
2011	1,641,838	876,000	876,000
2012	695,058	590,000	570,000
2013	872,683	400,000	400,000
2014	677,128	578,390	542,390
TOTAL	29,917,859	30,583,917	30,405,412

The global Sai corporation has not only moved money but depended on the movement of people too. The presence of many Indian surnames on the contributor list of the SSSA signals the important role that South Asian immigrants have played in the global Sai Baba corporation. As Sai Baba's following among middle-class professional Indians grew after Indian independence, these same middle-class professionals often sought employment overseas. The doctors, engineers, and scientists who made up "the upwardly mobile, well educated and Western-influenced" middle-class devotees of Sai Baba became part of the post-1965 immigration of Indians into the United States.[49] By 1967, one out of ten university graduates in India went overseas. "These emigrants represented 11 percent of the country's annual production of scientists, 10 percent of physicians, and 23 percent of engineers."[50] They also came from the same class as Baba's devotees, and when those devotees immigrated to the United States they brought Baba with them. The United States accepted these immigrants because its government sought specialized labor for engineers and scientists during the Cold War. Global conflict paved the way for Baba's devotees to immigrate to the United States.

Along with Indians immigrating to America, the Sai corporation has also relied on the movement of middle-class Americans back and forth to India. The first Sai Center in the United States began as a bookshop in Tustin, California, founded by Elise and Walter Cowan. The Cowans were one couple in a community of Americans who encountered Sai Baba during travels to India in the 1960s and 1970s. Indeed, devotees claim that Sai Baba raised Walter Cowan to life after he died of a heart attack in India.[51] John Hislop, the first president of the Satya Sai Baba Council of America, met Sai Baba in India in 1968. In 1971, playwright Arnold Shulman published his account of his travel to India and encounter with Sai Baba, simply titled *Baba*.[52] Likewise, psychiatrist Samuel H. Sandweiss published his devotional narrative, *Sai Baba: The Holy Man ... and the Psychiatrist*, in 1975.[53] Hislop's, Shulman's, and Sandweiss's narratives share a common structure. They were all men unsatisfied with the Christianity or Judaism they grew up with. So, after a period of seeking, each ended up in India, where they met Baba, and then they returned home to establish his devotion in America.

In August 1974 Elise Cowan wrote Sai Baba asking him to travel to America and visit his devotees. Rather than make the trip himself, Baba sent writer and devotee V. K. Gokak, who had been working at the Sri Sathya Sai College. Gokak headed to New York in September of that year and spent a month touring the country, visiting the budding Sai Centers in America. Gokak's account of his trip paints a picture of a community of middle- and upper-middle-class white American devotees who found Baba in India and brought his devotion back with them. Professors, doctors, lawyers, writers, and other educated professionals populate Gokak's visit.[54] Thus, Baba's devotees in America and India have shared a similar educational, professional, and class background. The Americans were part of a larger American culture of seeker spirituality. As sociologist Robert Wuthnow described it, "In the 1960s, many Americans, having learned that they could move around, think through their options, and select a faith that truly captured what they believed to be the truth, took the choice seriously, bargaining with their souls, seeking new spiritual guides, and rediscovering that God dwells not only in homes but also in the byways trod by pilgrims and sojourners."[55] These American seekers found Sai Baba.

As the nation-state of India liberalized its economy and entered postcolonial global markets, Sathya Sai Baba attracted a following of middle-class devotees with a message that blessed consumerism and capitalism. These same middle-class Indians constituted the post-1965 influx of South Asian immigrants to America, and they brought Baba with them. Meanwhile, middle-class American seekers who could afford the trip headed to India in search of new spiritual truth and found Sai Baba there. When they returned they brought Baba with them. From a global perspective, middle-class people crisscrossed the globe between India and America as the Sai Baba organization built itself into a multinational corporation.

The global Sai Baba corporation also circulated commodities. Beginning in the 1960s, the foreign devotees who traveled to Baba's ashram in Puttaparthi bought pictures, postcards, books, and items related to the godman to bring home with them. A commercial district around the ashram that marketed goods to a global community of devotees grew in the 1970s and peaked in the 1990s. The SSSO took an interest in this market for Sai Baba goods and began to sanction certain goods and to direct devotees visiting Puttaparthi toward the SSSO's own bookshops. Tulasi Srinivas has described how the market for Baba goods intersected with larger global economic forces:

> By the mid-1990s the Euro-American and South East Asian devotee base increased exponentially, and the trade in Sai objects boomed. Rising devotee numbers and easier access to Puttaparthi coupled with the liberalization of the Indian economy and entry of every kind of currency into the Indian market led traders to set up money changing centers in Puttaparthi sponsored by foreign banks that devotees would recognize, such as HSBC, Swiss Bank, and ING Orange.[56]

The growth of devotees around the world meant the global circulation of Sai Baba commodities and the influx of foreign money into the SSSO.

Outside of Puttaparthi, the SSSO controls a network of Sai bookshops that sell Sai Baba goods to overseas devotees. It is no coincidence that the first Sai Center in America began as a bookshop. Sai goods are central to devotees' practice. Srinivas described the basement shrine of a devotee in Maryland:

> In one corner stood an empty wooden thronelike chair draped with a bright red and gold sari. Behind it the entire wall (which ran forty feet) was covered in floor to ceiling mirrors, in the center of which a life-size photograph of Sai Baba hung. In front was a small altar with the bouquet of silk flowers and a bowl of fruit and an incense burner. The room smelt of the Nag Champa incense, though to be Sai Baba's favorite. . . . Other walls of the room held garlanded and framed picture of Sathya Sai Baba at stages of his life. . . . In front were a series of small tables on which stood images of Krishna, Rama, the Buddha, Hanuman, Jesus Christ, Shirdi Sai Baba, and Sathya Sai Baba.[57]

Along with photographs and images, devotees can buy videos of Baba singing and speaking, audio recordings of his discourses, books and educational curricula, and coloring and activity books for children. Though they are run by volunteers and appear to be stand-alone shops, the Sai bookshops are actually controlled by the SSSO and function as distribution channels for Sai goods.[58] The local shops in Tustin, California, or Toronto, Canada, are storefronts for the multinational Sai Baba corporation, circulating money and goods around the globe.

Though the Sai Baba corporation has grown into a multinational organization, Sai Baba himself was quite critical of Western culture and Western materialism. Similar to Vivekananda, Baba filled his speeches with "a basic dichotomy between the 'spiritual East' and the 'material West'—a fundamental spilt between an idealised image of India as the land of religion, mysticism, and inner truth, and the West as the land of material progress but also of atheism, immorality and spiritual decline."[59] While Baba toned down such rhetoric for his international audience, the dichotomy between spiritual East and material West reflected an ambivalence in the attitudes of his devotees.

Euro-American Baba devotees turned to him in the 1960s and 1970s because they wanted a "spiritual" alternative to American materialism. Meanwhile, Indian American devotees have come to America in search of material gain but bring their spiritual godman with them. Urban has argued that Baba's East/West distinction functions, like Vivekananda, as a nationalist call for renewing the Hindu Indian state, but in America it functions to attract materially affluent Euro-American devotees, on the one hand, and to connect Indian American immigrants to the Hindu nation, on the other. The Sai Baba organization is one example of how Indian American religion takes part in Hindu nationalism back in India. As Appadurai notes, "The overseas movement of Indians has been exploited by a variety of interests both within and outside India to create a complicated network of finances and religious identifications, by which the problem of cultural reproduction for Hindus abroad has become tied to the politics of Hindu fundamentalism at home."[60] Like other multinational corporations, Sai Baba's organization exists outside of the nation-state while also taking part in the politics and maintenance of the nation-state.

While scholars such as Smriti Srinivas and Hugh Urban have accounted for the global expansion of Sai Baba's organization, studies of Sai Baba in America have failed to make the connection between Sai Baba's devotees in America and the multinational Sai Baba corporation. Even in Tulasi Srinivas's

In the Presence of Baba: Body, City, and Memory in a Global Religious Movement the author approaches her chapter on a Sai Center in Atlanta as a case study and does not tie it back to the larger movement.[61] Likewise, both Chad Bauman's and Norris Palmer's chapters on Sai Baba in America focus on the practices and meanings in individual Sai Centers.[62] While all these studies use the term *global* to describe the Sai Baba organization, approaching Sai Baba's organization as the multinational corporation that it is reveals the scope of its "globalness" while also revealing the global forces of economics, neoliberal markets, labor, and immigration that made a global godman like Sai Baba possible. In short, Sai Baba's organization is even more global than it first appears when it is recognized as a multinational business.

The Business Turn as Redescription

Recognizing Sai Baba's organization not as a "global religious movement" but as a multinational corporation with business interests around the world represents the most important consequence of the business turn in the study of American religions: redescription. The need for redescription in the study of religion is summarized nicely in Bruce Lincoln's final thesis on method:

> When one permits those whom one studies to define the terms in which they will be understood, suspends one's interest in the temporal and contingent, or fails to distinguish between "truths," "truth-claims," and "regimes of truth," one has ceased to function as historian or scholar.[63]

While historians of American religions have often taken the step Lincoln calls for and moved past describing religions in terms of so-called insiders to explaining and redescribing them, such redescription frequently fails when it comes to discussions of money and business. As Sai Baba and Vivekananda show, religion is business. Any organization that moved the amount of money, goods, and people around the world that Sai Baba's organization has would be considered a business by most observers. Yet that label is often avoided if the money, goods, and people involved are categorized as "religion." Rather than using business as a metaphor or simile for Sai Baba's organization, saying, "Sai Baba is *like* an entrepreneur," I have argued that Sai Baba *is* an entrepreneur. This redescription then opens up space to recognize how Sai Baba's multinational corporation has been shaped by global trends in economic markets, immigration, and nationalism.

The "business turn" in American religious history must collapse the distinction between business and religion. Earlier work on religion and business analyzed the "commodification" of religion or posited "the religious" and "the economic" as two domains that somehow encounter one another.[64] Other work used the free market as a metaphor for explaining pluralism and changes in the practices and identities of Americans.[65] More recent work has sought to highlight the role of business in religion or argued that business functions as religion.[66] Yet in each of these approaches "religion" is a stable thing in the world. "Religion" shapes, is influenced by, or is like business. Such approaches treat "religion" as a sui generis category in which certain practices, discourse, beliefs, institutions, or people are essentially "religious."

But when the business turn collapses religion and business, the scholar's job shifts and she must pay particular attention to how "religion" is constructed as a category. For example, in the cases of Vivekananda and Sai Baba, the category of "religion" is rarely invoked. Baba in particular claims that his divinity is more universal than any "religion." Both of these entrepreneurs used the English word *spirituality* when describing themselves and their organizations. They both constructed this category of "spirituality" to buttress nationalist claims to the unique Hindu identity of the Indian nation, to raise money from foreign devotees, and to support social reforms in India. Collapsing religion into business by redescribing Sai Baba's organization as a multinational corporation and identifying Vivekananda as an entrepreneur opens up the ways that both men used discourses of "religion" and "spirituality" to construct their global business networks.

The spiritual/material split Vivekananda and Sai Baba posited between India and the West mirrors the split between religion and business in much of the scholarship on religion and business. In both cases, the dichotomy protects an essentialist definition of religion or spirituality from infringement by the material. The next step in the business turn is to dismantle the dichotomy of religion and business. Religion is business.

Notes

1. Krishnalal Shridharani, *My India, My America* (New York: Duell, Sloan and Pearce, 1941), 96.
2. Ibid., 97–99.
3. Max Weber, *The Religion of India: The Sociology of Hinduism and Buddhism*, trans. Hans H. Gerth and Don Martindale (New York: Free Press, 1958), 113.
4. Ibid., 332–333.

5. Thomas A. Tweed, "Buddhism, Art, and Transcultural Collage: Toward a Cultural History of Buddhism in the United States, 1945–2000," in *Gods in America: Religious Pluralism in the United States*, ed. Charles Lloyd Cohen and Ronald L. Numbers (New York: Oxford University Press, 2013), 195.

6. Andrea R. Jain, *Selling Yoga: From Counterculture to Pop Culture* (New York: Oxford University Press, 2015), 47.

7. Arjun Appadurai, *Modernity at Large: Cultural Dimensions of Globalization* (Minneapolis: University of Minnesota Press, 1996), 32.

8. Thomas Tweed, *Crossing and Dwelling: A Theory of Religion* (Cambridge, MA: Harvard University Press, 2006), 60–61.

9. Thomas Tweed and Stephen Prothero, eds., *Asian Religions in America: A Documentary History* (New York: Oxford University Press, 1999), 5.

10. Prema A. Kurien, *A Place at the Multicultural Table: The Development of an American Hinduism* (New Brunswick, NJ: Rutgers University Press, 2007), 41.

11. For yet another example, see Vasudha Narayanan, "Hinduism in America," in *Cambridge History of Religions in America*, ed. Stephen J. Stein (New York: Cambridge University Press, 2012), 3:331–356.

12. Richard King, *Orientalism and Religion: Postcolonial Theory, India and "the Mystic East"* (London: Routledge, 1999), 106–108.

13. Philip C. Almond, *The British Discovery of Buddhism* (Cambridge: Cambridge University Press, 1988).

14. Thomas A. Tweed, "Theory and Method in the Study of Buddhism: Toward 'Translocative' Analysis," in *Buddhism Beyond Borders: New Perspectives on Buddhism in the United States*, ed. Scott A. Mitchell and Natalie E. F. Quli (Albany: State University of New York Press, 2015), 7.

15. Swami Vivekananda, *The Complete Works of Swami Vivekananda* (Calcutta: Advaita Ashrama, 1985), 5:36.

16. Carl T. Jackson, *The Oriental Religions and American Thought: Nineteenth-Century Explorations* (Westport, CT: Greenwood Press, 1981), 249.

17. Carl T. Jackson, *Vedanta for the West: The Ramakrishna Movement in the United States*, Religion in North America (Bloomington: Indiana University Press, 1994), 33.

18. Vivekananda, *Complete Works*, 6:254–255.

19. Ibid., 6:255.

20. Ibid., 5:12.

21. Ibid., 6:251.

22. Ibid., 6:235.

23. Jackson, *The Oriental Religions and American Thought*, 26.

24. Marie Louise Burke, *Swami Vivekananda in the West: New Discoveries*, 4th ed. (Kolkata, India: Advaita Ashrama, 1998), 5:1.

25. Vivekananda, *Complete Works*, 6:423.

26. Ibid., 6:424.

27. Peter van der Veer, *Imperial Encounters: Religion and Modernity in India and Britain* (Princeton: Princeton University Press, 2001), 47.

28. Ibid.

29. Joanne Punzo Waghorne, "Beyond Pluralism: Global Gurus and the Third Stream of American Religiosity," in *Gods in America: Religious Pluralism in the United States*, ed. Charles Lloyd Cohen and Ronald L. Numbers (New York: Oxford University Press, 2013), 233.

30. Agehananda Bharati, "The Hindu Renaissance and Its Apologetic Patterns," *Journal of Asian Studies* 29, no. 2 (February 1970): 277.

31. Ibid., 276.

32. Ibid., 287.

33. William R. Hutchison, *The Modernist Impulse in American Protestantism* (Oxford: Oxford University Press, 1982).

34. C. J. Fuller, *The Camphor Flame: Popular Hinduism and Society in India* (Princeton: Princeton University Press, 1992), 177–178.

35. Lise McKean, *Divine Enterprise: Gurus and the Hindu Nationalist Movement* (Chicago: University of Chicago Press, 1996), 1.

36. Ibid., 2.

37. Lawrence A. Babb, *Redemptive Encounters: Three Modern Styles in the Hindu Tradition* (Berkeley: University of California Press, 1986), 161–162.

38. Tulasi Srinivas, *Winged Faith: Rethinking Globalization and Religious Pluralism Through the Sathya Sai Movement* (New York: Columbia University Press, 2010), 59.

39. Hugh B. Urban, "Avatar for Our Age: Sathya Sai Baba and the Cultural Contradictions of Late Capitalism," *Religion* 33, no. 1 (January 2003): 82.

40. Ibid., 83.

41. Srinivas, *Winged Faith*, 235.

42. Smriti Srinivas, *In the Presence of Sai Baba: Body, City, and Memory in a Global Religious Movement* (Leiden: Brill, 2008), 129, 135–136.

43. Srinivas, *Winged Faith*, 248–249.

44. Ibid., 251.

45. Ibid., 252.

46. International Sathya Sai Organization, "Guidelines for Centers and Groups," August 2012, 5, http://us.sathyasai.org/council/Guidelines2012Sep.pdf.

47. Urban, "Avatar for Our Age," 81.

48. International Sathya Sai Organization, "Guidelines for Centers and Groups," 12.

49. Urban, "Avatar for Our Age," 81.

50. John M. Liu, "The Contours of Asian Professional, Technical, and Kindred Work Immigration, 1965–1988," *Sociological Perspectives* 35, no. 4 (Winter 1992): 676.

51. John Hislop, *My Baba and I* (San Diego: Birth Day Publishing, 1985), 28–31.

52. Arnold Shulman, *Baba* (New York: Viking Press, 1971).

53. Samuel H. Sandweiss, *Sai Baba: The Holy Man ... and the Psychiatrist* (San Diego: Birth Day Publishing, 1975).

54. Vinayak Krishna Gokak, *Bhagavan Sri Sathya Sai Baba: An Interpretation* (New Delhi: Abhinav, 1975), 255–299.

55. Robert Wuthnow, *After Heaven: Spirituality in America Since the 1950s*, new ed. (Berkeley: University of California Press, 1998), 57.

56. Srinivas, *Winged Faith*, 304.

57. Ibid., 282.

58. Ibid., 305–306.

59. Urban, "Avatar for Our Age," 85.

60. Appadurai, *Modernity at Large*, 38.

61. Srinivas, *In the Presence of Sai Baba*, 292–332.

62. Chad Bauman, "Sathya Sai Baba: At Home in Midwestern America," in *Public Hinduisms*, ed. John Zavos et al. (Thousand Oaks, CA: Sage, 2012), 141–159; Norris W. Palmer, "Baba's World: A Global Guru and His Movement," in *Gurus in America*, ed. Thomas A. Forsthoefel and Cynthia Anne Humes (Albany: State University of New York Press, 2005), 97–122.

63. Bruce Lincoln, "Theses on Method," *Method and Theory in the Study of Religion* 8, no. 3 (1996): 227.

64. R. Laurence Moore, *Selling God: American Religion in the Marketplace of Culture* (New York: Oxford University Press, 1994); Robert Wuthnow, *God and Mammon in America* (New York: Free Press, 1994).

65. Wade Clark Roof, *Spiritual Marketplace: Baby Boomers and the Remaking of American Religion* (Princeton: Princeton University Press, 1999); Roger Finke and Rodney Stark, *The Churching of America, 1776–2005: Winners and Losers in Our Religious Economy*, 2nd ed. (New Brunswick, NJ: Rutgers University Press, 2005).

66. Timothy E. W Gloege, *Guaranteed Pure: The Moody Bible Institute, Business, and the Making of Modern Evangelicalism* (Chapel Hill: University of North Carolina Press, 2015); Kathryn Lofton, *Oprah: The Gospel of an Icon* (Berkeley: University of California Press, 2011).

67. Data from IRS Form 990.

7

Hunting Buffalo in Oklahoma

NATIVE AMERICAN CASINOS, CONSTRUCTED IDENTITIES, AND PORTRAYALS OF NATIVE CULTURE AND RELIGION

Angela Tarango

ON A WARM and soggy late June morning in 2014 my research assistant, Isaiah Ellis, and I left our hotel and headed toward the Choctaw Casino and Resort in Durant, Oklahoma. In the very front of the casino there was a large bowl-like structure containing multiple torches made of metal. Isaiah said to me that according to the casino website it was supposed to represent the "eternal flame" of the Choctaw nation. The flame, alas, was not visible, perhaps because of the heavy mist in the air. We walked into the casino and immediately were confronted with the pinging sounds of electronic gambling machines, as well as a giant statue of a white buffalo. "We've found the white buffalo," I said to Isaiah, "Oddly though, it seems we found it among the Choctaw."

The white buffalo statue, as it turned out, was more than a statue.[1] It had a light, water, and sound show that went with it. Behind the giant white buffalo was a large waterfall. Every thirty minutes a light show would begin behind the water and the cascade of water would intensify, along with booming music that seemed to be trying to simulate thunder or buffalo hoofbeats. As the buffalo "roared," the light show would intensify, flashing in red, purples, and oranges, and the waterfall would increase in volume and velocity. The show lasted about ten minutes and repeated every thirty minutes, according to a posted sign. As Isaiah went to seek permission to take pictures of the buffalo, I stood in front of it contemplating why it was we had found the white buffalo among the Choctaw, a tribe that had been forcibly relocated to Oklahoma from Mississippi and Alabama, when it was a spiritual symbol associated with the Sioux tribes of the northern Plains. Why had the Choctaw put a white buffalo in the front entryway of their casino? What did this say about how Native Americans chose to represent their identities to the average American, whose only point of contact with Native people would be the casino? Why the white buffalo? And why in a casino?

Project

In the past three decades, Native American casinos have experienced exponential growth in the American capitalist marketplace. The growth has led to unprecedented economic power among some tribes to boost tribal members' quality of life, along with severe critiques both within and outside of the tribes of "casino Indians" as well as what some view as economic opportunism by Native Americans. Casinos have become known colloquially as the "new buffalo"—a new economic enterprise that contains the potential to lift tribes out of dire economic straits. While much has been written on the economics, sovereignty issues, and politics of Native American casinos, only a few authors have written about how tribes use their casinos to address their own culture, and thus Native religious and cultural symbols. Aside from a few studies on the Mashantucket Pequots and their immensely popular Foxwoods casino, few have addressed the construction of cultural and religious capital through cultural representations at casinos among Native tribes outside of New England.

This chapter will address how culture is constructed by three Oklahoma tribes through their concerted depictions of specific and pan-Indian tribal cultures in their casinos. Casinos are an interesting place of cultural cross-pollination, in that they are often one of the few places where non-Natives experience some form of Native representation. Especially in Oklahoma, where casinos are usually conveniently located off major highways and just over state lines, it is not uncommon to see a myriad of license plates from many nearby states in the parking lots. In this chapter I examine the examples of the Choctaw Casino Resort in Durant, the Cherokee's Hard Rock Casino in Tulsa, and the Downstream Casino Resort, owned by the Quapaw nation, in Miami to see how these tribes map tribal identity and try to evoke their "Indianness" through visual representations of culture. During my trip to Oklahoma I visited twenty-one casinos, but I have chosen to focus on these three in order to contrast three distinct forms of cultural representation and what it may mean for Native constructions of nation among these Oklahoma tribes.

My method, which focuses mostly on visual aesthetics, came about mainly because of necessity. The Oklahoma tribes maintain strict research protocols. A researcher who wishes to interview anyone on tribal land must first meet with the tribal anthropologist, present her project to the chiefs, and go through the tribe's own institutional research board along with the separate institutional research board of the scholar's institution, and then the tribe still retains the editorial rights over all published work. I discovered these protocols only a month before the trip, so I could not interview any tribal members as to why the casinos were constructed with certain symbols. I also could not ask how tribal members felt about the usage of such symbols. I could only go to each casino, take photographs, and observe them for myself; thus my work took shape as a multiple-locale visual ethnography. In no way do I wish to examine "authentic" (a term that is fraught and problematic) versus "inauthentic" forms of Native representation. Instead, by visiting the casinos as a typical American observer, I aimed to tease out how tribes create culture, explore how they claim and reclaim the Oklahoma landscape, and examine how their constructions of culture help us to understand modern Native identities.

I begin the chapter by addressing how gaming traditionally functioned in Native life and how the casino fits into that history. I then move on to lay out a short economic and political history of Indian gaming and how it has affected Native communities, especially in Oklahoma. Then I address the Choctaw, Quapaw, and Cherokee casinos, explore their individual depictions of culture, and talk about the ramifications of reconstructing tribal identity in the casino era. I will also parse some of the issues brought up by scholars who have engaged this issue directly.

Even though Oklahoma is not the original homeland of any of the three tribes, all three grapple with the problem of Oklahoma as homeland, and they do so in different ways. The Choctaw wholeheartedly embrace their new sacred land, Oklahoma, with little reference to their previous homeland, while the Cherokee try to educate the public about their pre-removal history in the Southeast through specific uses of artifacts in their casino. In contrast, the Quapaw take the middle ground by celebrating their distinct culture and old homeland through recognition of their pottery tradition, but also stake their place as a people who have not disappeared, by displaying photographs of actual Quapaw people in the casino. The Choctaw "adopt" the buffalo. The Cherokee do not, and their casino is one of the very few not to have any buffalo motifs. The Quapaw invoke the buffalo but also manage to proudly display their own culture. Therefore, the adoption or non-adoption of the buffalo as a cultural symbol in these three tribes represents three different ways of coming to terms with a removed identity in a twentieth-century capitalist framework. The tribes' varied approaches toward images of the sacred also signal a protectiveness against intruding on the sacred. These tribes only obliquely refer to traditional Native religions, thus creating identities that are both open about their own unique histories and guarded—reflecting a push-pull among the tribes of how much of their culture should be exposed to the prying eyes of outsiders.

The histories of the Choctaw, Quapaw, and Cherokee tribes are bifurcated—once they lived in areas very different from Oklahoma, then they were forced to a new land. Both the Choctaw and Cherokee also left behind some members, thus splitting up their people. The Quapaw tribe, in contrast, is small in number compared to the other two and far less well known. All three tribes are forced to construct two identities: the first being their historical identity, the second being their new Oklahoman identities. In bucking the trend of depictions of casino buffalo, the Cherokee try to embed a more historicized identity that embraces their pre-removal roots, while in their casino the Choctaw adopt their new homeland wholeheartedly by embracing the buffalo and make no reference to their original land. The Quapaw display a distinct fusion of Oklahoma with tribal history and stake their place as a people who will not be wiped from history. Thus we have different examples of how three removed nations sacralize their new land: the Cherokee and the Quapaw choose to link one history to another in their own distinct ways, while the Choctaw choose to embrace their new land and evoke a new identity. Although they visually create these identities, all three tribes are clearly uncomfortable with granting the sacred wide exposure within the casino, even though traditional games among many tribes were undertaken for sacred purposes. The depictions of tribal identities in casinos acknowledge the postmodern identity of removed nations that are torn between two lands, two histories, and two stories of nation that are trying to adapt to a fast-growing economic reality in Indian country.

Traditional Gaming

Gambling among Native American peoples has ancient roots within tribal societies. As Paul Pasquaretta asserts, "An estimated 130 tribes from 30 different linguistic stocks played dice game of various kinds centuries before

European settlement."[2] He goes to explain that "unlike Euro-American games of chance, which function as secular rituals and foster acquisitiveness, individual competition, and greed, traditional Native American games of chance are sacred rituals that foster personal sacrifice, group competition and generosity."[3] One of the main examples he points to is the Haudenosaunee's (Iroquois) *guska'eh*, the peach stone game, which is played during the *midewiwis*, or the Midwinter Ceremony, to symbolize the struggle of the Twin Gods to win control over the earth—it is meant to help balance out nature and to give joy to creation. The main point of the game not to win goods (like in Euro-American gambling) but to play with the right attitude, and in that process play for the good of the community itself.[4] As Pasquaretta notes, fruit pits are placed in a wooden bowl, which is smacked against the ground or a rock. The players bet on how the pieces will fall. In the myth surrounding the game, "Skyholder chose to play with the heads of several small birds he had created. By killing the birds and playing with their heads he gained the crucial advantage he needed to defeat his powerful twin. In this way he retained his right to govern the earth."[5] Thus the game must always be played in the proper manner and in "right attitude" to commemorate the importance of balancing the community when reenacting this cosmic struggle between the Twin Gods.

Traditional gambling games were also usually team competitions, with members of the tribes choosing representatives who had the best technique. This was the case with the Iroquois bowl game. Typically the game was "normally contested between neighboring communities or different clans within a particular community. The Victory belonged to both the gambler and his clan or nation."[6] Gambling practices also encouraged the redistribution of wealth among Native tribes and were useful in managing natural resources. Certain Eastern Woodland dice games such as *hubbub* served this role. "Within a classless society gambling losses and gains contributed to the fair and equal distribution of the group's communal resources."[7] The gambling helped to sort out who would use what resources; among some tribes, sachems would even play and lose all their own "wealth," which "served to counter the centralization of authority."[8]

Indian gaming intrigued many anthropologists, especially in the nineteenth and early twentieth centuries. At the turn of the century, Frank Cushing and Steward Culin compiled a massive study of Native games, both the sacred and those that were undertaken for fun or war play. Published in 1907, Culin's volume classified thirty-six different forms of games that were played by Native peoples, solidifying the idea that gaming, in both its gambling and sports forms, was a central part of Native life. It also emphasized that many of the gambling games served to redistribute wealth and were rooted in sacred myth. As Culin notes in his introduction:

> References to games are of common occurrence in the origin myths of various tribes. They usually consist of a description of a series of contests in which the demiurge, the first man, the culture hero, overcomes some opponent, a foe if the human race, by exercise of superior cunning, skill, or magic. Comparison of these myths not only reveal their practical unity, but disclose the primal gamblers as those curious children, the divine Twins, the miraculous offspring of the Sun, who are the principal personages in many Indian mythologies.[9]

Aside from being an integral part of sacred mythologies, traditional gaming is also explored by many modern Native American authors, with references to it in popular novels such as Leslie Marmon Silko's *Ceremony* and Louis Erdrich's *Love Medicine, Tracks,* and *Bingo Palace.*[10] In both mythology and literature, traditional games have always been a way of life, with games and cultural identity each helping to construct the other.

Although gambling was a sacred part of Native society, especially pre-contact, it was not at all like its modern incarnation of Vegas-style slots, bingo halls, electronic gambling machines, and pull tabs, which serve to (attempt to) enrich the individual over the communal. Yet while the actual style of modern gambling may be heavily individualistic and driven by a desire for wealth, a number of arguments could be made that the implementation of casino gambling has allowed some tribes to become more self-sufficient, more efficiently manage the resources that they have, and flex their political sovereignty and rights. So while modern casino gambling no longer reflects the sacred, like the ancient bowl games, and fosters materialism and individual self-interest, it can also be used to rebuild tribal identities and as a way to hold on to land and to create new identity, as seen with the Pequots of Foxwoods, as well as some of the Oklahoma tribes featured in this chapter. We will see how gaming has helped the Chickasaw and Cherokee revitalize their cultures, so in a sense casino gambling can sometimes function in a way that is beneficial to the community. And through the depictions of culture in the modern Oklahoma casino, we see that gaming and constructions of identity through casino aesthetics (instead of through myth and literature) continue to allow tribes to remake their postmodern identities.

Oklahoma Casinos

Oklahoma tribes have not been as extensively studied by scholars of Native American casinos as their northeastern cousins. Part of this is geography; the Mashantucket Pequots and their amazingly successful Foxwoods casino are located in the heart of the Northeast megalopolis and therefore are more visibly imprinted in the minds of Americans when they think "Indian casino." Oklahoma casinos tend to be smaller, as a whole—sometimes just a small room filled with machines next to a smoke shop, gas station, or travel plaza, and more often a modest-sized casino, with the occasional hotel attached to it. They also tend to pull from local communities: they seem to be a vacation destination for midwestern Americans, most of whom seem to come from Oklahoma or the neighboring states of Kansas, Texas, Missouri, and Nebraska. The clientele was more ethnically mixed than one might expect—when Isaiah and I visited the Oklahoma casinos we noted a sizable white clientele, along with African Americans and Asian Americans, specifically Vietnamese and Chinese Americans.

Oklahoma does have one giant Vegas-style casino, Winstar World Casino and Resort, which is located just over the state line of Texas off I-35. Winstar boasts a mile-long casino floor and Vegas-style entertainment, and it is a themed casino, revolving around "city" themes such as New York or Paris. There are almost no markers of Native identity at Winstar, which is owned by the Chickasaw nation, except for one very obvious marker of sovereignty that confronts casino-goers as they walk through the door: a sign that states, "Welcome to the sovereign and self-governing lands of the unconquered and unconquerable Chickasaw Nation!" The sign is a strong statement of political sovereignty, but it is the only indication that you are entering a Native American–owned casino. This was, however, the case for all of the Chickasaw casinos that we visited on our trip—they tended to have few outward markers of Indian culture.

In Oklahoma, Native American gaming is spread across the entire state, with the exception of the panhandle. Native American gaming in general is classified in three groups, the first being Class I, which includes traditional games and social games; Class II, which includes bingos, pull tabs, and lotteries; and Class III gaming, which includes table games and slots (Class III games are usually referred to as "Vegas-style" gaming.). Although Class III games get the most attention in studies of Native casinos, in Oklahoma Class II is the area with the fastest growth and greatest popularity— unsurprising to me, given the size of the bingo halls that I encountered in my research trip.[11]

Native gaming initially became legal as a result of *Seminole Tribe of Florida v. Butterworth* (1983). In that case, the Seminole tribe's bingo hall offered prizes over $100, which exceeded the state limit in terms of prize money. When the state of Florida tried to obtain regulatory control over Seminole bingo, the tribe sued the state. The Fifth Circuit Court of Appeals ruled that the Florida bingo statute was "civil/regulatory" rather than "criminal/probatory" and found that that the Florida Seminole were not subject to the state's statute. This opened the door to high-stakes bingo and other forms of gambling run by the tribe. Indeed, the Seminole tribe of Florida became one of the most successful Native American casino operators in the world, leading to their eventual purchase of the entire Hard Rock enterprise.[12]

The second major court case that helped spur the growth of Native American casinos was *California v. Cabazon Band of Mission Indians* (1987). The Cabazon band promoted bingo and card games on their reservation in the early 1980s, and the state of California and Riverside County tried to enforce state and local regulations limiting the tribe's control over the games. The Cabazon band sued, and the case made it to the U.S. Supreme Court, which ruled that since the state of California allowed bingo and card games, which were civilly regulated by the state, the games were subject to tribal jurisdiction and not state regulation. "*Cabazon* demonstrated the tribal and federal interest in upholding tribal self-determination, emphasizing the federal government's interest in Indian self-government, including the goal of encouraging tribal self-sufficiency and economic development."[13]

Since the *Cabazon* decision confirmed the role that tribal governments had over gaming regulation, Congress acted to placate state concerns by drafting and passing the Indian Gaming Regulatory Act (IGRA) in 1988, which balanced the regulatory roles between the tribes and state governments, while still allowing for tribal sovereignty. The IGRA classified gaming into the three categories mentioned above, and then set the regulatory limits for each class. Class I games are totally controlled by the tribes, as they are seen as traditional forms of gaming, with minuscule or nonexistent purses. Class II games are regulated primarily by the tribal governments with federal oversight in the form of the National Indian Gaming Commission (NIGC). Finally, Class III games are supposed to be regulated through individual agreements between the tribes and the states, therefore allowing for the possibility of sharing regulatory jurisdiction with tribes over Vegas-style gaming. Therefore IGRA allows for tribal sovereignty along with shared oversight by the federal government and the state.[14]

The National Indian Gaming Commission is the federal regulatory oversight agency for Indian gaming and is housed within the Department of the Interior. The commission plays the main federal role in regulating Indian gaming, developing Indian gaming in general and monitoring Class II gaming. The NIGC reviews and approves of all gaming ordinances, as well as all contracts with outside management companies, including the needed background checks that are maintained to keep Indian gaming out of the hands of organized crime. It also oversees the proper licensing of "key employees" at casinos and cross-checks their histories against FBI records. Therefore, the NIGC isn't simply another federal oversight committee—it is key for the smooth operation and management of Indian casinos.[15]

Class III gaming only began in Oklahoma in 2005, when the state of Oklahoma passed a referendum allowing for Vegas-style gambling on tribal lands.[16] Previous to that, Indian tribes in the state heavily focused on Class II gaming. Since 2005, more than one hundred casinos have started offering Vegas-style gambling (usually attached to the already popular bingo halls), and Oklahoma now trails only California in the amount of Indian casino revenue that it generates annually, with $2.9 billion.[17] Overall, the state's gaming contracts with the tribes have netted the state $105.9 million in revenue. This has led to the state's thirty-eight federally recognized tribes becoming, as a group, the state's fifth-largest employer. The Chickasaw tribe (which owns and operates the Winstar casino) on its own employs 11,800 people and has an $800 million budget thanks to its incredibly popular casinos.[18]

In Oklahoma, however, gaming is only one piece of the economic pie. For the Chickasaw, gaming naturally helps expand their tourism draw, which also feeds into their other industries, including the manufacture of fine chocolates. In 2010, the Chickasaw nation opened the Bedré Fine Chocolate factory, which is right off State Highway 7. Prominent signage alerts highway drivers that they are near the factory and notes where they should exit to visit it. The factory has drawn more than a quarter million visitors since its opening, and the tours are quite popular. The tribe bought the company in 2000 and moved the factory to its lands. It is the only tribe in the United States to own a chocolate company, and the candies are sold in upscale retailers across the state. The chocolate company, the nearby Chickasaw-owned Artisan Hotel Resort and Spa, (which has a small casino in it), and the Chickasaw Welcome Center, Cultural Center, and Recreation Area all draw thousands of visitors every year and offer the tribe diversified revenue beyond just casinos in order to support themselves and preserve their culture.[19] The promotion of this corner of Oklahoma near the Arbuckle Mountains, journalist Anne Barajas

Harp observes, "may give the best perspective on what the Chickasaw Nation is offering along the road now known as Chickasaw 7: Oklahoma, in all its thorny past, natural beauty, and promise for a people who have claimed the land of their removal and are bringing it to others."[20]

Gaming has also helped other tribes diversify their economic holdings and spur economic growth. With the advent of Vegas-style gambling and its acquisition of the Hard Rock Casino in Tulsa, the Cherokee Nation has managed to pump money back into social services and cultural preservation. One such example of this is the restoration of the old Cherokee National Supreme Court building, now a museum, in Tahlequah, Oklahoma. The building, which had been left to decay, houses a museum that "offers a sense of both the importance of the rule of law throughout Cherokee history and the power of the written word as delivered in both English and Cherokee by the *Cherokee Advocate,* the first newspaper in Indian Territory, whose offices were inside."[21] Under the administration of the current principal chief, Chad Smith, "the Cherokees have tripled the sizes of the tribe's health-care system in ten years, transformed historic Sequoyah Schools in Tahlequah into a highly sought-after boarding school for more than four hundred Native American students and created more than five thousand new jobs."[22] For Smith, gaming helps allow the Cherokee Nation to maintain both its sovereignty and its history— it allows for the tribe to invest in itself and in the maintenance of its own culture. This trend fits that of most tribes in Oklahoma. Generally, when managed carefully, gaming has allowed a large number of Oklahoma tribes to invest in other industries, to improve tribal social safety nets, and to begin to offer better economic opportunities to their people. In this way, casino gaming in Oklahoma does serve a societal purpose, not unlike traditional gaming, which distributed wealth among tribal members. Although the data pool is small and somewhat incomplete, most social scientists agree that gaming among Native tribes has introduced economic advantages to the tribes who use gaming as a way to invest back into their communities.[23]

Casinos and Constructions of Culture
Choctaw

The Choctaw casino sticks out of the flat landscape of Durant, Oklahoma, like a ship on a calm horizon. Aside from the cluster of torches in the front, designed to be symbolic of the sacred fire, it looks like a mostly unimpressive, curved hotel tower.[24] When we walked through the front doors we noted that an etching of the Great Seal of the Choctaw was on the door. Inside the Great

Seal are a bow and arrow and a pipe, all common enough symbols of Native American identity. The lobby of the casino, while containing the aforementioned white buffalo and its water, light, and sound show, was decorated in warm earthen tones. In front of the white buffalo were wood-grained coffee tables cut in the shape of leaves surrounded by rich red chairs. From the coffee tables, visitors had a clear view of the white buffalo and its show, and we could see a few gamblers milling about in that area, counting cash or checking smartphones.

The white buffalo itself was a feat of engineering for the designers of the casino. The tribe collaborated with a Las Vegas firm, Worthgroup Architects, to create it, which is not an unusual partnership in Indian casinos; the Mohegans did a similar thing by partnering with the Rockwell Group in designing their casino, Mohegan Sun. The white buffalo weighs 1,200 pounds and is seven feet tall. The glass installation behind it, which comprises the waterfall and light sequence, was created entirely of handmade tiles that took ten people more than twelve hundred hours to piece together.[25] Together, the buffalo and the water/light/sound show are hard to miss and demand the visitor's immediate attention. What is odd is that the white buffalo stands in front of the casino without any explanation by the Choctaw. It is simply there, to be consumed and seen by visitors, who are left to come up with their own interpretation as to its meaning. Perhaps the Choctaw meant it to be this way, because in an article in *Oklahoma Today* in which the white buffalo is mentioned as a sign of Native culture within the casino, it is simply reported to be "a sacred symbol of vast abundance." Satisfied with this answer, the writer of the article does not explore the deeper meanings behind the legend of White Buffalo Woman.

Traditionally, White Buffalo Woman, or Ptesan-Wan, appeared to the Lakota people as a holy being. There are multiple versions of the story, but it is generally agreed that she brought the Sioux the sacred pipe and sacred knowledge. She is also said to have brought the sun dance, the sweat lodge, and the vision quest, and to have given the Sioux useful knowledge for survival. Initially she appeared as a beautiful woman, but also as a white buffalo, which are regarded as sacred by Plains tribes, because they were given to them by the Creator and sustained their traditional way of life.[26] Generally the myth is one that is shared by Plains tribes, and is well known in the Native American world. None of this, however, is explained in front of the Durant Casino's white buffalo. Also, it leads an observer to ask why the Choctaw would choose to put up a white buffalo. A southeastern tribe, they were forcibly relocated to Oklahoma; they were not indigenous to the southern Plains. The Choctaw certainly knew of the Sioux story, and Native peoples have never been exclusive about myths that are borrowed, repurposed, or reinterpreted, but the reasons for the usage of the white buffalo remained mysterious.

As I mulled various questions at the foot of the Choctaw white buffalo, Isaiah urged me into the casinos in order to explore the depictions of culture on the casino floor. The North Casino itself continued with the earthen color schemes—shades of red, brown, and ocher predominated. The casino was designed for visitors to follow a main "path" through the casino floor, and wooden and stone motifs were integrated into the beams supporting the casino ceiling. Several lights hung from the beams, their covers depicting rural Oklahoma motifs, including farmland, shocks of hay, trees, and the increasingly ubiquitous buffalo. On the actual casino floor we encountered a taxidermied Texas longhorn, which Isaiah and I also found puzzling, and right outside the bathrooms we found pictures evoking the rural landscape, tornados, and other spectacular incidences of high Plains weather. The bathrooms themselves were womb-like, with red sinks, red stalls, and a dark wooden floor, and were marked by large "tornado shelter" signs.

The lobby of the main hotel shared a lobby with the casino itself, so we could not go further into that hotel, but nearby was a smaller, less flashy, more economical-looking hotel. Called the Choctaw Inn, its outside was constructed in a Southwest style, faux adobe, with the symbol of the four directions etched into the outside walls. Inside, the earthen color scheme predominated again in brown and tan, and we encountered yet another depiction of buffalo, this time a painting, over the water fountains near the lobby restrooms. Closer to the Choctaw Inn but connected with the North Casino by a walkway, the South Casino had a design style similar to that of the North Casino—natural color schemes, but the colors were lighter, with more orange accents. It was a bit brighter compared to the North Casino, and the buffalo motif carried over into the bathrooms, where buffalo were depicted running above the sink's mirror. Also in the South Casino was what Isaiah and I christened the "Vietnamese corner": an oddly decorated section with umbrellas and light-up birdcages with signs in Vietnamese and English and Vietnamese-themed electronic games. Advertised there was a "Vietnamese singing contest" with a prize, like a Choctaw-Vietnamese version of *American Idol*. Even though it was relatively early in the morning, we did see a few older Vietnamese people playing some of the electronic gambling games.

Aside from the Vietnamese corner, where the Choctaw were clearly catering to a specific demographic who come to their casino, the Plains and buffalo motif was felt most heavily at the Choctaw casino compared to the other casinos that we toured in the summer of 2014. In his article on representation at Foxwoods, scholar John Bodinger de Uriarte notes that "it is not so much how the identity of the Mashantucket Pequot is imagined and maintained as it is how the identity at Mashantucket is imagined and projected, both to the community at Mashantucket and to its industries' tourists and visitors."[27] In the case of the Choctaw, they clearly imagine and project a certain identity in their main North Casino—one that is strongly tied to the imagined Oklahoma landscape and buffalo. The pictures of the Oklahoma land in the casino do not actually mirror the topography of the land outside of it—the Choctaw live in a hilly, green section of Oklahoma that is dotted with lakes and streams (trucks trailering boats were a common sight on the roadways in the area). And while the color scheme certainly invoked the rich soil of Oklahoma, the area around Durant is not the expanse of plains that we would later encounter on the border with Kansas. Nevertheless, the Choctaw clearly wished to evoke the "idea" of Oklahoma—that is, the imagined Oklahoma of plains, buffalo, and tornados—and they were successful in doing so in the casino.

In creating an "imagined" landscape, along with adopting the Lakota's white buffalo, the Choctaw are asserting a "new Plains" identity. The Choctaw's original landscape and sacred lands were very different from the lands they now live on. This "new Plains" identity publicly grapples with the land they currently live on and makes the southern Plains a new part of their ever-evolving identity. Although it is the new face of the tribe, however, this assertion of a "new Plains" identity is not a disavowal of their southeastern roots; it instead points to the elasticity of Choctaw community and Choctaw sacred land. Here on the Oklahoma land, the Choctaw have reassembled their tribe after their trail of tears. In the reassembling they have made their new land sacred in their own way by claiming the animals, colors, and weather of that land in their most public economic enterprise: the casino. In doing so, they have constructed this new identity of who they are as Choctaw. In Durant, Oklahoma, the white buffalo is the symbol of the rising economic and social power of a tribe that had to remake itself in the shadow of the horrors of removal.

Quapaw

Racing ahead of severe weather and forbidding skies on the fifth day of our road trip, Isaiah and I found ourselves at the Quapaw (pronounced "O-Gah-Pah") nation's casino, the Downstream Casino Resort near Miami, Oklahoma, on a very muggy and tornadic afternoon. The Quapaw's casino sits tucked up in the corner of Oklahoma that touches Missouri and Kansas (you literally enter and exit Missouri on the roundabout that takes you into the casino). It is a modern, new building, and one of the first things that you notice are the signs reminding you that you are on sovereign tribal land and subject to Quapaw laws. In front of the casino sat a giant tipi, its outer shell dangerously whipping and crackling in the high winds that were preceding the storms. Because it had started to rain lightly, we moved very quickly into the main casino/resort lobby, where we were greeted by an impressive Quapaw motif: a giant abstract pot in the middle of the lobby that spanned from the floor to the ceiling. It was an intricately styled motif made of curving ironwork, and beautifully tasteful, much like the rest of the casino/resort lobby, which was dimly lit and filled with images to examine.

It is thought that originally the Quapaw were from the Ohio Valley but were forced further south by Iroquois tribes fighting over hunting land. They eventually settled on the western side of the Mississippi, in the present-day state of Arkansas (the state is named after a variation of the tribal name, Akansea), where they came to be known as the "downstream people."[28] The name of the casino and resort is clearly a reference to the meaning of their tribal name. Like the Cherokee and Choctaw, the Quapaw were removed to Oklahoma in the 1830s. The Quapaw were, according to the display cases that filled the main entrance lobby, renowned pottery makers. In the main lobby was an carefully curated, extensive collection of archaeological finds of Quapaw pottery. Of a variety of styles and motifs, the pots were labeled with the location in which they had been found, and explained with care. Near the pottery was a two-paragraph explanation of the significance of pottery in Quapaw culture. All of the pots were from the period before their removal to Oklahoma, with dates ranging from 1000 CE to 1700 CE and some going far back enough to be from before their migration to Arkansas. The emphasis on pottery explained the giant ironwork pot motif in the middle of the casino—the Quapaw were clearly stressing a key component of their culture that existed before they came to Oklahoma, and displaying it for all those who came to their casino to see. Their pots harked back to a pre-migration and pre-removal period, and gave most visitors a sense of where the tribe was from and of an art that tribal members clearly held in great esteem. By showcasing their pottery, the Quapaw were directly tying their new industry (the casino) to their old industry (pottery) as well as to land and history. If the Choctaw's casino was the "new buffalo," than the Quapaw's casino was clearly the "new pottery."

While I browsed the pottery, Isaiah discovered another fascinating section of the lobby—the seating area. Dotted throughout the whole seating area were pictures of past and present tribal members. These included family portraits, formal portraits, informal pictures, and military photos. They spanned from the nineteenth century to the modern era. Many of the photos were labeled with the names of the individuals pictured, some carried explanations (especially the military photos) or short histories, and all were of Quapaw people. It gave the lobby the feeling of a people that were still very much a part of Oklahoma culture. Through the use of the photos of actual past and present tribal members the Quapaw made a loud statement. These were not "disappearing Indians" or just "historical Indians." These photos announced a vibrant tribe that was very much still a part of American society.

The bathrooms in the lobby were labeled "men" and "women" in English and in the Quapaw language. Like in the other casinos we had seen on the trip, they were also tornado shelters, which was a relief given that the skies had been swirling and turning greenish all day. Off to the side of the hotel lobby was the Buffalo Grille, with a giant highlighted buffalo sign; the Ma-ko-shaw coffee shop (I think the name was supposed to be Quapaw for "coffee shop"); and the Nee spa, which offered "herbal" treatments for relaxation and purification of the skin. Just outside of the casino doors was a well-landscaped pool area, which was full of visitors, especially children, splashing about that afternoon despite the weather. Isaiah noted that the pool had special lifts installed so that the disabled and elderly could get in and out of it easily, and that the casino and resort were well designed in general in terms of disability access. The pool and spa gave this particular casino more of a family-friendly feel, especially compared to the Cherokee casino, which doesn't let people under twenty-one anywhere near the casino doors. In fact, it seemed that one could come to Downstream and mostly enjoy the spa, food, and resort facilities, and not even have to spend much time in the casino at all.

The inside of the actual casino contained a water and leaf motif, again clearly evoking the "downstream" history of the Quapaw. The carpet on the outer part of the casino referenced water, with curving lines of blue, while the carpet in the inner part of the casino exploded in a leaf motif of various browns. The ceiling was paneled in transparent browns, which gave it a warm, womb-like setting, like in the Choctaw casino, and invoked the Oklahoma landscape. The columns around the casino were paneled with wood carved in geometric patterns. Just behind the casino and resort is a conference center, which looked mostly like generic conference rooms with the exception that portraits of Quapaw people continued in here, much like in the lobby.

Behind the main check-in desk of the hotel hobby was a huge mural portraying certain moments in Quapaw history and referencing the four directions (a cosmological symbol), the pipe, and aspects of what seemed to be Quapaw myth. Next to it was a display case with Quapaw pipes, eagle feather fans, and other tribal artifacts.

We had found the buffalo among the Quapaw, with the reference to the Buffalo Grille and its large sign, and we had also found a reference to Oklahoma Plains identity in the giant tipi that stood outside the casino. Yet the majority of the casino was clearly carefully curated to feel distinctly Quapaw. It evoked both their pre-removal lives on the western side of the Mississippi as the "downstream people" but also their pre-migration lives through the pottery artifacts preserved from archaeological sites in the Ohio Valley. The portraits of actual tribal members in the lobby and in the conference center very much tied the casino to the actual members of the tribe. To me this was the most telling aspect of the casino—the Quapaw, a small tribe that many people had probably never even heard of, were announcing via their casino that they were still here, still a part of American society. Although small in number, they had not "disappeared," and through their casino they asserted their identity as a tribe. Of all the casinos that we saw during out trip across Oklahoma, the Downstream Casino Resort most seamlessly navigated the complex identities of removed Oklahoma tribes. They managed to weave together their many histories of migration and removal and create a mostly cohesive narrative, while also visually invoking the "new Plains" identity through the use of buffalo and the tipi. Through their casino the Quapaw people assert that despite being a small nation, they have a rich history and language that they are fighting to preserve. The visitor can see that the downstream people are willing to serve American culture through a capitalist enterprise, the casino, but also that they use that enterprise to reassert their own identity.

Cherokee

The Cherokee casino that Isaiah and I decided to visit was the Hard Rock Cherokee casino in downtown Tulsa. We wanted to see what a large urban casino complex looked like, off the main tribal lands. The Hard Rock is a massive complex that clearly caters to an upper-middle-class, mostly white clientele who come to the casino to enjoy its luxurious hotels and adult entertainment. Unlike every other casino that we visited in Oklahoma, where the law is that you must be eighteen to gamble, at the Hard Rock you must be twenty-one to even enter the casino grounds. This rule was also strictly enforced, with the guards regularly carding people as they walked in. This meant that it is exclusively an adult playground, with no children or teen-agers to be found near the casinos. The age restriction presented a problem, however, as Isaiah was only twenty at the time, and I had to leave him sitting outside on a bench to scout the interior of the casinos. Hard Rock also was stricter about the use of the camera than the Choctaw and Quapaw casinos had been—we could not take pictures of the interior, so we settled on mainly photographing the outside and the parking garage.

The Hard Rock Tulsa has multiple hotel towers, and two main casino complexes. The main two casinos and hotel tower look like most other Hard Rock franchises, and nothing immediately jumps out at the observer that this is a Native-owned casino, even though the Seminole Tribe of Florida owns the Hard Rock casino corporation. The other casino appeared temporary, essentially a high-end, durable tent-like structure in an oblong shape. On the outside of the tent was a red and black tribal-looking design, thus making it the only "Indian"-looking building visible from the parking lot. The main casi-nos were also accented with red and black on the outside, but it looked more modernist than "Native." A Cherokee worker told me the tent-like casino was called Cabin Creek and that it was specifically constructed for country music acts that came to Hard Rock. The inside of Cabin Creek looked fairly stan-dard for a casino, with electronic games, a stage for music acts, and a cashier. But when I approached the cashier's stand I realized that it was constructed as a fake log cabin. It seemed to be a nod to the Cherokee's pre-removal way of living, as log cabins were popular among tribal members who lived in the mountains of the Southeast. It could, however, have simply been a nod to this casino's "country" theme and more working-class clientele. The people who were gambling in Cabin Creek appeared to be less well-off compared to more flashily dressed gamblers in the main casino.

The main casino consisted of two separate casino floors. The casino that the main entrance funneled visitors into was full of glitz and Hard Rock man-ufactured glamor. It was two stories tall, though it felt much taller thanks to the vaulted ceilings. Aside from the main casino floor, poker rooms and other rooms (likely for off-track betting) were on the second floor. This casino looked like any casino you would see in Vegas. To the left of the main casino sat another casino, which appeared to be much the same but with one excep-tion: in the middle of the casino floor sat a giant abstract iron sculpture in the shape of a tree that reached up all the way to the casino ceiling. There were glowing orange panels in the cutouts, and the sculpture radiated color out in concentric circles. The giant "tree" was clearly invoking something botanical and natural, like a tree-of-life motif, but when I first saw it I puzzled over how to link it specifically to Cherokee culture. Again, like with the Choctaw's white buffalo, there were no explanatory signs or any references to the tree within the casino, and because it was directly on the casino floor I was unable to take a photo of it.

The hotel lobby, which was right off to the side of one of the casinos, was the first place where I viewed direct signs of Cherokee culture. It had dimly lit display cases of pottery, baskets, and some paintings. Some of the art was labeled with the artist's name, and next to several of the names was the designation "Cherokee National Treasures." Again, the display case was simply there; I could not find an explanation of the art inside, nor did I see any dates. From the hotel lobby Isaiah and I worked our way over to the parking garage, which gave us a delightful surprise; the garage was labeled by floor and section not only in English but also in Cherokee, using both English transliteration and the Sequoyah syllabary. The elevators were marked in this way as well. We noticed that the principal chief of the nation had his own parking spot right next to the elevators, and that his SUV was there—with his name and title on the side in both English and Cherokee using the Sequoyah syllabary.

It was also through this back entrance to the main casino complex that I encountered the most overt display of Cherokee culture. Right by the entrance from the parking deck I was directed to a display section overlooking the second floor of the main casino. This section was filled with historical pieces from the period 1690–1790. All of the artifacts were pre-removal, and it was set up as a museum display, with small placards near each piece giving its approximate date of creation and other information. There was also a guard watching over the display cases and a placard warning against photography. The cases contained beautiful baskets, paintings, masks, clay figurines, turtle rattles, dolls, and multiple vases shaped as turtles. Turtle, in old Cherokee myths, is a sacred animal, as he balances the world on his back. All of the pieces were obvious archaeological artifacts or collector's finds, and they were carefully curated to showcase pre-removal art that evoked the homelands of North Carolina, Tennessee, and Georgia. The curator had clearly spent much time, money, and care to build a narrative of Cherokee life before removal through the various artifacts on display. This display was a serious museum piece of Cherokee culture and life that the tribe funded and placed inside its casino. Though it was tucked into the back of the casino, some visitors did stop and look at several of the pieces before they hustled off toward the gambling.

The Cherokee's Hard Rock casino is part of a larger franchise, and this shapes much of the interior of the casino and its design. It looks very much like other Hard Rock casinos, with its emphasis on classic rock figures and bands, the Hard Rock display cases, and the Hard Rock shop in the front. While almost every other casino Isaiah and I visited displayed buffalo in one form or another, the Cherokee did not. The main "Cherokee" aspects of the casino focused on actual artifacts, and the majority of these artifacts were from the pre-removal period, thus reminding visitors and viewers of their southeastern history and gently hinting at their removal from their original lands. Along with these artifacts were the subtle reminders of culture on display in the parking garage in the form of directions and places marked in English and Cherokee in the Sequoyah syllabary. The parking garage, of all places, reminded visitors that they were in not just any Hard Rock casino, but a distinctly Cherokee one.

The Cherokee have chosen to make their mark as a tribe that owns a vibrant, expensive casino, having thrown in their lot with another tribe, the Seminole, who own Hard Rock. The Cherokee casino asserts their past in a way that is not "imagined" but is instead tangibly real. With the tree-of-life motif in the center of the second casino, and the references to their southeastern mountain life in Cabin Creek, the Cherokees seem to also have tried to integrate certain "Native" markers into their casino design. The use of the museum exhibit also clearly delineates a particularly Cherokee material culture that existed before coming to Oklahoma. In fact, the motif of an imagined Oklahoma itself doesn't exist at the Hard Rock casino; it is missing along with the buffalo. Instead the sense visitors get from the casino is of a vibrant, well-off tribe that nurtures artists and holds a position of power in the state. This is a tribe that has the audacity to put up signage in its tribal language and alphabet on the parking deck. Why would the Cherokees need an imagined Oklahoma of buffalo and flat plains when their huge, expensive, glittering casino sits just outside of downtown in busy, very real Tulsa?

Conclusion

Actual buffalo are rather uncommon in Oklahoma. They can mainly be found out in the panhandle region, which has no Native American casinos, or among some of the patches of tallgrass prairie that still exist near the state line with Kansas. But in the world of Oklahoma casinos, they are everywhere. Even though this chapter discusses only three casinos, the majority of the twenty-one casinos that I toured contained references to buffalo.

In the Choctaw's beautiful new casino in Durant, Oklahoma, the buffalo points to a "new Plains" identity—as well as to adoption of Oklahoma as a new homeland, a new beginning for a removed southeastern tribe. The white buffalo in the front also asserts the casino's status as the "new buffalo"—an economic engine of opportunity for the tribe; in this sense the buffalo is a symbol of abundance, as *Oklahoma Today* suggested. In the case of the Cherokee, the buffalo are missing from their Hard Rock casino; instead the Cherokee assert their material culture and history. With the museum displays and the displays of Cherokee art, the Cherokee show visitors specific aspects of their history, especially since the majority of the artifacts are from the pre-removal period. Instead of a buffalo, the visitor sees a giant tree in the middle of one of the Cherokee casinos, and in another casino a log cabin, which refers to their southeastern mountain roots. And among the Quapaw, the buffalo is tucked away in a food establishment. The Quapaw tribe uses the casino to explain their own complicated history and assert themselves as a people who haven't disappeared. In their case, the buffalo is a nod to what is expected in an Indian casino, but the majority of the casino revolves around pottery, which refers to their past as skilled artisans and as a people who had migrated to the Southeast from the Ohio Valley and then were eventually removed and forced to grapple with Oklahoma as their new land.

Hanging over the three tribes is the ugly history of removal. All were forced from their lands and walked their own trail of tears. All faced the brutality of a government that wanted them gone. All of them had to come to terms with the fact that they now live on the southern Plains. At the end of it all, these tribes were left with Oklahoma, a land that was given to them not by their Creator but by Andrew Jackson, and the alien prospect of becoming Westerners. Their casinos reflect three ways of approaching their new narratives in the twenty-first century. The Choctaw wholeheartedly evoke Oklahoma through its landscape and animals, even if it might be an "imagined" version of it, and even if it is only for the benefit of white tourists. The Quapaw stubbornly hang on to their pre-migration and pre-removal history, both with the name of their casino and the artifacts and design within it. Moreover, unlike the two other tribes, which are large and well known in the American imagination, the Quapaw, through their use of photos of tribal members in the casino, assert that they have not disappeared. Finally, the Cherokee painstakingly and publicly maintain their linkage to their pre-removal history though preservation of material culture in a carefully curated museum exhibit, also for the benefit of the white tourist gaze.

Although all tribes refer to the sacred, all do so obliquely: the Choctaw with the white buffalo, the Cherokee with the tree of life, and the Quapaw with the display of religious artifacts (pipes, sacred fans) and a mural that invokes their cosmology. None of the tribes really explain these religious artifacts or images, leaving the public to make up their own mind, or even notice them at all. The fact is, non-Natives historically have misunderstood Native religions, which has led many tribes to shield their sacred symbols and artifacts. Given, too, the fact that many sacred artifacts have been stolen by museums and collectors, and the occasional hostility outsiders show toward traditional religion, it is a wonder that these images or artifacts are even displayed in casinos at all. The average American casino-goer is not likely to be well versed in traditional Native religions, and will simply observe Native religious symbols without really understanding what he or she may be seeing. Yet one cannot separate traditional religion from Native culture, and if the tribes wished to imbue the casinos with their own understandings of culture, they were bound to use religious imagery and objects. So the lack of explanation in the casino is likely a protective measure. Because the Choctaw, Cherokee, and Quapaw are constructing new cultural identities for themselves, their religious symbols have to be there—they are just left to silently speak for themselves and to be interpreted by the observer.

In all three examples the tribes are creating a specific public image that caters to non-Natives, while at the same time framing the way they want their own histories to be understood. Even as they do this, the casinos are also vibrant displays of wealth—they proclaim that the Choctaw, Quapaw, and Cherokee are becoming economic powers to reckon with. They herald the beginnings of a new history of modern Native identity that is shaped and created by the tribes themselves. Finally, the casino buffalo, like the images of many modern tribes, defies easy classification. It is both visible and invisible in the Oklahoma casinos, much the way Native people are perceived in modern America. Native Americans are depicted as "disappearing" when they really are continually engaging American culture. Native people, however, through how they engage outsiders economically and culturally, will continue to define the meaning of both the visible and invisible casino buffalo for themselves.

Notes

1. In this paper I use the term "buffalo" colloquially. The proper name for the animal is the American bison, but many Americans, including Native Americans, refer to it as a "buffalo."

2. Paul Pasquaretta, "On the 'Indianess' of Bingo: Gambling and the Native American Community," *Critical Inquiry* 20, no. 4 (Summer 1994): 698.

3. Ibid.

4. Ibid., 699.

5. Ibid.

6. Ibid., 700.

7. Ibid.

8. Ibid.

9. Stewart Culin, *Games of the North American Indian* (New York: Dover, 1975), 32.

10. Eileen M. Luna-Firebaugh and Mary Jo Tippeconnic Fox, "The Sharing Tradition: Indian Gaming in Stories and Modern Life," *Wicazo Sa Review*, Spring 2010, 28.

11. Kenneth W. Grant II, Katherine A. Spilde, and Jonathan B. Taylor, "Social and Economic Consequences of Indian Gaming in Oklahoma," *American Indian Culture and Research Journal* 28, no. 2 (2004): 99.

12. Ibid., 103–104. Also see Jessica Cattelino, *High Stakes: Florida Seminole Gaming and Sovereignty* (Durham, NC: Duke University Press, 2008.)

13. Grant, Spilde, and Taylor, "Social and Economic Consequences," 104.

14. Ibid., 105.

15. Ibid., 106.

16. James McGirk, "Game Stories," *Oklahoma Today* 63, no. 4 (July/August 2013): 26.

17. Tom Lindley, "New Indian Country," *Oklahoma Today* 60, no. 4 (July/August 2010): 54.

18. Ibid.

19. Anne Barajas Harp, "Spirit of a Nation," *Oklahoma Today* 60, no. 4 (July/August 2010): 56.

20. Ibid., 61.

21. Lindley, "New Indian Country," 57.

22. Ibid.

23. For more information on the positive economic effects of casinos, see Gary C. Anders, "Indian Gaming: Financial and Regulatory Issues," *Annals of the American Academy of Political and Social Science* 556 (March 1998): 98–108; Nicholas Moellman and Aparna Mitra, "Indian Gaming in Oklahoma: Implications for Community Welfare," *Journal of Socio-Economics* 45 (2013): 64–70; Katherine Spilde and Jonathan Taylor, "Economic Evidence on the Effects of the Indian Gaming Regulatory Act on Indians and non-Indians," *UNLV Gaming Research and Review Journal* 17, no. 1 (XXXX): 13–30.

24. All observations on the casinos in this chapter were completed between June 24 and June 30, 2014, and were noted in the recorded or written notes of either Angela Tarango or her undergraduate research assistant, Isaiah Ellis. All of the photos used for research in this chapter were taken by Isaiah Ellis.

25. McGirk, "Game Stories," 28.

26. "The White Buffalo Woman," in *American Indian Myths and Legends*, ed. Richard Erodes and Alfonso Ortiz (New York: Pantheon Books, 1984), 47–52. Also see Black Elk's depiction of the myth: Joseph E. Brown, *The Sacred Pipe: Black Elk's Account of the Seven Rites of the Oglala Sioux* (Norman: University of Oklahoma Press, 1989).

27. John J. Bodiger de Uriarte, "Imagining the Nation with House Odds: Representing American Indian Identity at Mashantucket," *Ethnohistory* 50, no. 3 (Summer 2003): 551.

28. See the Quapaw Nation's website, https://www.quapawtribe.com.

8

St. Homobonus Leads the CEOs

DOING GOOD VERSUS DOING (REALLY) WELL

Paula M. Kane

EARLY INTERPRETERS OF Max Weber's famous 1904 work, *The Protestant Ethic and the Rise of Capitalism*, concluded triumphantly that capitalism began and flourished only in Protestant regions of Europe following the Reformation because Catholics lacked the commercial spirit that sparked capitalism and were indifferent to seeking profit systematically.[1] They further disparaged Catholics for their characteristic indolence or hedonism. Today these scholars and their Protestant forebears would be perplexed by the appearance of St. Homobonus as the patron saint of businesspeople and the model for America's Catholic corporate commanders. To be sure, the saint has been unheralded and unmentioned in the United States, except in executive quarters. Homobonus, known as an honest Italian merchant of the twelfth century, lived and died in Cremona, where he helped the poor and was made a saint just two years after his death. His image has been resurrected quite recently in the United States by new organizations serving Catholic business elites, such as Legatus, founded in 1987. The saint's statuette and holy cards are sold now as novelties for Catholic CEOs, who accord him anachronistic credit for proving that personal virtue and the free market can flourish together, even though Homobonus died well before the birth of capitalism.[2] Yet despite their devotion to this little-known medieval saint, it appears that wealthy American Catholics have embraced something different that Weber could not have foreseen: a Calvinist ethic conveyed through a Jansenist piety in newly minted organizations to serve very rich Catholics.[3] Perhaps wealthy Catholics, too, have found an elective affinity with capitalism.[4]

Has an identity shift occurred among elite Catholics? At the time Weber's essay appeared, most American Catholics, as historians have well documented, were living in impoverished conditions as immigrants in the nation's cities. Too much money and too many opportunities were never the problems of the tenement dwellers of the nineteenth and early twentieth centuries. The gradual assimilation of the two major waves of Catholic immigrants (the Germans and Irish of the 1840s–1850s, and the Hungarians, Italians, Lithuanians, Poles, and Slavs of 1880–1924) into American society was demonstrated in their eventual upward mobility, apparent especially in the 1960s as earlier forms of discrimination in banking, housing, insurance, and newspapers faded. Within the American Catholic community, success was largely due to the end of a Catholic siege mentality; the passage of the G.I. Bill, which created an educated middle class out of World War II veterans; suburbanization, which allowed Catholics to leave urban ethnic enclaves for new housing developments; the income mobility that accompanied new white-collar jobs; a lowered birth rate; and the adoption of middle-class values. But this story of assimilation is already more than fifty years old. It is time to address the situation of some extremely successful descendants of those Catholic immigrants and the presence of a Catholic financial elite that is determined to make its mark on cultural, economic, and political life through its own "business turn" that merges faith with corporate influence.

Studies of Protestant wealth, beginning with sociologist E. Digby Baltzell's *The Protestant Establishment* in 1964, have indexed American prosperity and success among the nation's WASP elite.[5] (Indeed, Baltzell popularized the acronym, and charted the WASP elite's characteristic anti-Semitism while mostly ignoring Catholics.) Catholics received slight notice in his preceding volume on the social elite of Philadelphia, where Baltzell wrote of the descendants of mostly English and Welsh settlers: "Glancing back to the turn of the century, when a flood tide of immigrants came to these shores from southern and eastern Europe, to say nothing of the Irish Catholics who came earlier, one wonders if this American democracy has not produced somewhat of a caste situation at the upper-class level. Or are the talented and powerful descendants of the immigrants going to be assimilated into some future upper class way of life and social organization?"[6]

No Baltzell has emerged to put American Catholic elites under a microscope, although there has been increased attention to the relationship between spirituality and the marketplace.[7] Post-assimilation Catholic wealth has been understudied in the past half century, and it hardly registers as a category in scholarship. Search the indexes of scores of narrative histories of American Catholics in vain for entries on affluence, attitudes toward wealth, or millionaires and billionaires.[8] By focusing here on the beliefs and activities of a cohort of Catholic top-tier earners, I aim to consider how Catholic cultures in the United States have changed due to the presence of a very successful elite and its embrace of the secular marketplace and its "rules." Instead of a narrative of triumph through hard work, or tales of ups and downs on the rungs of the corporate ladder, America now has many exemplars of such individuals and families who enjoy the success of previous generations, who have more than succeeded, and who have perhaps lost connections to their ancestors' working-class or even middle-class status.

Does the situation of contemporary Catholics present an unexpected twist on the Weberian thesis of a work ethic and capitalism? Today's Catholic CEOs—the Busches, Hannas, Langones, Monaghans, and others—offer persuasive evidence that Weber was wrong about the entrepreneurial energies of Catholics. But at the same time, has religion been the price for their upward mobility? Do they embody Weber's conviction that secularization follows upon capitalist success? Perhaps not. These wealthy Catholics protest the Protestantization of Catholic culture and speak of a "tsunami of secularism"[9] inundating the nation, but their own Catholicism remains intact, although out of date—derived from Tridentine piety, it is the very type that was superseded by the documents of Vatican II, and is linked to conservative politics. Still, this new Catholic elite imagines its select role as infusing the business world with Catholic principles.

Further, these select Catholics illustrate standard theories of class formation and maintenance—the myriad ways in which rich Americans scheme with each other by founding institutes and adding legitimacy to their economic dominance by attaching powerful leaders (clergy and conservative intellectuals) to shape electoral and economic policies that favor them. It seems a contradictory situation: that rich Catholics in America now represent Protestant (and even libertarian) principles to a relentless degree, despite the anti-Calvinist pre–Vatican II piety that they seem to prefer, and despite the more progressive elements of Catholic social teachings that have inspired the faithful since the 1890s, but which some wealthy Catholics are trying now to reclaim for conservatives.

There is a gap in Catholic historiography about religion and personal wealth, a topic that has been treated more often by Protestants, perhaps due to the impact of Weber's thesis and the dominant position of Protestants in colonial and early American history that led to capital accumulation and their consolidation as an upper class. By contrast, Catholics, in the accounts of some Catholic historians, have held a countercultural position favoring the need to prioritize the common good rather than to seek personal gain at all costs. Against Weber's view of Catholics as lazy, disorganized, and unable to work incessantly, a living insider's critique of Catholics may offer a better explanation: Catholics, from the outset in the early twentieth century, were liberal *only* on economic issues, and remained conservative on moral and cultural ones.[10] This claim would explain rich Catholics' obsession with the free market and antiabortion measures at the same time, reflecting a mixed outlook on the proper role of the state in both economic and private matters. That contradiction aside, wealthy Catholics do not seem puzzled by claims that the age of "core beliefs" has ended, as they remain tied to an essentialist view of Catholic tradition that fails to reflect post–Vatican II doctrine and that is now staging new conflicts with the current pope, Francis I (born Jorge Mario Bergoglio in Argentina in 1936).

As historians of religion and of American society have demonstrated, Irish Roman Catholics are second only to Jews in terms of their economic success as immigrants to the United States, despite their initial exclusion from the economic and social mainstream by Protestants.[11] Moving forward one century, to the 2000s, this chapter investigates several dimensions of Catholic history that are challenged by the presence of an affluent, even super-rich Catholic elite in the United States, many of whom trace their ancestry to Ireland. To evaluate the impact of very affluent Catholics upon America, I shall first address the formation of networks of Catholic corporate wealth represented by two recently created organizations: Legatus and the Napa Institute. Next, I shall evaluate their attempts to affect higher education through the foundation of research facilities dedicated to espousing a neoliberal economic creed in hopes of producing future generations of like-minded Catholics.

Legatus, an organization for corporate executives to help them "influence the world marketplace," and its allied associations (such as its college outreach arm, called FOCUS), have existed since 1987, when they were created by Thomas S. Monaghan (b. 1937), the former head of Domino's Pizza. The Napa Institute, established in 2011 by a Legatus member, culls an even more elite segment of rich Catholics. Legatus emerged after Monaghan sold Domino's Pizza in 1998 to Bain Capital (founded by Bill Bain and Mitt Romney in 1984 as a private equity firm. With new income and time, Monaghan intended to focus on

advocacy, especially of prolife causes. He has been involved with Operation
Rescue, Right to Life, and Priests for Life.[12] Soon after he went on to create
a political action committee (PAC) called the Ave Maria List to target elec-
toral campaigns. The Center for Public Integrity reported that in 2002 this
PAC, through a second group, gave 100 percent of its money to Republican
candidates.[13] Monaghan has also founded a conservative Catholic school,
Ave Maria University, then moved it from Michigan to its own Florida town,
which he intended to control; a law school was likewise moved from Ann
Arbor to Ave Maria's southern campus. Because the law school had failed in
Michigan and was ranked last in many national categories of educational eval-
uation, its existence as a competitive school of law has not been promising.[14]
The university itself offers majors in a variety of fields, including business/
management, as well as Catholic Studies, whose curriculum, as listed on the
institution's website, leans heavily toward theological topics, with courses
in ancient and medieval theology more typical of a seminary—Augustine,
triune God, sacraments, Thomas Aquinas, and electives in Scholastic Latin
texts. The Catholic studies major is "aligned" with *Ex Corde Ecclesiae*, the
controversial 1990 apostolic constitution of Pope John Paul II that led many
Catholic institutions to dispute the pope's attempt at intellectual control
of the Church through academic life and his conflation of "the intellectual
search for truth" with adherence to Catholic doctrine. The most galling feature, according to defenders of academic freedom, was the requirement that
all theological faculty at Catholic schools obtain a *mandatum* from the local
bishop establishing their fitness to teach Catholic principles. Among other
things, *Ex Corde Ecclesiae* mandated that a majority of Catholic school faculty members be Catholic, and that all members of its governing boards be
committed to its Catholic identity. Ave Maria has embraced the document
without question and has thoroughly endorsed its ideology along traditionalist lines. For example, its economics major includes the study of Catholic
social teaching, but only as mediated by conservative thinkers George Weigel
and Michael Novak.

Monaghan's goal with Legatus (the name means "ambassador") is to organize Catholic business leaders as "ambassadors for Christ in the marketplace."
This cohort, who must qualify to be invited to join, is meant to reflect upon
"how Catholic truth and values can help you meet the ethical challenges
you face on a daily basis." The group's activities and outlooks are chronicled
in detail in the association's monthly magazine, also called *Legatus*, which
sports on its masthead the slogan "To serve God and money." In its pages,
predictably, are articles touting the wonders of the market, but the ideology

that emerges from its other columns suggests an organization that believes Americans are engaged in culture wars against Islam, secularism, and an "advancing Culture of Death."[15] Advertisements in its pages suggest that it *is* possible to serve God and money, by investing in Ave Maria Mutual Funds. To its credit, the June 2016 issue of *Legatus* included one article on entrepreneurship that attempted to address corporate responsibility toward employees and society, in light of Milton Friedman's claim in an often-cited article in the *New York Times Magazine* in 1970 that only profits matter to businesses in a free society. The author suggested that in addition, corporations should consider other elements in their mission statements, including the three elements of "creating, supporting, and rewarding" not only the owners but also customers and employees.[16] Following the bank collapses, credit crisis, and real estate crash of 2008, at least one article in *Legatus* argued for business ethics to avoid becoming "a hollow exercise in compliance to avoid legal liability."[17]

Following the visit of Pope Francis to the United States in September 2015, *Legatus* made the comparison between the pope's expressed concern for the poor and that of his namesake, St. Francis of Assisi, but went on to reassure readers, "Of course, there is nothing intrinsically wrong with expensive suits and spacious offices; they have a legitimate place in most corporate cultures."[18] Reminders that although you may be super-rich, you deserve what you have, have become constant in the magazine's pages, and even more so since the election of Pope Francis in 2013.

Legatus is largely the product of Patrick Novecosky, a western Canadian who has been the magazine's editor in chief since 2005. He now resides in Naples, Florida, one of the places that has attracted Catholic corporate leaders and their families, as well as Catholic retirees, and is a member of St. Agnes parish, established only in 2007. The Diocese of Venice, Florida, established in 1984, where St. Agnes is located, is growing quickly, adding parishes from corporate retirement havens where wealthy Catholics are clustered and from new suburban developments in southwest Florida. The diocese is also home to Ave Maria University, carved out of Corkscrew Swamp some twenty miles from Naples. The university has a quasi-parish oratory on its campus—the startling 100-foot-high building resembles a huge Quonset hut that towers over the flat Florida landscape.[19]

In its public face, the diocese of Venice has opposed the Affordable Care Act and gay marriage, and now focuses on defending Catholics' "religious freedom." These events signal a distinctly conservative tone emanating from the present bishop, Frank J. Dewane, installed in 2007, which is duly reflected in many of the Catholic institutions of central and southwest Florida. Local Catholics have not been pleased by Dewane's performance, however. In August 2014 Catholics involved with Call to Action, a progressive movement founded in 1976, were fed up with the bishop's regime and sent a letter to Pope Francis and to the apostolic nuncio exposing and protesting Dewane's bullying and oppressive behavior. Voice of the Faithful, the lay Catholic group founded in 2001 in response to revelations of sexual abuse by American Catholic clergy, also expressed its concerns about Dewane in a letter, as did ten priests in the diocese, in a gesture that is highly unusual for Catholics.[20] Appraising Dewane in business terms as "a man who operates more like a CEO of a large corporation than the shepherd of his community," the Call to Action letter had hundreds of signatures. In addition, opponents collected stories of abuse at the hands of the bishop of Venice, along with revelations of his lavish expenditures on his own mansion, his "outbursts of anger and sexism directed at students," cuts to the Catholic Charities budget, and firings of dozens of chancery employees who had reported sexual predators; all these created a hostile climate. The issue has yet to be resolved. Vatican officials initially made no response to the letters, but the nuncio was dismissed by Pope Francis in 2016, and there may be some progress made under the newly appointed nuncio.[21] In the meantime, the Venice diocesan website has made no mention of the conflict, and continues its round of reporting on every homily or speech delivered by Bishop Dewane as though nothing has changed. Ironically, Bishop Dewane has been obliged to alter his tone and message on some issues. In January, 2017 Dewane, now serving as Chair of the USCCB Committee on Domestic Justice and Human Development, sent a letter to Congress recommending against repeal of the Affordable Care Act, which the USCCB had previously opposed.

Tom Monaghan's enormous success in starting a corporation based upon the novelty of selling pizza through a delivery service, combined with his insistence on his Catholicity in the establishment of Legatus, calls to mind another founding member of that organization, a member of another powerful Irish Catholic entrepreneurial family whose wealth has compounded exponentially over the past 160 years: Joseph Peter Grace Jr. (1913–1995), of the Grace Corporation. Now headquartered in Columbia, Maryland, the Grace Corporation was founded in 1854 in Peru, where it produced fertilizers and gunpowder; it later moved its operations to New York City and added machinery, shipping, and banking concerns there to connect its South American imports to America markets. William Russell Grace, an emigré who fled the Irish famine, was the founder of W. R. Grace and Company, renamed Grace Brothers and Company when his brother joined him. Beginning as a merchant shipping and trading firm, today it functions as a chemical conglomerate with annual sales topping $2.5 billion. Unmasked as a ruthless and destructive entity by journalist Penny Lernoux in her study of North American versus Latin American public policy, the Grace family did not appear in a saintly or even ethical light.[22] The grandson of the founders, J. Peter Grace Jr., took over the business in 1945 when his father had a stroke, and ran it for forty-seven years. J. Peter was deeply influenced by the Irish Marian fanatic Father Patrick Peyton, whom he had met on a ship in 1946 and who impressed him by his holiness and his international Marian crusade. (In South America, Peyton's missionary work also attracted the attention of the CIA, which secretly funded the Rosary Crusade there.) After World War II, however, J. Peter Grace was involved in a darker crusade, called Project Paperclip, a CIA program to purge classified information from the dossiers of more than fifteen hundred German SS members and Nazi scientists (mostly in rocketry, aeronautics, medicine, and electronics) so that they could emigrate to the United States.[23] The Grace company hired some of them, and employed at least one chemist who had been convicted of war crimes at Nuremburg.[24] Under J. Peter Grace's tenure, the chemical company diversified further and developed several new separate divisions, including specialized health care.

Most recently, Grace Corporation emerged in February 2014 from a thirteen-year bankruptcy case stemming from claims of asbestos poisoning by residents of Libby, Montana.[25] Although the firm was acquitted of charges of knowingly exposing citizens to the hazardous substance and is no longer in the asbestos business, its reputation suffered. In the 1980s Grace had also been charged with contaminating groundwater in several sites in Massachusetts by improperly dumping carcinogenic chemicals. Grace Corporation represented the ruthless face of American transnational business in the Western Hemisphere from the 1950s to the 1990s. J. Peter Grace's religious activities, including service as president of the Catholic Youth Organization of the Archdiocese of New York, and his work with other charities seem like appendices to his executive career and a life of comfort and wealth. His connection to the strongly devotional style of the preconciliar church, via Father Peyton's Marianism, is reprised in Legatus by the members' absorption with pilgrimages and Catholic relics, which led them in 2010 to Oberammergau, Germany (the birthplace of Pope Benedict XVI), to see the passion play, and is echoed in the annual trips of the Napa Institute, which sponsored a private visitation to the shrine at Guadalupe, Mexico, among others.[26] For these Catholics, such events may fulfill the ascetic component of the Weber thesis, which under-girds and energizes the rational work ethic in capitalism.

To receive an invitation to join Legatus, one must be a business leader at the highest levels, not merely a branch manager or a franchise owner.[27] Attorney Tim Busch, for example, cofounder of the Napa Institute (discussed below), has belonged to Legatus since 1990. He describes its activities as a "game-changer" in his life, involving monthly meetings and the intention to make Mass, the sacraments, and the Rosary part of daily life.[28] The monthly chapter meetings, which include opportunities for the sacrament of reconciliation (still called "confession" here), Mass, and an inspirational lecture, are described by Monaghan as the "heart" of the Legatus experience.[29] As with the Napa Institute, Legatus members defend their financial principles, finding them worthwhile guides to their religious ones. Busch, for one, describes the free market system as "proven" to be the best in the world: "In places that are adopting free-market capitalism, we see people being raised out of poverty. That doesn't mean that there isn't more to do, but that capitalism creates an environment in which the ordinary person is most likely to prosper."[30] To that end, Legatus proudly reported on the founding of a new chapter in Austin, Texas, despite its reputation as "a solid blue city in a red state."[31] In Colorado, however, "the founding president of the Denver Legatus Chapter, John Saeman, and his wife, Carol, raised eyebrows in late November when they penned a *Washington Post* op-ed that said their belief in Pope Francis's vision of Catholic social teaching motivates their activities in Catholic charities and also motivates their financial support for Freedom Partners, a nonprofit founded by billionaires Charles and David Koch to defend the free market system."[32] That Catholic millionaires would support the Koch brothers represents the consolidating power of capitalism to unite the dominant class in the present day. Likewise Tim Busch has expressed admiration for the Koch brothers, who are partners in his donation to the business school at Catholic University, while they in return claim to admire Catholic social teaching.

When asked about Catholics he admires, Tim Busch named Carl Karcher (1917–2008), a Catholic farm boy from Ohio and a political conservative who founded the fast-food hamburger chain Carl's Jr. Like Busch, Karcher, father of twelve children, spent most of his life in affluent Orange County, California. In 1978 Karcher became newsworthy as the largest donor in the effort to enact Proposition 6 (the Briggs Initiative) in California, legislation that would have banned gays and lesbians from employment in California's public schools. In 1989 Karcher paid a large settlement to the Securities and Exchange Commission in response to accusations of insider trading that benefited six family members immediately before the announcement of a 50 percent company loss.[33]

The Legatus summit meeting of 2015 illustrated that Catholic business leaders such as Karcher and Busch continue to form similar alliances with political and economic conservatives, regardless of their moral shortcomings: attending the meeting were Bobby Jindal, governor of Louisiana, who proposed deep tax cuts for state businesses despite already low rates, and Mike Huckabee, both of whom were at the time Republican candidates for president; Pam Stenzel, an abstinence-only activist who attended Jerry Falwell's Liberty University and frightens students with false information about birth control; and Cardinal Archbishop Timothy Dolan of New York, who, in his previous position in the archdiocese of Milwaukee, hid $59 million in a trust fund to prevent it from claimants of clerical sexual abuse.

At the moment, it appears that future of these Catholic procapitalist ventures hinges upon their willingness to embrace the welcoming and forgiving tone of Pope Francis on moral and social issues, and on the brewing debate over their founders' interpretation of Catholic social teaching in terms of business ethics and protection of labor and the environment. Legatus and the Napa Institute have made various efforts to spin *Rerum Novarum* for its 125th anniversary, although working conditions are much different now, in a global economy, than they were in 1891—a key difference that has not been clearly acknowledged. While the two organizations have endorsed the message of *Centesimus Annus* (1991), in which Pope John Paul II was kindhearted to capitalism, they are having a hard time with Pope Francis's latest documents, *Evangelii Gaudium* (2013) and *Laudato Si* (2015). Catholic Legatus members or those who support the Napa Institute are Americanized to the degree that they possess a thoroughly ethnocentric perspective on the economic systems being attacked or supported by popes, but, lacking any actual experience of socialism or communism, they are unable to imagine any alternatives to neoliberal capitalism. Without alternatives, Catholic elites and their families encounter and defend nothing but a gung-ho market mentality and their belief in its inevitability.

How will their free marketeering fit with today's secularized, post-Puritan patterns of self-valorization? Michael Budde, in his 1992 study *The Two Churches: Catholicism and Capitalism in the World-System*, pointed out that while John Paul II's *Centesimus Annus* gave a much stronger nod to capitalism than the prior papal documents that form Catholic social teaching, "the encyclical's impact on the Church will largely hinge on how effectively pro-capitalist groups employ it as a technological cudgel, and by whether its intellectual and ecclesial positions are adopted by John Paul's successors."[34] With Pope Francis, the answer is a clear no.

The second organization for well-heeled Catholics, the Napa Institute, was inspired directly by Legatus, but it is a much more ideologically driven organization that has taken up the procapitalist banner. Cofounded in 2011 by Legatus member Timothy R. Busch, founder of the Busch Firm which specializes in high net-worth estate planning and CEO of the Pacific Hospitality Group, which owns luxury hotels and resorts, and Robert Spitzer, a Jesuit priest, it is presently headed by Mike Brumley, the president of Ignatius Press.[35] (The press was founded by Father Joseph Fessio S. J. in 1978 to print and reprint titles espousing traditionalist Catholicism. The Jesuit Order does not endorse it, and Fessio has been reprimanded numerous times by his California province, most notably in 2002 when he launched a traditionalist Catholic college next door to the Jesuit-run University of San Francisco. Fessio was ordered to "have no role, public or private" at what became Campion College.[36]) The Napa Institute is overseen by a cadre of conservative American Catholic bishops, led by its ecclesiastical advisor, Charles Chaput, archbishop of Philadelphia. The institute focuses on defending Catholic principles in the public arena,[37] and allies itself with groups such as the National Organization of Marriage and the Papal Foundation (whose members must have given at least $1 million to the papacy over the course of a decade). Since 2011 the institute has held its annual assembly at one of Pacific Hospitality's California holdings, Meritage, a four-star resort connected with a vineyard also owned by Tim Busch. Busch, who has resided in Orange County, California, since 1982, grew up near Detroit, son of the founder of a chain of upmarket groceries in Michigan. After finishing law school he relocated to southern California.

The institute's website, napa-institute.org, contains a wealth of information about its intentions, strategic plan, members, and conferences. The site's masthead proclaims that it is "Equipping Catholics in the 'Next America,'" which might be mistaken for an alliance with America's futurists. The notion of preparing for the "next America" turns out to be a peculiar turn of phrase meaning that the members seek a return to the past as a weapon against the fearsome onslaught of secularism—never mind that secularism has been alive and well for at least five hundred years, since the Renaissance.

Since 2010 the Napa Institute has hosted an annual conference in California. The July gatherings feature programs of all-male speakers on a variety of topics, spun in traditionalist ways, with the aim of promoting limited government and preventing regulation that would impede their allegiance to the rhetoric of free markets. Its clerical patrons are ultraconservatives in the American hierarchy, such as Archbishop Chaput and Archbishop Salvatore Cordileone of San Francisco, both highly divisive leaders who devote themselves to opposing same-sex marriage, defending heterosexual marriage, and, in the latter's case, trying to control the private lives of parochial-school teachers through the language of their work contracts. The video that introduces the Napa Institute on its website prominently features clergy in their religious garb, making the sign of the cross, delivering sermons, and speaking about the need for ethical behavior. Nuns appear in full pre–Vatican II habits. Everyone speaks earnestly about the value of the Napa Institute's role.

The phrase "the next America" was used first by Archbishop Chaput in a 2010 article in the conservative journal *First Things* that helped catalyze the Napa Institute. However, instead of suggesting ways for the rich to serve the poor by dealing with the crying social injustices of the moment, which seems a logical target of potential philanthropists, the goals of the Napa Institute are to "defend Catholic principles," such as traditional marriage, the unborn, and "religious freedom"—the last being a charged category that has lately been used by the rich and powerful to represent themselves as victims of cultural attacks, including attacks upon their faithful Catholicism.

What the Napa Institute offers its members, beyond what Legatus has attempted, is personal access to powerful prelates, and vice versa.[38] For instance, in 2014 two cardinals and more than a dozen archbishop and bishops attended its annual conference. No doubt all of them benefited from financial gifts from the Napa Institute attendees, who received something in return. In April 2016, for example, cofounder Timothy Busch was honored in Rome by the North American College, alongside the just-dismissed papal nuncio Archbishop Carlo Maria Viganò, at a $450-a-plate dinner. Viganò had been speedily removed by Pope Francis as papal nuncio to the United States after the nuncio had arranged for the pope to meet Kim Davis, the Kentucky county clerk who refused to authorize a same-sex marriage certificate as an exercise of her First Amendment rights, at the very end of the pope's five-day American visit in September 2015. That meeting with Davis, hastily executed and widely regarded with horror by progressive Catholics, turned out to be a maneuver planned by Viganò and Rick Santorum, a conservative Catholic ex-senator from Pennsylvania with Republican presidential ambitions.[39]

The choice of Busch for the North American College's dinner indicates the conservative tit-for-tat relationship between rich Catholics and the bishops who have been accustomed to running things in the United States, at least during the papacies of John Paul II and Benedict XVI. The group's new relationship with Pope Francis is surfacing many tensions, given that Francis's positions on the economy and on the social inequality stemming from it explicitly reject their free market worldview. At the 2014 Napa Institute annual conference, the sumptuous surroundings conflicted conspicuously with the pope's criticism of free market economics and the self-congratulating behaviors of the rich. Pope Francis's 2013 exhortation, *Evangelii Gaudium*, criticized any economic system that "tends to devour everything which stands in the way of increased profits." Napa Institute members were clearly unhappy with the message, and some conference speakers tried to minimize the importance of the pope's message for them by subsuming Francis's words to those of previous popes who were less critical of capitalism. Napa commentators have strained to make their interpretations of the remarks and writings of Pope Francis reassure the wealthy that they need not change their attitudes or behavior.[40] The group has recently partnered with television (the conservative Catholic Eternal Word Television Network, or EWTN) and print media (EWTN purchased *the National Catholic Register*) to reach as many Catholics as possible. If the Napa Institute group constitutes the Catholic 1 percenters of the contemporary United States, they were surely well represented among the 366 people attending the 2015 conference.

Not surprisingly, perennial Catholic conservative George Weigel is on Napa's board of directors. A longtime "distinguished senior fellow" of the Ethics and Public Policy Center, and an apologist for the compatibility of Catholicism and capitalism, Weigel writes a weekly column that reflects views shared by many members of the Napa Institute. In a March 11, 2016 posting, after condemning the reputations of Hillary Clinton and Bernie Sanders (at the time the leading contenders for the 2016 Democratic presidential nomination), Weigel portentously announced that America would benefit from a reconstructed political culture leavened by "Catholic social doctrine," the very element of the postconciliar Catholic Church that Weigel regularly ignores and willfully misinterprets. His vision of Catholic social teaching could not be further from what is being said by Pope Francis, and Weigel's discernible mission is to reassure the rich, not to comfort the poor. The Pope, on the other hand, has stated clearly that "some people continue to defend trickle-down theories which assume that economic growth, encouraged by a free market, will inevitably succeed in bringing about greater justice and inclusiveness in the world. This opinion, which has never been confirmed by the facts, expresses a crude and naïve trust in the goodness of those wielding economic power and in the sacralized workings of the prevailing economic system. Meanwhile, the excluded are still waiting."[41] Despite the pope's clear-cut message of "no to a financial system which rules rather than serves," Archbishop Chaput heard something else; he asked his Napa Institute audience, "What concretely does Francis believe about economic justice? He's never offered his systematic thoughts about it or the policies that promote it. And, frankly, we can sense some ambiguity in this thinking."[42]

In March 2016, at Catholic University's new Busch Business School, the Napa Institute celebrated the 125th anniversary of *Rerum Novarum,* which is regarded as the first papal document to treat the labor question and income inequality. It also recognized the twenty-fifth anniversary of Pope John Paul II's encyclical *Centesimus Annus.* At a three-day conference, perversely, the Napa program included no representatives of labor and no workers, and it discussed no issues involving actual work. The goal of the conference seemingly was to commandeer the tradition of Catholic social teaching in defense of the laissez-faire principles and entitlement of Napa Institute members, now bending in a libertarian direction. For the same anniversary, Tim Busch offered a guest piece in *Forbes* about "reviving Catholic principles in business," speaking of the great chance to apply Christian principles to the economy through the Catholic University business and economics school that he funded. Yet in 2016, even the task of defining and identifying who is a "worker" is a problem. In the service sector, which has increasingly dominated growth in the American economy during the past forty years, many Americans work without the expectation of protections from labor unions, are obliged to work abusively long hours, and must endure the isolation of an each-worker-for-himself attitude. These workers have been treated more and more like a commodity. The service sector is expected to account for nearly 80 percent of all American jobs and output by 2018, as opposed to the former dominance of manufacturing or agriculture. To give one telling statistic from 2014, "in 1939 the services to manufacturing employment ratio was 2.1:1. Today it is 9.9-to-1."[43]

Even with the impact of the economic recession in 2008, more and more jobs are located in service sector fields where wealthy Catholics are already well represented as CEOs: financial and business activities, health care, leisure and hospitality, and management. Hence, while they are the first to cite Pope Leo XIII's defense of private property as the cornerstone of society, Napa Institute Catholics have little contact with actual laborers and the working class, and regard papal messages mostly as defenses of private ownership and unregulated "freedom in the economic sector." They do not see a problem with the neoliberal economic claim that the free market protects individual freedoms, because they have not been on the losing end of that economy. Furthermore, such discussions of business ethics at conferences held by Catholic business leaders seemingly depend upon an older, paternalistic family-firm model, in which the owner knows all his employees, rather than the globalized corporations and widely dispersed (and often feminized) workforces that define today's economy. The disparity between the two models might explain the mismatch between the rhetoric of morality and ethics so ardently idealized by Napa Institute members and so imperfectly realized in daily life.

Richard Marens, for one, has argued that Catholic social teaching could be effective during the nineteenth century because it addressed the visible employer-worker relationship in an industrializing Europe dominated by a Catholic working class. In the late twentieth century, Pope John Paul II "moved beyond Leo's somewhat paternal focus on the relationship between worker and employer" to address a far different stage of capitalism: postindustrial, global, anonymous. If the church fails to convincingly address this stage, Marens argues, there will be less incentive for business leaders to follow Catholic social teachings, even when they find them appealing.[44] Furthermore, while it could exhort employers to treat their workers more fairly, the Church can no longer establish the rules of the game in a world of global corporations. One portion of its social teaching leaned toward nostalgia for the feudal, agrarian past, spawning communal projects by groups such as the Catholic Worker (especially the contributions of Peter Maurin and the creation of self-sustaining farms), as well as mildly progressive reforms for industrial labor, focusing on unionism, insurance, health regulations, and a living wage.

Together, Legatus and the Napa Institute suggest two variant directions being pursued by wealthy American Catholics—business leadership in Legatus, and the overt shaping of policy by Napa—as they understand their role in the economy and in terms of Catholic doctrine as presented by papal teaching, at least until the installation of Pope Francis. The Napa Institute, as I have noted, consists of supremely rich Catholics who try to connect their devotional style of Catholic piety—sponsored pilgrimage trips with prominent conservative clergy to visit famous relics—to their mission of "education, adoration, and networking." Through Napa's gatherings they meet like-minded people in business with the aim of creating "one of the greatest apologetic conferences in the world." Ironically, although Napa members are more financially secure than most American citizens, they represent themselves as victims, pronouncing Christianity as under attack from the challenge of atheism, immigration, and secular materialism while they paint themselves as advocates for fellow Catholic victims of these social forces. In addition to considering these two organizations as models of recent developments for rich Catholics, I turn now to a discussion of the synergy between such groups and corporate capitalism, to highlight their intentions to shape Catholic higher education, the training ground for tomorrow's elites.

Catholic conservative groups have made strenuous efforts here. Catholic schools (from elementary school through university levels) were once thought to be a bulwark against the loss of Catholic identity. Indeed, the Catholic parochial school system was created precisely to address the needs of immigrants. Catholic colleges and universities did likewise, but now these schools perform the recruiting functions for corporate capital formerly attributed to the WASP establishment. The earnest graduates of Catholic schools in accounting, finance, management, and marketing are being taught to be just as ruthless and profit-minded as their peers in secular institutions. Despite the inclusion of rhetoric by Catholic higher education about morals-based learning, if rich Catholics believe in these claims by Catholic institutions, then why do many of them send their children to secular institutions, particularly the top-ranked Ivy League schools?

Between 2012 and 2014 the Napa Institute organized three symposia that revealed how it intends to shape Catholic higher education. In partnership with Catholic University's new Tim and Steph Busch School of Business and Economics, the Institute hosted an invitation-only gathering themed "Liberty and Solidarity: A Conference on Catholic Social Doctrine and the Economy" on the university's campus in Washington, D.C., in September 2014. Speakers included the business school's dean, Andrew Abela, who emphasized the economic value of the family. Cardinal Peter Turkson (b. 1948), a Ghanaian who is president of the Pontifical Council for Justice and Peace, was also present.[45] In other settings since the conference in which he has reflected on Pope Francis's encyclical letter, *Laudato Si*, Turkson has been unsparingly critical of Catholic neoconservatives. One commentator noted the contrast between the pope's approach and Turkson's speeches, and the lack of interest in justice in the conduct of business by Legatus and the Napa Institute.[46] The latter's approach still reflects a stockholder mentality, which defines success as the highest return on investment, versus a shareholder model for success, which rewards all who are involved in the venture on the basis of their common interests.

The prime example of wealthy Catholics investing in promoting their procapitalist, antiregulation business ideology, the Busch School of Business and Economics, established in 2013, enrolls mostly undergraduates at present. The $47 million donation from the Busches and others is the largest in Catholic University's history. The couple has also made a separate $15 million gift to aid the business school. The Koch Brothers Foundation has given $1 million in support of the university's call for research in "principled entrepreneurship." There has been a lot of publicized resistance against the Busch and Koch monies, generated by faculty, staff, and others connected with the university.[47] Tim Busch claims that he wants to revive Catholic social teaching in business practices, but his version of it is not recognizable in most Catholic circles, while the methods of the Koch brothers have directly opposed many principles at the core of Catholic social teaching, such as care for the environment (Koch Industries has a terrible environmental record and the brothers fund many organizations that deny climate change); support for the rights of workers to have union representation and to employ collective bargaining (most recently the Koch brothers generously funded Governor Scott Walker's plan in Wisconsin to strip public employees of those things); and support for programs that help the poor and vulnerable (the Koch brothers' political agent, Americans for Prosperity, has fought Medicaid expansion in several states, which is intended to help the working poor, pregnant women, disabled Americans, and the elderly living in nursing homes).[48]

The question of political influence and financial power over universities is one place where the interventions of the wealthy are an obvious attempt to eliminate any barriers to their personal and corporate financial profits for generations to come. But a parallel shift has happened within Catholic higher education that may be abetting these targeted donations from the Koch brothers, the Busches and others. The decline of the liberal arts, which were traditionally central to the mission of Catholic institutions, may be one marker of Catholic disinterest in academic disciplines that are perceived as not profitable for employment prospects and therefore not attractive to today's students. Catholic schools have been asking themselves why more students opt for undergraduate majors in economics and finance than classics and theology. The answer is that students apparently believe in the promise of a secure job following from those majors, and also that they are respond to pressures from parents who are footing the large tuition bills for their college attendance. Of the eleven largest Catholic colleges and universities in the United States, whose enrollments range from 12,000 to 29,000 students, all have business schools. While some programs are older, like that of St. Louis University, which dates from 1910, or Notre Dame's, from 1921, others are more recent, like that of Regis University in Denver, which just established its business school in 2015. In that year, 182 Catholic colleges and universities offered business degree programs. There are 184 management programs at the same institutions, and at least 127 programs in marketing.[49]

One dimension of Catholic conservative outreach has been to convince Catholic students to attend only Catholic schools, where the rhetoric of "Catholic values" is cited to add value or appeal. While it has often been the richest conservative Catholics demanding that Catholic institutions to define themselves increasingly as "orthodox," they have tended to understand orthodoxy primarily as limited to issues of sexual morality, leaving the arena of economic justice ignored. Economic, gender, and racial justice issues have generally been neglected in these conversations, which may help account for the flourishing of undergraduate majors and graduate programs in business, as they pose no challenges to faith.

Using the present moment as an opportunity to assess the cultural and political influence of a very assimilated affluent Catholic population in America has suggested several forces at work: first, that the American identities represented by the very rich Catholics, nicknamed "neo-Catholics" by one author, rather than opposing Weber's notion of a Protestant work ethic, directly parallel the ideology of successful Protestants in a capitalist economy.[50] The wealthy in both Christian traditions support free market principles, lower taxes on the rich, and conservatism as embodied in the Republican Party, and they have even spawned libertarian factions hoping to do away with pesky government interference and regulation as well as gut state-funded programs to fight poverty and help immigrants. On the one hand, big-money Catholics of the twenty-first century may represent merely the latest version of American conservatism with a religious tinge, playing the same role as Opus Dei or the Knights of Malta did for Catholics in previous American decades and administrations. As Catholics have moved further and further from their immigrant origins and their minority status in America, assimilation has increased conservative emphases among Catholic elites while decreasing their affective bonds to less affluent citizens. On the other hand, the formation of new groups such as Legatus and the Napa Institute make use of WASP tactics that have long proved effective for the dominant classes: the use of economic power to fund political candidates who support them, the control of media to push their message, and the establishment of research centers and institutes to promote their dedication to one economic theory and model. In fact, many of the Catholics discussed above applaud the single-minded focus of the Koch brothers and have even modeled their organizations upon them, rather than looking to Catholic associations and traditions that might also provide inspiration.

Like conservative American Protestants, wealthy Catholics are founding and endowing foundations, institutes, and research centers, and making business connections via invitation-only private organizations created to applaud themselves. Their associations foster economic libertarianism but work to destroy legislation and advocates of labor and of the poor. There is seemingly little difference between this cohort of very affluent Catholics and conservative groups such as the Koch brothers' Americans for Prosperity, the American Enterprise Institute (whose president, Arthur C. Brooks, is a Catholic), the Olin and Scaife Foundations, and the so-called "Koch network," which now includes, along with Charles and David Koch, Catholics Tim Busch and Kenneth Langone (b. 1935), the co-founder of Home Depot, who is among the richest Americans, with a net worth of over $2 billion.[51] Like conservative Republican elites, Langone has worked, most recently as a director of Yum! Brands fast food corporation, to prevent an increase of the minimum wage and the unionization of its employees and the farmworkers who provide the meals for Kentucky Fried Chicken and Taco Bell.[52] The Koch brothers have joined Catholic elites in giving money to Catholic University, and they have provided Catholics with a template for influencing U.S. politics through their financing of political and policy organizations, especially free market groups, including their notorious American Legislative Exchange Council (ALEC), the Cato Institute, and the Mercatus Center at George Mason University in Fairfax, Virginia. The Koch brothers, as funders of the Tea Party and ALEC, have influenced the growing libertarian sentiment among wealthy Catholics.[53] A Catholic neoliberalism seems the predictable result of the emphatic embrace of the market ethic. The surprising election of Donald Trump as American President in November 2016, can only bring satisfaction to those Catholics in investing, insurance, and petrochemical industries who will gain financially from the potential dismantling of the Affordable Care Act and the elimination of many environmental and financial regulations, as promised by the candidate.[54] However, Trump's crony style of capitalism—rewarding family and allies while punishing dissident voices— does not mesh well with the morally-tinged "servant"-style capitalism that Catholic millionaires claim to represent. Moreover, Trump's contempt for the public sphere and of government-funded social welfare programs will target millions of Catholics who support them and have benefited from them for the last seventy years. Trump will also target immigration, impose limits, or bans on particular populations of immigrants, and generate fear toward

Catholic migrants, notably Mexicans, as well as Muslims. On the horizon, the prophetic voice of Pope Francis and the struggle among Catholics over the interpretation and implementation of Catholic social teaching will continue to provide challenges to the class privilege and political machinations of the American Catholic elite.

Notes

1. See Philip E. Hammond and Kirk R. Williams, "The Protestant Ethic Thesis: A Social-Psychological Assessment," *Social Forces* 54, no. 3 (1976): 579–589.
2. Paul J. Voss, "(Re)Introducing St. Homobonus of Cremona," *Legatus*, October 1, 2015.
3. Do not confuse my use and interpretation of Weber with that of Catholic conservative and Tea Party defender Samuel Gregg of the Acton Institute, who has written a biography of Maryland colonist Charles Carroll of Carrollton, the lone Catholic to sign the Declaration of Independence, claiming Carroll as the first Tea Party member. Samuel Gregg, *Tea Party Catholic: The Catholic Case for Limited Government, a Free Economy, and Human Flourishing* (New York: Crossroad Publishing, 2013).
4. Weber uses the term "elective affinity" three times in *The Protestant Ethic* and elsewhere in his other sociological writings. It implies the process by which two cultural entities enter into relationships that mutually reinforce each other.
5. E. Digby Baltzell, *The Protestant Establishment: Aristocracy and Caste in America* (New York: Random House, 1964). Baltzell was not an egalitarian social visionary. He lamented the "decline of authority in America in the twentieth century" (380), which to Baltzell meant the loss of an upper class who created standards to which "the rest of society aspires" (381). While admiring an elite leadership as vital to American society, Baltzell did admit that Anglo-Saxonism had lost its own authoritative reach when it excluded too many others "based on ethnic or racial ancestry" (382).
6. Baltzell, *The Protestant Establishment,* quoted on xiii.
7. For example, Craig Martin, *Capitalizing Religion: Ideology and the Opiate of the Bourgeoisie* (London: Bloomsbury, 2014); Jan Stievermann, Philip Goff, and Detlef Junker, eds., *Religion and the Marketplace in the United States* (New York: Oxford University Press, 2015). On Catholics between the 1890s and 1960s, two contrasting perspectives appear in David J. O'Brien, *American Catholics and Social Reform: The New Deal Years* (New York: Oxford University Press, 1968), who applauds progressive figures in Catholic social thought, and Kevin E. Schmiesing, who mostly ignores liberal and pro-labor Catholics to concentrate on conservatives, in *Within the Market Strife: Catholic Economic Thought from Rerum Novarum to Vatican II* (Lanham, MD: Lexington Books, 2004). For an account that includes the 1960s and discusses the ideological framing of both perspectives, see Craig R. Prentiss, *Debating God's Economy: Social Justice in America on the Eve of Vatican II* (University Park: Pennsylvania State University Press, 2010).

8. Some narrative histories telling this story include Jay P. Dolan, *The American Catholic Experience: A History from Colonial Times to the Present* (Garden City, NY: Doubleday, 1985); James J. Hennessey, *American Catholics: A History of the Roman Catholic Community in the United States* (New York: Oxford University Press, 1981); James M. O'Toole, *The Faithful: A History of Catholics in America* (Cambridge, MA: Belknap Press of Harvard University Press, 2008).

9. The phrase was used by Washington, D.C., Cardinal Archbishop Donald Wuerl, in his pastoral letter of May 2015. Lisa Bourne, "We Need Strong Catholic Identity to Face 'Tsunami of Secularism': Cardinal Wuerl," LifeSiteNews.com, May 20, 2015.

10. This is the contention of Peter Steinfels, the former "Beliefs" columnist for the *New York Times* and the former editor of *Commonweal* magazine.

11. See, for example, Charles R. Morris, *American Catholic: The Saints and Sinners Who Built America's Most Powerful Church* (New York: Times Books/Random House, 1997); and O'Toole, *The Faithful*.

12. On Bain Capital's nasty reputation and methods, see Matt Taibbi, "Greed and Debt: The True Story of Mitt Romney and Bain Capital," *Rolling Stone*, September 13, 2012. Taibbi claims that Romney heralded a seismic shift in American economics, where wealth is created out of transactions and takeover deals, which generate wealth only for the parties involved without generating any prosperity outside the deal, which is funded by taxpayer-subsidized debt.

13. Betty Clermont, *The Neo-Catholics: Implementing Christian Nationalism in America,* (Atlanta, GA: Clarity Press, 2009), last page of chap. 11 in unpaged Kindle edition. Clermont speculated that Catholics would soon replace evangelicals as conservative standard-bearers.

14. Mariah Blake, "How and Eccentric Right-Wing Pizza Billionaire's Attempt to Build Catholic Law School Ended in Disaster," *Alternet*, September 8, 2009. Ave Maria Law School hoped to train neoconservative lawyers for government jobs, especially during the administration of President George W. Bush.

15. Brian Fraga, "Ready, Set, Kill," *Legatus*, June 1, 2016. The article is an attack on parliamentary sponsored bills to permit euthanasia and assisted suicide in Canada.

16. Andreas Widmer, "Social Responsibility in the Corporate Context," *Legatus*, February 1, 2016.

17. John Della Costa, "Signs of Unsettling Times," *Legatus*, March 1, 2009. The author directs a Canadian consultancy group called the Centre for Ethical Orientation, based in Toronto.

18. Lance Richey, "A Tale of Two Francises," *Legatus*, November 2, 2015.

19. Thomas Monaghan engaged architect Fay(e) Jones (1921-2004) to design the Oratory. Jones was best known as an apprentice of Frank Lloyd Wright and as the creator of the striking Thorncrown Chapel (1980) in Eureka Springs, Arkansas.

20. Tom Roberts, "Priests' Letter to Nuncio Denounces Bishop," *National Catholic Reporter*, June 20–July 3, 2014.

21. The letter and many comments appear in "Stand Against Injustice in Florida Diocese," September 9, 2014, http://cta-usa.org/swfl/#.

22. Penny Lernoux, *People of God: The Struggle for World Catholicism* (New York: Penguin Books, 1990), 290–297. Lernoux relates Grace's power as a Catholic layman to his position as a Knight of Malta, with other like-minded anticommunist, anti-affirmative-action, antienvironmental, pro-Reagan Knights.

23. See Annie Jacobsen, *Operation Paperclip: The Secret Intelligence Program to Bring Nazi Scientists to America* (New York: Little, Brown, 2014). The best-known arrival from Germany was aerospace engineer Werner von Braun.

24. "J. Peter Grace, Ex-Company Chief, Dies at 81," *New York Times*, April 21, 1995.

25. A documentary film about the health crisis in Libby, Montana, attributed to the W. R. Grace Company's mining of vermiculite for its insulation product Zonolite, aired on the PBS show *P.O.V.* on August 28, 2007.

26. In September 2017 the Napa Institute "Counter-Reformation pilgrimage" will be a atrip to Spain and Fatima, Portugal, the center of an international Catholic ultraconservative movement related to the Marian shrine there. The Fatima cult is one of the founders of modern Catholic fundamentalism.

27. The initial requirement for Legatus membership was limited to CEOs or presidents of corporations that had at least 50 employees. Annual dues were $2500.

28. Jim Graves, "The Man Behind Catholic U's Largest Donation Ever," *Catholic World Report*, May 19, 2016.

29. Thomas Monaghan, "The Monthly Chapter Meeting," *Legatus,* May 1, 2015.

30. Graves, "Man Behind Catholic U's Largest Donation Ever."

31. Patrick Novecosky, "Deep in the Heart of Texas," *Legatus*, May 1, 2015.

32. Dan Morris-Young, "Napa Institute Gathers US Church's Well-Heeled and High Ranking Devout," *National Catholic Reporter,* December 15, 2014.

33. "Carl N. Karcher, 90, Founder of Carl Jr.'s Hamburger Chain, Is Dead," *New York Times*, January 13, 2008.

34. Michael L. Budde, *The Two Churches* (Durham, NC: Duke University Press, 1992), 52. All papal documents cited or mentioned can be found at w2.vatican.va/content/en.html.

35. Information on Busch and the Busch Firm comes from Jim Graves, "The man behind Catholic U's largest donation ever," *The Catholic World Report*, May 19, 2016.

36. Don Lattin, "The pope has a friend in local priest,editor/Conservative Fessio clashed with liberal Jesuits at USF," *San Francisco Chronicle*, May 21, 2005.

37. Morris-Young, "Napa Institute Gathers."

38. Ibid.

39. Joshua J. McElwee, "Francis Replaces Vatican Ambassador Vigano Days After He's Lauded by US Bishops," *National Catholic Reporter*, April 12, 2016.

40. One Napa Institute speaker is Tim Gray, who cites Deuteronomy and Leviticus as privileged biblical sources for information on ending poverty, and who also describes the Sermon on the Mount as the "Magna Carta of social justice." Morris-Young, "Napa Institute Gathers." None of Napa's members have cited Mark 10:17–27: "How hard it will be for those who have wealth to enter the kingdom of God!"

41. Pope Francis, *Evangelii Gaudium*, ch. 2, #54.

42. Morris-Young, "Napa Institute Gathers."

43. Doug Short, "The Epic Rise of America's Services," *Business Insider*, September 1, 2014.

44. Richard Marens, "Timing Is Everything: Historical Contingency as a Factor in the Impact of Catholic Social Teaching upon Managerial Practices," *Journal of Business Ethics* 57, no. 3 (March 2005): 285–301, 286.

45. Morris-Young, "Napa Institute Gathers."

46. One example is Turkson's lecture at the University of the Andes in January 2016. See coverage by Michael Sean Winters, "Cardinal Turkson on Business Vocation," *National Catholic Reporter*, January 8, 2016.

47. Kevin Clarke, "Scholars Warn CUA over Koch Clash," *America*, December 16, 2013. Charles Koch has also given money to fund research centers at the business schools at the University of Kansas, Florida State University, George Mason University, and the University of Maryland, which has alarmed faculty and alumni who believe that Koch is supporting research that only supports his economic positions. Some protesters have joined the efforts of the UnKochMyCampus movement (see www.UnKochMyCampus.org) that emerged to remove Koch's personal influence upon hiring and curriculum decisions at colleges and universities through his stated goal to support only defenders of free enterprise capitalism. Jim Tankersley, "Charles Koch's $200 Million Quest for a 'Republic of Science,'" *Washington Post*, June 5, 2016.

48. Clarke, "Scholars Warn CUA over Koch Clash."

49. Source: best-catholic-colleges.com, accessed May 29, 2016.

50. The term is used by Betty Clermont in her book *The Neo-Catholics*.

51. In December 2013, Langone criticized Pope Francis's negative comments about free market capitalism. In a conversation with Cardinal Timothy Dolan of New York to express his concerns about the pope, Langone said: "You want to be careful of generalities. Rich people in one country don't act the same as rich people in another country."

52. Joe Conason, "Rich Catholics Threaten Pope Francis—Because He Frightens Them," *Alternet*, January 3, 2014.

53. David Koch was the Libertarian Party's vice presidential candidate in 1980, for example.

54. Since this chapter was submitted, several notable events have occurred that bear on this topic. First, in May 2016 Pope Francis delivered an apostolic exhortation on the family called *Amoris Laetitia* (The Joy of Love), whose chapter 8, on the pastoral care of civilly divorced Catholics, now living in new relationships, caused controversy among Catholic traditionalists. A group of four cardinals even formally expressed their doubts about the authoritativeness of the document, in which Pope Francis recommends loving discernment on a case-by-case model for each "irregular" family situation, and advises kindness toward non-traditional same sex couples

and families. The dissident cardinals were strongly rebuked by the pope. Second, the election of Donald Trump as U.S. President has revived the hard right wing in American politics in social and economic issues. His numerous anti-government and anti-regulatory positions and free marketeering are aligned with the interests of some Catholic conservatives, but his plan to defund social services for the poor and vulnerable, to revoke the Affordable Care Act, and to blatantly defend the rights of corporations above those of ordinary citizens, may not sit well, even with wealthy Catholics who now often represent the same social conservatism as Protestant evangelicals and fundamentalists.

Afterword

James Hudnut-Beumler

THE "BUSINESS TURN IN AMERICAN RELIGIOUS HISTORY" turns out to be so much more than even the capacious title of this volume promises. Indeed, no single title could adequately capture the constellation of contributions to the many ways in which its readers can profitably think about the history and practice of religion in America. Here I wish to lift for further appreciation some of those contributions as they relate to how historians and others think about and write about religion after "the turn," and to suggest future directions for investigation that might emerge from the scholarship engaged in the foregoing chapters. Collectively these historical essays pose the methodological question of why we have been studying religious activities, particularly in the United States, without attending to their business aspects. Individually they offer parts to a tool kit of useful approaches for study without ever reducing religious history's humanistic mode of inquiry to some crass utilitarian calculus. Finally, several of the chapters strike an effective critical balance between recounting a history and laying bare the compromises that organized religious organizations have been willing to make in an advanced capitalist society in order to succeed for their own sake and even serve as chaplains to the economic order. The variety of these essays provide multiple paths forward.

The Theological Origins of American Religious History

A waggish view of the clergy holds that a minister, priest, or rabbi is someone who went to work serving God so as not to get his (or her) hands dirty with money. It is the kind of joke that lay leaders at churches and synagogues tell each other just before they get down to the business of setting their religious leader's salaries—thereby a kind of commentary on people who do not live wholly in the world by people who live all too much in the world of work and money. This divide between holy precincts and people, on the one hand, and the secular domain, on the other, goes far back in Western culture, at least as far as Solomon's Temple in Jerusalem, where ordinary coinage needed to be exchanged for temple money, which could then be used to purchase sacri- fices and make offerings to support the work of the temple's priests and other Levites. The sacred/mundane distinction in various instantiations has been with us ever since. A religious leader who talks too much about money is sus- pect (at least until recently in the United States with the rise of the prosperity gospel). The religious realm, we are taught, is "supposed to be" about religious ideas, theology, and interpretation of scripture. Yet as the authors in this book amply demonstrate, religion in America (among other places) is also about buildings, mission projects, book enterprises, radio shows, evangelistic and missionary schemes, and lay participation in philanthropy. Indeed, to the ves- try or temple board joking about their religious leader's salary and where it comes from, it is all religion—worship, prayers of the funeral, the deep intro- spection, a fund-raising campaign for a new orphanage, and the meeting they are in that evening. Therefore, most of the people who have been religious in the history of the United States (i.e., lay participants) have a holistic expe- rience of religion. Why, then, has American religious history been written primarily from the frames of intellectual history and institutional history? It is doubtless because ministers, priests, rabbis, and the people they in turn educated were the primary interpreters of the American religious experience and they wrote from the clerical perspective.

For more than two centuries, the chroniclers of the American religious experience shared the mentality of the pulpit more than that of the pews. Even with the eclipse of denominational history and the rise of evangelical- ism, as Daniel Vaca notes, the historiographical practice of thinking in terms of theology and institutions continued. Vaca writes, "[George] Marsden and other avowedly evangelical historians inspired a tradition of historiography that focused especially on identifying theological or institutional criteria that situate Christians within that unity's ostensible boundaries." Vaca further compares the use of evangelical history's repeated definitions with the four- fold criteria of "conversionism, activism, biblicism, and crucicentrism," defin- ing evangelicalism within that earlier moment of religious history known as "church history." Newer movements in American religious history have attended to the media employed by particular groups, such as tracts and print culture in the nineteenth century and hymnbooks (to stick with evangelicals for a moment). Other studies have followed R. Laurence Moore's argument that religion has not so much disappeared as been commodified, with the result that we could see that religion and the market were being mixed, such that morally it seems as though religion was losing its soul. The contribution of Daniel Vaca's chapter on this point is to let us see that from the beginning in the American Tract Society to Zondervan's juggernaut years of the 1980s and right down to televangelists today, evangelicals are not being used, subverted, or having their witness diluted. They are just working the Lord's business in a new way.

If there is a character in religious studies that looms Zelig-like throughout all discussions of religion and economics it is Max Weber, whose 1905 book *The Protestant Ethic and the Spirit of Capitalism* is much invoked in a kind of comic book version that has allowed scholars to say something (usually about Protestant avarice, or selfishness, or Catholic laziness) with more basis in prejudice than fact and then to stop thinking about the topic in its entirety.[1] One of the real dangers of universalizing Protestants, Calvinist worldly asceticism, Catholics, and even capitalism is that the things these terms denote actually change, subtly over brief periods of time and dramatically over long periods of time. For this reason, Timothy Gloege's opening discussion of how both economic thinking and religious thought changed separately and together over the course of more than two centuries of national history makes fascinating reading and a worthy historicist advance over the religion scholar's usual resort to Weberian truisms. As Gloege points out, in modern societies we play several "games" simultaneously, and while each game, be it political, religious, economic, cultural, or ethnic, has its own rules, they are permeable to one another. The genius of Weber's original proposal was that he saw how one form of Christianity (Calvinism) could inspire work and thrift via anxiety about one's state of salvation, which in turn led to the preconditions and sustenance of capitalism. What Gloege offers American religious historians is a much more sophisticated substitute for Weber's thesis—a dynamic, multifactor account of how the assumptions of one game lead into another and affect others over time. Concretely, it is these differences over time that account for why fundamentalism failed to capture the hearts and minds of the American Protestant majority in the fundamentalist-modernist controversy over the first decades of the twentieth century and then succeeded more than half a century later with the business methods, kindly words, attractive brands, and niche marketing that came in with later market segmentation.

The 1920s fundamentalists tried to "take over" denominations; in the 1980s they "started" Christian churches; and by 2000 they had ended up with the largest share of the nation's Christians. Religion changed, but so did business, and their relationship *together* made a difference that changed the course of American religion.

The Business Turn as a Big Idea in American Religious History

The study of American religion renovates itself by changing its perspective on its subject matter. It is, I think, not too early to think of the business turn as a "big idea" in the practice of American religious history. What I mean by "big idea" is a perspective that allows historians in a given place and time to rethink what is going on in a broad sweep of the American religious experience. To get at why the business turn offers such a prospect, let me briefly consider some other such big ideas of the past. Taking things no further back than Sidney Mead's provocative idea that America was a "nation with the soul of a church," we can note the close association of American religious identity with democracy, an intellectual preoccupation of the last century's middle decades. Also in the eclipse of denominational history, Martin Marty saw things whole again in *Righteous Empire* by depicting all of American religion as a two-party system of conservative and liberal blocs stretched across all religious traditions. Not surprisingly, postwar twentieth-century American intellectual life was conducted under the influence of communism from outside, and the grand battle for supremacy between liberalism and domestic conservatism lent itself to these kinds of readings.[2]

Big ideas come and go as times change. Only with the fall of Soviet communism in Europe in years after 1989 did the right-left key lose its magic ability to open any and every lock. Scholars soon found a new panacea in thinking about religion in terms of the market. Just as market economics had triumphed over centrally planned socialism, so markets were the key to explaining every human behavior, however small or large. Sociologists Roger Finke and Rodney Stark put the ideas of University of Chicago economist Gary Becker to work in *The Churching of America*, which represents a strong version of market thinking about religion.[3] Robert Wuthnow, Jay Demerath, and Peter Dobkin Hall all represent thinkers who wrote voluminously in the 1990s about religion as a philanthropic entity poised between markets and governments.[4]

When big ideas don't come from the headlines or from other divisions of the university, they have often come via other colleagues in the study of religion. Thus Catherine Albanese brought an insight from the history of religions' emphasis on the big and little traditions into the American scene and taught us to see the everyday religion of Elvis adoration as well as the official Catholic Mass.[5] The emphasis on seeing Native American religious practices, popular-culture dimensions of religion, and hybrid immigrant religious experience (to name just three) as central and equally important to any description of the American religious experience has generated other big ideas and projects on lived religion, the retelling of U.S. religious history (in which we learn one cannot tell the whole story, only parts), and, I would argue, the business turn.[6] It is a continuation of a long interest in "history from the bottom up," yet I think that, like other big ideas in America religious history, it is in part a product of its own times. We live in an age of FICO scores, financial scandals, Occupy Wall Street, and the get-rich preaching of Joel Osteen and Creflo Dollar. Meanwhile, *the* Donald Trump, elected President in 2016, was a businessman with no experience in elective office who beat out senators and governors for his party's nomination. Not since the 1920s has business seemed as integral to American life or explanatory of its culture.

Like an earlier fine collection called *Belief and Behavior*, this collection is premised on the simple but rare conviction that what people *do* is disclosive of what they actually think, mean, and believe.[7] Of course the method works for people who leave buildings or ledgers instead of letters, emails, or diaries. But it works also for people who do leave literary remains, sometime confirming their voiced intentions and sometimes undercutting their pious rhetoric. And speaking of pious rhetoric, we used to say that "the purpose of history is to let the dead speak." Not all the informants in this book are dead, of course, yet one cannot help but be impressed that the authors have found ways to let not just their words speak but their actions as well. The fundamental big idea throughout this volume is that religious actors' business activities are religiously purposive. With that in mind, let us see where the commitment to examine the business activity led the authors to fresh discoveries.

One of the most striking contributions the study of religion in America via the business turn has to offer is from the vantage point gained when one departs from formally religious sites of activity. The clearest example of this in the book occurs in Angela Tarango's decision to look for Native American representations—including sacred symbols—in Oklahoma casinos. The audacity of the first move here is not to be missed. A casino is the last place most Native American religious scholars trained in the folklore and anthropology traditions would want to go to for the "religiously authentic." Casinos are products of the late twentieth century and hybrid accommodations with the dominant white American culture's pension for glitz and gaming. Yet in the eyes of Tarango the casinos of the Choctaw, the Cherokee, and the Quapaw become extraordinary access points to how Native American identities are variously remembered, created, and even invented by the various nations. The Choctaw's adoption of the white buffalo, more characteristic of the Lakota Sioux, is a stunning representation of the Choctaw's ability to fashion a new symbolism representative of their at-homeness in Oklahoma. For the Cherokee, the tragic removal in the Trail of Tears and the southeastern original home of the transplanted nation are on display in historic documents and in linguistic reminders of past cultural accomplishments, even on the signs of men's and women's restrooms. The Quapaw, meanwhile reach back a millennium to a golden age of trans-Mississippian artistic genius to share their story—they are the people known for their extraordinary pottery and ceramics and not for the number of times they were forced to move (before and after European contact). Taken together, this is really a remarkably exciting amount of information about how Native American experience and memory are still being worked out and shaped in the present. One wonders how many other contemporary stories are just below the surface of every historical site one encounters throughout the nation.

An example of using just such a willingness to look at the records is Deborah Skolnick Einhorn's account of the rise of Jewish women's philanthropy focused on the eastern cities of New York, Boston, and Philadelphia in the early decades of the twentieth century. Even though historians have been asking "Where are the women?" since the late 1960s, Einhorn takes a fresh look by going back to the business records of early Jewish federations and community-wide campaigns. The story she tells reminds us that new occasions, particularly crises such as World War I, are the instigators of social change. If Jewish philanthropy prior to World War I was a matter of a few rich men being asked to do everything, the war spirit asked everyone to do their part. Women quickly concluded that everyone meant them, too, and what Einhorn finds is how quickly they sprang into action to found women's divisions of philanthropic efforts and how quickly they began to raise significant sums. Einhorn's work is significant because, as she herself notes, the subsequent histories of Jewish federations usually leave the women out or minimize their contributions (and the sums they raised). Indeed, this mobilization has never gone away since, but it is the copious business records of women's organizations and subdivisions we may have to look to if we are to find the full story. These records used to be plumbed by people who wrote institutional histories, but they should be interesting afresh to scholars focusing on questions of women's agency and the history of gender, not to mention Jewish life in the twentieth century. With both Tarango's and Einhorn's work the business turn's mode of looking at ordinary business activities of an identified group of people and their institutions allowed each to find jewels in what others might have dismissed as sand and rock.

Follow the Money, Measure the Flows

Another theoretical direction the big idea represented by the business turn in American religious history augurs is the determination to get beyond American isolation and to measure the flow of ideas, money, and people globally so as to understand what is happening with religion and America more completely and dynamically. This book contains two different examples of such efforts to think globally. David King and Michael Altman utilize globalist versions of the business turn to blow up or at least extend received historiographies about Americans and overseas Christian activity and Asian religions in America, respectively.

Using the concept of tracking flows of people, funds, and ideas allows King to contest and complicate several worn-out storylines all at once. When accounts are given of the relationship between American Christians and Christians in other lands, there is, as King more delicately notes, a tendency to tell the story in terms of a transfer of Christianity from the global North to the global South over time, or to depict it as an artifact of the decline of mainline Protestantism, or the rise of conservatism or pentecostalism in the two-thirds world, or to write of the tourist economics of mission trips taken by wealthy first-world Americans to seek authentic Christian experience anywhere but North America. To all of these competing and ideologically fraught tropes, King brings the concept of tracking the flows to tell a more interesting story. Just as money and food move all across the world, so too do people of faith, people's money to support faith programs, and ideas about faith. Importantly, they do not just move in one direction. Numerically declining North American Christians are intimately involved (through sending money, traveling, and sponsorships) with some of the sites of Christian vitality in the Southern Hemisphere. Meanwhile, ideas did not just travel from 1950s seminaries to present-day Ugandan churches; there are flows coming back this way as well. King's work, therefore, helps us think about things such as American

Anglicans with Rwandan bishops. King's work makes me wonder how much we have missed in other instances because we have so often tracked only the one-way flow of ideas in religious history, never stopping to measure the other ways religious people engage in intercultural exchange.

Michael Altman helps us understand that Christians were not the only people engaged in the cross-cultural religious exchange goods and services. As Altman sees it, "the business turn in the study of Asian religions in America means taking a global view of networks and circulations." So, like King, he seeks to interrupt the center-periphery construct (which simultaneously tells the Westerners at the center that they are guilty and that they are the most important) in favor of a truly global exchange view, meaning that the critical terms in Altman's case must shift quickly to seeing "Asian religions *and* America" in place of "Asian religions *in* America." Once again it is the flows that are important. Following the money, trade, and labor takes Altman to some truly fascinating individuals, such as Swami Vivekananda, who came to the World Parliament of Religions in 1893 with a universalist version of Vedanta philosophy, aiming not to be a missionary but a fund-raiser. Vivekananda had plans for India, expressed via the Ramakrishna Mission in India, and to finance them he had to sell Indian spirituality to Americans. He turned out to be just the first of many global gurus and "godmen CEOs" working a complex trade between India and America. Just how complex the trade could get is hinted at when Altman discusses followers of Sathya Sai Baba: "Anglo-American Baba devotees turned to him the 1960s and 1970s because they wanted a 'spiritual' alternative to American materialism. Meanwhile, Indian American devotees have come to America in search of material gain but bring their spiritual godman [Baba] with them." Altman asks us to see Sai Baba as an entrepreneur, to fully take advantage of the business turn, and to get beyond describing religious entities only in terms of insider religious language. Putting King and Altman together for a moment, the emphasis on following the money, on watching what religions do in this world rather than attending to their claims about some other world, pushes one of those boundaries established by religious scholars concerning the practice of American religious history. The boundary between practitioners and scholars has been reinforced as a friendly fence for decades by interpretations that privilege the religious adherents' own accounts of what is going on. The business turn opens up the possibility that that the most compelling interpretations of what is going on are (at least in part) beyond the direct experience of individual insiders themselves.

Capitalist and Religious Zealotry

Two of the chapters in the volume take on the role that religion plays in favoring or opposing capitalism in American life up to and including the present. Matthew Bowman's chapter explains the Mormon ambivalence (in the genuine sense of being of two minds) about capitalism. Paula Kane, for her part, writes about the rise of enormously wealthy Catholic CEOs and their organizations dedicated to finding perfect compatibility between free market capitalism and Catholic social teachings. Though Bowman's and Kane's chapters focus on very different kinds of protagonists at first—a Mormon con man in Bowman's case and wildly successful CEOs in legitimate businesses in Kane's—there are some features of the stories each tells that makes one aware of the changes in focus wrought by the business turn. In each instance it is an account of business leaders and what they want from religion-and-business (which they see as an indivisible entity dedicated to the good) that drives the narrative. So what the business turn means first is an important shift of the protagonists of American religious history away from religious founders, bishops, theologians, and saints to entrepreneurs and CEOs—religious adherents who believe that their success in business translates to a seat at the religious leadership table in some way, shape, or form. Indeed, nothing could be more American, it would seem, once we have read Kane and Bowman unpack their stories, then to see that in America capitalism and Christianity can be made into a powerful alloy by the very individuals who spend the most time trying to be good in both domains.

The pleasure in reading Kane's and Bowman's chapters qua American religious history comes from the differences that emerge because of the historical differences in the religious experiences of the two groups. Bowman's Mormons arrive by their notable affinity for multilevel marketing and get-rich capitalism on the basis of a long elision of nineteenth-century liberal economics with other truths taught in the gospel. But they are also the people who set up alternatives to the cruelties of the market in the "bishops' storehouses" that provide for the needs of poor members even to this day in every Mormon ward. Modern-day Mormons are living heirs to elaborate traditions of building Zion collectively *and* supporting the acquisition and protection of individual wealth. In like manner, Kane's modern-day Roman Catholic super-CEOs and their clerical allies know they came out of the immigrant Catholic tradition of small, less powerful Americans, which they celebrate. Emotionally they identify with widows and orphans, but now they themselves are rich. They loved John Paul II and his celebration of individual dignity in the face of communist collectivism, but Pope Francis is not singing their tune. Still, being wealthy, and having bishops, archbishops, cardinals, and theologians at their sufferance, they can afford to create an American Catholic infrastructure in their own image to preach the virtues of Catholic economic neoliberalism. Their colleges and law schools and clubs for like-minded businessmen can glorify wealth as good and baptize its getting while narrowing the interpretation of Catholic social teaching to be only about personal virtues, being charitable, and maintaining a hard line on sexuality- and abortion-related issues. The twisting of Leo XIII's labor encyclical from one teaching a responsibility of owners to workers into a blanket defense of global capitalism clearly stirs Kane's passions, as well it should. She provides a great deal of narrative backstory to make the ideological shifts intelligible. So does Bowman, and indeed these chapters possess elements of insider journalism: they use the business turn to let readers inside organizations (and minds) to see "how the sausage is being made." It is not always pretty, but it is fascinating. It would be hard to read these chapters and come away saying that "religion is just religion," a benign separate sphere that has no effect on individuals' lives other than on their spiritual notions. Instead, the heuristic effect of the business turn in these and other chapters is to open readers' eyes to the ways that religions are implicated in other domains of American and global life that affect even those who do not share the faith of their adherents.

If the business turn in American religious history succeeds beyond this book, it will succeed as it has in these chapters, by demystifying the human— sometimes humane, sometimes otherwise—aspects of organized religious life. While one can imagine that opening the business affairs of religious actors and organizations might hold a promise for religious history akin to telling a small child to cut his drum open to see what makes the sound inside, the reverse proves true in these capable hands. The editors and contributors are to be congratulated on demonstrating methods, perspectives, and techniques in religious history that should bear fruit for the understanding of religious life, past and present, for years to come.

Notes

1. Max Weber and Talcott Parsons, *The Protestant Ethic and the Spirit of Capitalism* (Mineola, NY: Dover, 2003).
2. Sidney Earl Mead, *The Nation with the Soul of a Church*, ROSE 10 (Macon, GA: Mercer University Press, 1985); Martin E. Marty, *Righteous Empire: The*

Protestant Experience in America, Two Centuries of American Life: A Bicentennial Series (New York: Dial Press, 1970).

3. Roger Finke and Rodney Stark, *The Churching of America, 1776–1990: Winners and Losers in Our Religious Economy* (New Brunswick, NJ: Rutgers University Press, 1992).

4. Robert Wuthnow, *The Restructuring of American Religion: Society and Faith Since World War II*, Studies in Church and State (Princeton: Princeton University Press, 1988); Robert Wuthnow and Helmut K. Anheier, eds., *Between States and Markets: The Voluntary Sector in Comparative Perspective* (Princeton: Princeton University Press, 1991); N. J. Demerath, ed., *Sacred Companies: Organizational Aspects of Religion and Religious Aspects of Organizations*, Religion in America Series (New York: Oxford University Press, 1998); Peter Dobkin Hall, *Inventing the Nonprofit Sector and Other Essays on Philanthropy, Voluntarism, and Nonprofit Organizations* (Baltimore: Johns Hopkins University Press, 1992); Peter Dobkin Hall, *The Organization of American Culture, 1700–1900: Private Institutions, Elites, and the Origins of American Nationality*, New York University Series in Education and Socialization in American History (New York: New York University Press, 1982).

5. Catherine L. Albanese, *America, Religions, and Religion*, 5th ed. (Belmont, CA: Thomson/Wadsworth, 2013).

6. David D. Hall, ed., *Lived Religion in America: Toward a History of Practice* (Princeton: Princeton University Press, 1997); Thomas A. Tweed, ed., *Retelling U.S. Religious History* (Berkeley: University of California Press, 1997).

7. Philip R. VanderMeer and Robert P. Swierenga, eds., *Belief and Behavior: Essays in the New Religious History* (New Brunswick, NJ: Rutgers University Press, 1991).

Index

Affordable Care Act, 110, 204–5, 217
Albanese, Catherine, 227
American Hebrew, 143–4
American Tract Society, 22, 24, 30, 225
    business techniques of, 26–7
Anglicanism, 3, 65, 82, 230
Apple. *See* Jobs, Steve
Aquinas, Thomas, 203
Augustine, St., 203
Ave Maria University, 203–4

Baba, Sathya Sai, 158
    claims to divinity of, 164
    following of in the United States, 166–70
    as a global entrepreneur, 163, 165–6
Bakker, Jim and Tammy, 12
Baltzell, E. Digby, 200
Bauman, Chad, 171
Benedict XVI, Pope, 206, 211
Benson, Ezra Taft, 115–22, 124
Book of Mormon, 109, 117–18, 120
Borg, Mrs. Sidney C, 145
Brekus, Catherine, 39
Brigham Young University. *See* Young, Brigham
Buddhism, 1, 13–14, 158, 169
    in American economics, 156

Busch, Tim, 201, 207–10, 212, 214–15, 217
Bush, George W., 98
Businessman's Revival, 7, 11, 28

Calvinism, 199, 201, 225
capitalism, 14–16, 58–9, 62, 231–2
    in the Cold War, 11
    among evangelicals, 30, 35, 48–9, 56, 63–5
    development of in postbellum America, 51, 53
    and the New Deal, 60
    See also Catholicism; global Christianity; Mormonism
Catholicism, 8–10, 15–16, 26, 65
    and capitalism in America, 199–200
    within corporate America, 201–18
    presence of within American conservatism, 207–13
    See also global Christianity
Catholic University, 207, 212, 214–15
Centesimus Annus (1991). *See* Francis I, Pope
Christensen, Doug, 122–3
Christianity Today, 33, 62
Church of Latter-day Saints, the. *See* Mormonism
Civil War, 9, 29, 52

Clinton, Bill, 98
Clinton, Hillary, 211
Cold War, 2, 75, 90, 167
  economic and religious consequences
    of, 11, 85
  as a launching pad for global Christian
    missions, 86, 88
  and Mormonism, 116, 118–19
Compassion International, 72, 86
Covey, Stephen R., 122–3

Dewane, Frank J., 204–5
Dollar, Creflo, 227

Edinburgh Conference (1910), 83
Eisenhower, Dwight, 116
Engel, Kate Carte, 28
Enlightenment, The, 3, 7, 48–9
evangelicalism, 3, 21
  American historiography and
    definitions of, 22–4, 38
  business characteristics of, 29,
    31–2, 36, 39
  and corporate America, 11, 22,
    52, 54, 63
  described as distinct from business, 25
  and individualistic economics,
    48, 63, 65
Evangelii Gaudium (2013). *See* Francis
  I, Pope

Falwell, Jerry, 64, 208
Federal Council of Churches, 55,
  57, 60–1
Finney, Charles Grandison, 6
  and religious entrepreneurialism, 6–7
Francis I, Pope, 202, 204–5, 207, 213–14
  social teaching of, 208–9, 211, 218, 232
Francis, St., 205
Fuller, Charles, 60–1
Fuller Theological Seminary. *See* Fuller,
  Charles

fundamentalism, 14–15, 47
  association with business, 25, 31, 47–8,
    52–3, 62–5
  historiography of, 47–8
  and Lyman Stewart, 55, 60
  and *The Fundamentals*, 48, 55–6, 60–1

Ghana, 72, 97, 214
global Christianity
  and American culture, 73–6
  and Catholicism, 87–8, 90, 93
  as a challenge to American
    evangelicalism
  ecumenical aspects of, 87–8, 90
  humanitarian-missionary
    organizations contribute to, 72,
    86, 92–3
  and Latin America, 73, 75, 79, 89, 92–3
Godbe, William, 113–15, 117, 120
Grace, Jr., Joseph Peter, 205–6
Graham, Billy, 20, 85, 89
  and Billy Graham Evangelistic
    Association, 84
  and religious marketing and
    media, 11, 62
Great Depression, 9, 58–9

Hinduism, 1–2
  in American economics, 15, 155, 158–61
  construction of as a category, 157–8
  as a spiritual commodity in
    America, 160–1
Hobby Lobby, 14, 39
Homobonus, St., 199
Huckabee, Mike, 208

IBM. *See* Watson, Thomas J.
India, 15, 85, 156–72
Islam, 39, 75, 78, 204

Jackson, Andrew, 5, 112, 195
Jakes, T. D., 12

Jenkins, Philip, 74
Jewish Exponent, 140–3, 151
Jindal, Bobby, 208
Jobs, Steve, 1, 14
   and Buddhism, 1–2
   and Hindusim, 1–2
Jones, Bob, 59
Judaism, 15, 37, 87–90
   and business practice in
     America, 131–2
   and the Federation of Jewish
     Charities, 136–49
   as financially deceitful, 131
   impact of World War I upon,
     136–40
   and philanthropy in America, 136
   and women in business, 133–49

Karcher, Carl, 207–8
Kennedy, John F., 116
Kladder, Peter, 20–1, 25, 33, 35
Koch brothers, the, 207, 215–17
Koerber, Rick, 108–11, 114, 119–20,
   122, 125–6
Kohut, Rebekah, 143, 153

labor, 6, 46, 50
   and America's market economy, 51–2
   and Asian religions in America, 158,
     163, 167, 171
   in Catholic social teaching, 208,
     212–13, 217
   in Christian businesses, 12
   in global Christianity, 72, 97
   See also Mormonism; Weber, Max
Laudato Si (2015). *See* Francis
   I, Pope
Legatus, 16, 199, 202–10, 213–16
Leo XIII, Pope, 212–13, 232
Lincoln, Bruce, 171
Loeb, Mrs. Arthur, 141–2
Lofton, Kathryn, 9, 23, 39

Marsden, George, 23, 47
Marty, Martin, 226
Maxwell, John, 12, 94
McDannell, Colleen, 39
McKay, David O., 119–20
McPherson, Aimee Semple, 11
Mead, Sidney, 226
Methodism, 2, 5, 7–8, 31, 89
Monaghan, Thomas S., 201–3, 205, 207
Moody, Dwight L., 11, 32, 54, 123
   and evangelical business practice,
     29–33, 52–3
Moody Bible Institute. *See* Moody,
   Dwight L.
Moore, R. Laurence, 7, 25, 225
Moreton, Bethany, 39
Mormonism, 6
   capitalist and anticommunist themes
     within, 118–20
   Church Welfare System of, 115, 123–5
   economic variation of, 112–15, 120–1
   and initial contrast with capitalism, 111
   and monetary schemes, 109–10
   and popular financial literature, 122–3

Napa Institute, 16, 202, 206–11
National Association of Evangelicals,
   23, 61, 64
National Council of Churches, 13
Native Americans, 176
   Cherokees, 15, 177–81, 185, 189–96,
     228
   Choctaws, 15, 176–9, 185–96, 228
   gaming culture of, 177–81, 183
   and identity construction in casinos,
     181, 186, 188, 191, 195–6
   Pequots, 177, 181–2, 188
   Quapaws, 177–9, 188–92, 195–98, 228
Nauvoo theology, 114–16, 122–3
neoliberalism, 39, 80, 217, 232
New Deal, 9–11, 13, 60, 123–4
New York Times Magazine, 204

Nibley, Hugh, 115, 120–2, 125
Noll, Mark, 76, 81

Obama, Barack, 98, 119
Osteen, Joel, 12

Parrish, Warren, 112–15, 117, 120
Paul II, Pope John, 203, 208–9, 211–13
Peale, Norman Vincent, 11, 35
Pentecostalism, 12, 31, 229
    and corporate Christianity, 58–9
    global presence of, 72–4, 78–80, 93
Pew, J. Howard, 33, 62
Pirsig, Robert, 13
Presbyterianism, 5, 7, 72, 89
prosperity gospel, 9, 12, 59, 72, 75.
    See also fundamentalism;
        Roberts, Oral
*Protestant Ethic and the Rise of
    Capitalism, The. See* Weber, Max
Protestant Reformation, 199
Prothero, Stephen, 157

Quakerism, 3, 54, 56

Red Cross, 137, 140
Religious Right, 38, 47, 64, 75
Republican Party, 16
    conservative Catholic involvement
        with, 203, 208, 210, 216–17
    presence of conservative evangelicals
        in, 64–5
Rerum Novarum (1891), 208, 212
Roberts, Oral, 12, 59
Robertson, Pat, 12, 64, 94
Rockefeller, Jr., John D., 83, 87
Roman Catholicism. *See* Catholicism
Romney, Mitt, 110, 202
Roosevelt, Franklin Delano, 60, 87, 123

Sanders, Bernie, 211
Santorum, Rick, 210

Scofield Bible, 54
Shridharani, Krishnalal, 155
Skousen, Cleon, 116–20
Smith, Adam, 35
    and *Wealth of Nations*, 35, 48
Smith, Joseph
    communal economics of, 110
    personal finances of, 111–12
Social Gospel, 8–9, 29, 83, 86, 88
Stout, Harry, 81

Truman, Harry, 62, 85, 87
Trump, Donald, 217, 227
Tweed, Thomas, 156–8

United Nations, 87–9, 98
Urban, Hugh, 154, 170

Vatican II, 201–2, 210
Vivekananda, Swami, 158
    arrival in America of, 158–60
    fundraising efforts of, 160–1

Walmart, 12–13, 16, 39
Warfield, Benjamin B., 55
Warren, Rick, 94
Washington, Booker T., 9
Watson, Thomas J., 2, 5
Weber, Max, 78, 207
    and Catholicism, 199–202, 216
    and non-Christian global
        religions, 156
    and Protestant work ethic, 16, 125
Wheaton College, 61
Wilson, Woodrow, 83, 137
World Parliament of Religions, 159,
    161, 230
World Vision International, 72, 86, 96
    and American exceptionalism, 84–5
    extensive resources of, 81–2
    and impact of global
        Christianity, 92–3

World War I, 56, 83, 136–9, 142, 145,
147–8, 228
World War II, 11, 15, 84–9, 149, 206
Wuthnow, Robert, 73, 76–7, 97, 168, 226
Wycliffe Bible Translators, 84

yoga, 155–6
Yogananda, Paramahansa, 2
Young, Brigham, 113–15, 120–1, 123–4
communal economics of, 110–11

Young Men's Christian Association,
29, 52, 83
Youth for Christ, 62, 84

Ziglar, Zig, 12, 122
Zondervan Corporation, 12, 25,
32–8, 225
as a public corporation, 33–6
and the relationship between
evangelicalism and business, 20–1